THE NEW COMPLETE
Pressure
Cooker

THE NEW COMPLETE
Pressure
Cooker

Get the best from your electric or stovetop model

Jennie Shapter

Photography by Jon Whitaker

LORENZ BOOKS

CONTENTS

Introduction

Whether you have just bought your first pressure cooker or already have one and want to extend your repertoire, this book will take you through all the basics – how pressure cookers work, the differences between stovetop and electric types, accessories, equipment and cookware, care and cleaning, troubleshooting, and getting the best from your pressure cooker, as well as providing you with lots of exciting recipes to try.

Long gone are the days of noisy vessels clanking away and the family story of grandma's pressure cooker exploding. Now there is a wonderful array of pressure cookers to choose from. All are very easy to use and have safety uppermost in their design.

The first acknowledged attempt at a pressure cooker is credited to a French physicist called Denis Papin in 1679. He invented a vessel called a 'steam digester', which used the same principles as today's modern cookers – an airtight cooker that uses pressure from steam to raise the boiling temperature of the water within, thus resulting in a quicker cooking time.

Various attempts were made from then onwards, and around 1939 the first saucepan-style pressure cooker appeared in New York. The production was temporarily halted during the 1940s as the aluminium

was needed during World War II. In the 1950s, many models appeared in both aluminium and stainless steel; this resulted in some inferior products, and the popularity of the pressure cooker began to wane due to its lack of reliability. However, the pressure cooker returned with greater safety features and ease of use, and the benefits of healthy meals, speed and fuel efficiency have meant it has once again found favour in the home.

Not only is there a range of stovetop pressure cookers with many different features available, including options of cooking at different pressure, but there is also a range of programmable electric pressure cookers that are gaining in popularity.

It is easy to feel overwhelmed by all the options, but this book is designed to help you get the best results no matter which cooker you decide to buy or already own.

The recipes have been tested on both electric and stovetop cookers. In addition, since there is a range of pressures offered by different pressure cooker manufacturers, each recipe has been tested on two different pressures. Electric pressure cookers mainly operate at lower pressures than the stovetop models.

The recipes have been tested on cookers within a range of 11.5–12psi/80–82kPa or 7–8psi/50–55kPa when tested on High. A few recipes need more gentle cooking, so these have been tested on Low at 7–8psi/50–55kPa or 5.8psi/40kPa. For both High and Low settings, the lower pressure timings are given in brackets.

Below and below right: Both electric and stovetop pressure cookers produce good results – it is your choice as to which best suits your needs. Electric models have pre-designated programmes, while stovetop models provide total flexibility.

Above: You can use a pressure cooker to make a classic French onion soup in just a few minutes.

Above: Substantial meals such as this sausage casserole are full of flavour when cooked in the pressure cooker.

Above: A pressure cooker is perfect for preparing vegetable side dishes such as these sweet potatoes with orange.

Some electric pressure cookers only have one setting but operate at 7–8psi/50–55kPa, so these can be used for recipes tested on High or Low. Use the longer time on High, and the shorter time on Low.

There are a few pressure cookers that work outside these settings. There are guidelines on pages 22–23 to adapt recipe timings for these pressure cookers. It is very important that you establish what pressure your cooker operates at. You should read your manufacturer's handbook or contact their helpline to confirm the operating pressure before trying the recipes in this book. The timings are guidelines only, and you should follow them in tandem with information from your own handbook which is specific to your pressure cooker.

The recipes have been tested on pressure cookers with a capacity of 5–6 litres/9–10½ pints/10½–12½ US pints. For small pressure cookers, the quantities may have to be pared down. Follow the instructions for maximum fill, according to the type of food.

RECIPE TIMINGS

The recipes in this book have been tested in both electric and stovetop pressure cookers. As the pressure varies between models, each recipe provides two timings to accommodate this. Remember to check your manufacturer's handbook to establish the pressure for your cooker before using the recipes.

• Where recipes are cooked on High, the first timing is for pressure cookers that cook at 11.5–12psi/80–82kPa, and the second timing in brackets is for pressure cookers that cook at 7–8psi/50–55kPa.

• A few recipes are cooked more gently on Low. In this case, the first timing is for 7–8psi/ 50–55kPa, and the second timing in brackets is for 5.8psi/40kPa.

Below: A beef pot roast in red wine with root vegetables can be prepared quickly while keeping all the flavours in.

Below: A pressure cooker makes it very quick and easy to cook salmon, as well as reducing any fishy odours.

Below: Desserts such as this chocolate and raspberry torte are extremely simple to make in a pressure cooker.

How a Pressure Cooker Works

Pressure cooking is a method of preparing food using water, or other liquid, in a sealed container where steam is produced. When foods are cooked in an ordinary pan, the temperature will not rise above the boiling point of the liquid, irrespective of the amount of heat applied to the cooker on the stove. With a pressure cooker, the air is expelled from the container and the steam from the liquid is sealed in, causing an increase in pressure and, in turn, temperature. This is identical for both electric and stovetop cookers.

Steam is essential to the process, so all recipes must include liquid, or the food must be cooked on a trivet, rack or basket with water added beneath, like when steaming food. Food is cooked more quickly because of the increased temperature and the effect of the steam being forced through the food, which tenderizes it. This is apparent with stews, where the effect of long braising times is achieved in a fraction of the time while still resulting in flavourful casseroles. Cooking time can be reduced by half to two-thirds of the time taken for conventional cooking methods. Most manufacturers recommend adding at least 250–300ml/8–10fl oz/1–1¼ cups of cooking liquid such as water, stock, wine or milk, as these all produce steam. For long cooking times lasting more than 30 minutes,

this needs to be increased. Also, when cooking foods such as dried pulses, extra liquid is required.

The pressure developed in the pressure cooker is measured in psi or pounds per square inch. Some manufacturers may use kPa or bar. The higher the pressure in the cooker, the higher the temperature and the faster the food will cook.

REACHING PRESSURE

All pressure cookers have a lockable lid which is fitted with a gasket. This seals the pressure cooker. Once meat or vegetables have been seared or sautéed and the liquid is added, the pressure cooker is ready for sealing. Many different foods, including pulses, steaming fish or desserts, are ready to seal and cook as soon as liquid is added to the base.

If the pressure cooker has more than one pressure setting, this is then selected and the pressure cooker is heated. For stovetop models, use a high heat until the pressure cooker reaches pressure, then reduce to just maintain pressure. This is automatic with an electric pressure cooker. Timings in the recipe begin at this time. Depending on the contents of the pressure cooker, the time taken to reach pressure can take as little as 1 minute to more than 10 minutes.

Left: A pressure cooker works by expelling air from the container and sealing the steam inside, thus causing an increase in pressure and temperature. Shown here are examples of electric pressure cookers.

Above: Different ingredients can be cooked at the same time, such as these eggs and foil-wrapped haddock.

Above: You can make a casserole by adding stock to chicken pieces before cooking at high pressure.

Above: Ramekins of crème caramel can be placed on a rack for cooking gently in an electric pressure cooker.

Pressure cookers have a visual pressure indicator to show they have reached pressure. This may be a valve cap with a coloured ring, or a coloured button or pin in the lid, which rises when under pressure. On electric pressure cookers, it is a metal valve or button.

You can set the time for a recipe with an electric pressure cooker at the start once the lid is closed, and it will count down once pressure is reached. Some stovetop cookers have their own timer; if not, you should use a separate one to time your recipe.

MAINTAINING PRESSURE

With stovetop models it is important to use the lowest possible setting to maintain pressure. Most pressure cookers give a gentle hiss. Excess heat results in loss of steam and liquid, and wastes fuel. If necessary, remove the pressure cooker from the hob for a short time if excessive steam is escaping. Make sure you keep the pressure cooker under pressure while it stabilizes. Gas cookers are quicker to react, but you may need to reduce an electric burner slightly early or transfer to another ring set on low after pressure is reached. Induction hobs tend to require a higher temperature to maintain pressure. This may result in loss of steam and liquid. All this is automatic with electric models.

REDUCING PRESSURE

There are two ways to release the steam and thus reduce pressure from the pressure cooker, as follows.
Quick Release This technique is used to quickly stop the food cooking. Electric cookers have a pressure or

steam release valve which is turned to the release or vent setting and the steam is quickly ejected. It is important to turn off the 'keep warm' mode, which many electric cookers automatically switch on after the cooking time is completed.

Stovetop cookers can be quickly released by one of two methods. Some have a pressure control valve which can be turned to the steam release setting. The other option is to place the rim of the cooker under tepid running water. Avoid covering the whole of the lid, as water may be sucked into the cooker.

It is important to follow the manufacturer's advice on how to release the pressure quickly, as this varies between models. Whichever method you are using, take care as the steam is extremely hot and will burn. Always point the valve away from you.
Slow or Natural Release This method lets the pressure and steam drop slowly and naturally. Most stovetop cookers refer to 'slow release', while electric models use 'natural release'. The lid may remain locked in place for up to 10–15 minutes, so the food carries on cooking. After a few minutes of slow/natural release, some recipes suggest releasing the remaining pressure using the quick release method, to release any remaining pressure. It is more likely that the food will still be under pressure in electric pressure cookers, as these take longer to release pressure naturally.

Slow or natural release is recommended for some foods and recipes, in particular foods with a large volume of liquid, or with a high starch content such as pulses, or milk-based recipes. Sponge puddings are more likely to drop if the pressure is released quickly.

Choosing a Pressure Cooker

It is worth taking your time when choosing a pressure cooker, and to select one that is right for your needs. There are a variety of sizes and shapes, different methods of sealing, different types of metals for stovetops, and of course the choice between electric and stovetop. The pressure can also vary between different models.

ELECTRIC VERSUS STOVETOP
Stovetop cookers will cook at higher pressure than most electric cookers, so if speed is all-important, then a stovetop cooker is probably right for you.

Most electric pressure cookers have one pressure level, while stovetop models vary between one to three different pressures. There is no one standardized pressure across the manufacturers, but several are similar. Electric cookers tend to have a shorter life than stovetop models. A top-of-the-range stainless steel stovetop pressure cooker can last almost a lifetime if it is looked after and the gasket is renewed periodically. However, if you like to keep up with the latest modifications, then longevity is less important.

An electric pressure cooker does most of the work for you, and for this reason, some cooks believe it is easier to use an electric pressure cooker. Once you have set the programme, you don't need to monitor it to check if the pressure is alright, although as with all electrical equipment, keeping an eye on it from a safety point of view is a good idea.

Electric pressure cookers can be placed anywhere where there is an power socket, while a stovetop model is always on the hob. If workspace is short, a hob model may be preferable.

When releasing the pressure slowly, the electric pressure cooker will take more time because the heat is contained within the body of the pressure cooker, for longer. The double wall construction insulates against heat loss and the pot cannot be removed from the heat source until the cooker has depressurized.

An electric cooker takes slightly longer to reach pressure, but is more efficient once pressure is reached due to the insulated construction.

Whether you opt for electric or stovetop, never leaves a pressure cooker unattended in the kitchen.

MICROWAVE PRESSURE COOKERS
A new addition to pressure cooking is the microwaveable pressure cooker. This combines the attributes of both cooking methods. The microwave oven becomes the energy source for the pressure cooker. It is a perfect alternative to a large pressure cooker if space is tight, or where a microwave oven is the only cooking equipment available, such as in a caravan or on a boat.

Like a conventional stovetop or electric model, the liquid will boil and produce steam and therefore develop pressure. The microwave pressure cooker becomes a sealed container that will not allow air or liquid to escape when properly sealed.

During cooking, the lid is kept firmly in place by the pressurized steam, and while under pressure the lid cannot be removed, so behaves in an identical fashion to electric and stovetop pressure cookers. By developing pressure, it will cook the food more quickly than by microwave alone, as well as keeping it moist. Microwave pressure cookers develop a pressure of around 4psi/28kPa.

Above: The Instant Pot is one type of electric pressure cooker, of which there are several on the market.

Above: This type of stovetop pressure cooker has a twist-lock handle that can be opened with one hand.

Above: Microwave pressure cookers are sold by a couple of companies, and different colours are available.

BENEFITS OF PRESSURE COOKING

• Foods cook faster in a pressure cooker than when using other methods, apart from a small quantity in the microwave oven. As the quantity of food increases in the microwave oven, so does the time. In a pressure cooker, the cooking times are determined by the size of an individual piece of food, not the overall quantity – 225g/8oz new potatoes will take the same time as 900g/2lb.

• Casseroles and stews can be made in well under an hour, making them quick and nutritious meals to prepare mid-week after work.

• Less liquid is required since there is little evaporation, so it takes less time to heat up. Along with the shorter cooking time, this means that less energy is required.

• Cooking smells are reduced as a minimal amount of steam is released, thus reducing the odours.

• Food does not need to be immersed in water, just sufficient to produce steam, so there is less leaching of vitamins and minerals relative to other forms of cooking.

• Several foods can be cooked together as there is no flavour contamination. You can add trivets and steamer baskets for more layering of foods.

• Pressure cookers produce recipes with dried ingredients such as whole grains and pulses, which can be cooked in a fraction of the time of conventional methods.

• A pressure cooker is an effective method when sterilizing glass jars for preserves and chutneys.

• In countries where high altitude affects cooking times, due to the lower pressure and therefore lower boiling point, the pressure cooker can considerably speed up the cooking times.

Above: Foods cook faster in a pressure cooker – casseroles can be made in less than an hour.

Above: Less liquid is needed than conventional cooking methods, because there is little evaporation.

Above: Vegetables can be cooked on a rack or trivet, or as shown with these artichokes, in a steamer basket.

Above: Several foods can be cooked together, such as these potatoes separated from a turkey mince.

Above: Pulses such as borlotti beans can be cooked much more quickly than when using ordinary cooking methods.

Above: A pressure cooker can be used for making preserves such as marmalade, jams and chutneys.

Stovetop Pressure Cookers

Stovetop cookers offer a range of options, including different capacities, heights and methods of operation, to suit the personal requirements of the cook.

SIZE

The size varies from 4 litres/7 pints/8½ US pints up to 7.5 litres/13 pints/16 US pints. If you are cooking for one or two, then a 4 or 4.5 litre will be sufficient. A 5.5 litre/9½ pint/11½ US pint or 6 litre/10½ pint/12½ US pint model is most suited to families and offers more flexibility, while the larger sizes are perfect for bigger families. Some of the larger models have a higher dome for bottling. Large pressure cookers tend to be tall as a necessary design feature for pressurizing. However, you can still cook smaller quantities in a large cooker.

DESIGN

There is a choice between aluminium and stainless steel. Aluminium is a good choice where cost is important. It is lightweight and conducts heat well.

With heavy use, it may stain and pit, although it is completely useable. Aluminium cookers are more prone to becoming warped over time. Stainless steel is considered the most durable and long-lasting, but is slightly heavier. If you are cooking on an induction hob, you will need a stainless steel pressure cooker. Stainless steel is often preferred for its looks, but it is not a good conductor of heat, so these pans are made with a layered base to eliminate this problem.

There are two main types of handles and lids on stovetop pressure cookers:

Twist-on lids with long handles These vary between models and are part of the locking system. There is a long handle on the lid and another on the pan base, which are offset when the lid is placed on the base and then aligned to seal. There are slots in the lid

Below: Three sizes of pressure cookers from those that serve one or two to a family-sized model. The pressure cooker at the back is an example of a high-dome cooker with a weighted pressure regulator.

Right: Three medium-sized pressure cookers, showing different controls and handles. All work in a similar manner. The version at the rear has a central fold-down locking handle, while the other two are locked by twisting the lid to align the handles.

that engage with flanges on the body. There are also markers on the lid and base to align the lid and body before twisting the lid. Many designs have a pull-back release button or lever in the lid, which needs to be engaged to enable you to open the cooker, so it cannot accidentally be opened. This also clicks on closing. Others have a safety bolt and spring built into the handle.

Side-handled cookers with jaws These have two side handles and a lid that locks on with jaws. The jaws are operated by twisting a central handle or folding the handle down. The jaws on the lid clamp down on the rim of the base and seal the cooker.

PRESSURE

Most stovetop pressure cookers are equipped with two pressure levels of around 11.5–12psi/80–83kPa and 7–8psi/48–55kPa. A few have a higher level of 14psi/100kPa and 8.7psi/60kPa. There is also at least one with a lower pressure of 5.8psi/40kPa. Traditional high-dome style pressure cookers also exist with 5lb/10lb and 15lb weights. Where stovetop cookers only come with one pressure, they are around 11.6psi/80kPa.

Above: This twist-on lid has long handles that seal the stovetop pressure cooker when they are aligned.

Above: This side-handled stovetop pressure cooker has a twisting central handle that operates the jaws.

Above: This side-handled cooker has a folding central handle to operate the jaws and lock the pressure cooker.

Above: A weighted pressure regulator on top of the cooker's lid indicates pressures of 5lb, 10lb and 15lb.

Above: A spring valve pressure regulator has a colour-coded knob that is visible when under pressure.

Above: This pressure regulator with a twist knob displays the symbols for different pressures and steam release.

All stovetop pressure cookers have a means of indicating and controlling the cooking pressure:

Weighted pressure regulator The classic form is a set of weights on the top of the lid, consisting of three parts that screw together to give the different pressures.

OPTIONAL EXTRAS

Before purchasing a stovetop model, first decide the size and which metal you prefer, then how many pressure levels you would like. Then look at the cookers that fit these criteria, and the optional extras.

Fold-down handles These make for easier storage; they can be useful when space is at a premium.

Integrated timer Most stovetop models do not include a timer, but it is possible to purchase one with a timer slotted into the handle. You can also remove it and pop it in your pocket, if you wish.

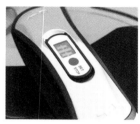

Above: Fold-down handles on the side of your pressure cooker keep it compact for storage.

Above: This integrated timer is slotted into the pressure cooker's handle, and is removable.

Spring valve regulator A short pressure indicator or pop-up valve will extend upwards from the cooker. Once this pops up, the heat is turned down to maintain the pressure required. This may be a central knob colour-coded for different pressures, and acts as the pressure indicator and regulator. It can also be pressed down to release steam quickly.

Twist knob regulator Others have a twist knob to set the cooker for the required pressure or to release steam and pressure quickly. These have separate visual indicator pins to show that the cooker is under pressure.

All methods are extremely safe, and the kind you choose is just down to personal preference.

USING AN INDUCTION HOB

You need to check whether the manufacturer states that their stovetop pressure cooker is suitable for use with an induction hob. Most aluminium pressure cookers are not compatible. You need to cook food at a higher temperature to maintain pressure on an induction hob, so this may cause a greater loss of liquid as steam. You may need to add slightly more liquid to the ingredients, or to the base of the cooker when steaming. Try the recipes as given, and keep an eye out. Possible problems are that it may be difficult to produce sufficient steam to keep the pressure cooker under pressure. If so, you may need to slightly increase the heat, however this may result in a sauce over-thickening and it may catch on the base of the cooker. Another possible problem is that the liquid required to steam when pressure cooking may become insufficient.

Electric Pressure Cookers

Providing a consistent heat source, electric pressure cookers don't take up space on the stovetop, and they are programmed with a timer to cook to exact times.

SIZE

Most electric pressure cookers have a 6 litre/ 10½ pint/12½ US pint capacity, although there are a few that contain 5 litres/9 pints/10½ US pints. The 6 litre models tend to be 1000 watts or even 1100 watts, but the 5 litre models are lower power so will take longer to cook.

DESIGN

All are quite similar to look at, the main difference being the control panel. The outside is brushed stainless steel and the housing is insulated to minimize heat loss. There is a heating plate and sensor on the inside of the base. A condensation collector is installed on the outer edge.

Inner pots These are usually made of aluminium with a non-stick coating. Care must be taken not to scratch this. Some are made from stainless steel.

Lids All the lids work in a similar fashion by rotating around 30 degrees to open or close and lock. These can be operated with one hand. Inside the lid is the

gasket. Some are attached to a metal disc, while others are held by a rack. There is also an anti-block shield in most cookers to protect the exhaust valve, and the float valve as well on some models.

On the top of the lid is the exhaust or steam release valve, which can be set to either seal or vent. Some models are much easier to read than others. The float valve, which pushes up as a visual indicator to show the pressure cooker is under pressure, is located in the lid.

Below: Examples of two electric pressure cookers: the left-hand version opens with a large handle, while the model on the right opens with a central handle.

Above: Stainless steel and non-stick inner pots for electric pressure cookers are easy to clean after use.

Above: Electric pressure cookers always have a steam release valve – this particular one is very clear to read.

Above: This shows the heating plate and sensor located on the inside of the base of an electric pressure cooker.

PRESSURE

Most electric cookers operate at one pressure only. This can be as low as 6psi, but on average they are around 8psi. It is possible to find a model with two pressure levels, one around 10.2–11.6 and the lower at 5.8–7.2, although the lower level is only on one programme.

CONTROL PANEL AND FUNCTIONS

This is the main difference between the electric pressure cooker models, apart from the pressures at which they operate. All have programmable menus with pre-set functions for soups, meat/stew and rice. Most also include functions for poultry and beans or pulses. Some include fish, vegetables, pasta, multigrain and desserts. These have pre-set times which the manufacturer suggests are ideal times, with adjustments up or down for longer or shorter cooking times that you may wish to set. Some of these pre-set functions are more useful than others.

Another option on some models includes a setting for meat with a rare/less, medium/normal or well/more options for large joints of meat. After selecting the

Below: The simple control panel of this electric model shows that it has fewer functions than some other models.

Below: This model has many functions, including sauté, with three temperature options and the manual function.

Above: The sauté function is useful for browning vegetables such as these shallots in butter and sunflower oil.

Above: You can cook whole fish in foil parcels using the fish setting on an electric pressure cooker.

Above: Rice pudding can be made in an electric pressure cooker using the manual or soup setting.

meat function, these extra functions can be engaged to alter the cooking time for a joint and the level of how well-done you would like your meat.

Sauté function More expensive models offer a specific function for sautéing meat and vegetables prior to pressure cooking. This produces a higher heat intended for browning. Some models offer the option of three temperatures as well. These allow for gentle simmering to reduce or thicken a sauce, a regular setting for sautéing vegetables, and a 'more' setting for speedier searing of meat and vegetables.

Below: If your electric cooker has a sauté function, use this for browning meat and vegetables prior to pressure cooking.

Manual function This is not commonly found on electric pressure cookers, but if you do find an electric model with a manual function, it can be useful because it allows the versatility of manually setting the cooking time from 1–120 minutes.

Delay timer This can be used when initial searing and sautéing is not required. The function selected can be delayed to suit your timetable.

If you have yet to select an electric pressure cooker, jot down a list of the main features that appeal and are important to you. Eliminate any models that do not have these, and this will narrow your choice. As a general rule, usually the more functions a model has, the more expensive it will be.

SPECIAL FEATURES

Extra functions can be found on some machines – often the more expensive ones – and include a number of non-pressurized cooking options.

Cake/bake Can be used to bake a single layer cake or a small loaf of bread.

Porridge A dedicated function that allows you to cook porridge. It may or may not be a pressurized programme.

Slow cook Enables you to use your pressure cooker as you would an electric slow cooker.

Yogurt Allows you to make yogurt from milk by providing optimum temperatures for this process.

Accessories and Useful Equipment

Many pressure cookers come with a trivet or steamer basket, although with the pricepoint often taking precedence, some manufacturers have chosen to make these optional extras. There are also a few pieces of kitchen equipment that will prove useful when cooking with a pressure cooker, several of which you may already have.

TRIVETS AND STEAM RACKS

The best form of trivet is a flat perforated disc with a rim on one side. This can be placed rim side down in the cooker, so food can be cooked clear of the cooking liquid, and different flavours will not mingle. It can be used as a shelf to divide different types of foods from one another, and it is also used as a stand on which to place bowls, basins and cake tins.

Some electric pressure cookers include a steam rack instead of a trivet, to be used in the same way. Another option is a trivet-like perforated shelf, which is located two-thirds of the way up the inner cooking pot.

STEAMER BASKETS AND DIVIDERS

These are accessories with some stovetop pressure cookers and are perforated baskets with one or two handles, and optional extras from others. You may also get an extra U- or V-shaped wire spacer to fix to the underside to raise the basket higher in the pressure cooker. Some manufacturers call this a trivet, but it does not work in the same way as the trivet mentioned above. Some steamer baskets have optional metal dividers to make separate compartments within the steamer basket.

ELECTRIC PRESSURE COOKER EXTRAS

Some electric pressure cookers include measuring cups and and rice spoons or paddles for stirring rice. A useful extra is a glass lid for covering the cooking pot when re-heating food, or as an option when pre-steaming.

TINS AND COOLING RACKS

Spring-form cake tins or pans are useful for dishes such as cheesecakes, to make for easy removal, while fixed-based cake tins are good for upside-down sponges and the chocolate torte on pages 226–7. An 18cm/7in tin is probably the largest size to fit in the cooker and allow space to insert and remove the tin, but check your model for size.

Loaf tins or pans with a capacity for 450g/1lb, or 900ml/1½ pint/3¾ cup loaf tins without a large rim, should fit in the pressure cooker and are necessary for meat loaves, nut loaves and pâtés.

An 18cm/7in round cooling rack is the perfect alternative to a steamer rack or trivet, if your pressure cooker does not have one. Some alternative suggestions on how you can improvise if you don't have a trivet include a metal lid from a large jar or a stainless steel pastry cutter. An upturned saucer or small plate can also work.

Below: A trivet can be included in some stovetop pressure cookers.

Below: Steam racks vary between models of electric pressure cooker.

Below: A basket with metal dividers is sold with some stovetop cookers.

Foil can be used to make a strip which acts as a handle to support a cake tin, pan or dish that needs to be lowered into the pressure cooker. Make sure that your piece of foil is long enough to go underneath and up both sides of the container.

DISHES, BOWLS AND BASINS

An 18cm/7in round ceramic dish with an approximate capacity of 900ml/1½ pints/3¾ cups is good for cooking desserts or potato dishes such as Dauphinois potatoes on pages 188–9.

Individual soufflé dishes are extremely versatile for cooking savoury dishes such as egg cocottes and desserts such as crème brûlée and crème caramel. Large soufflé dishes are perfect for pâté.

A metal bowl that will fit inside your pressure cooker is an option for containing rice and water inside the pressure cooker. You can use the steamer basket lined with foil if you wish.

A selection of heatproof glass and china pudding basins and bowls are ideal for both sweet and savoury puddings. The largest needs to fit the internal diameter of your pressure cooker, leaving just enough space to allow for placing the basin in and taking it out of the cooker. These need to be able to withstand temperatures up to 130°C/262°F.

HEAT DIFFUSER

This is a metal disc which can be used on a gas or electric hob to distribute heat evenly, for easy simmering. It will protect the pan from scorching or burning, and is ideal when cooking rice or risotto where liquid is absorbed, if this is a problem with your stove.

FOIL AND BAKING PARCHMENT

These are ideal materials for wrapping foods or for covering basins. They must be fitted securely on the basin and tied with string, so they do not come off during cooking and block the safety vents. Foil can also be used to make a strip which acts as a handle to support a cake tin or a dish, to lower and lift the item in and out of the pressure cooker.

TIMER

If you have a stovetop pressure cooker, you will probably need a separate kitchen timer since most do not have one built in. Even with electric pressure cookers, you sometimes need to cook for less or more time than you can set on the cooker. This will help you keep track. Timing is very important, as food can easily overcook.

Below: Cake tins or pans, a loaf tin and a cooling rack are needed for sponges, tortes and cheesecakes.

Below: Ceramic dishes, soufflé dishes, a metal bowl and heatproof pudding basins will all prove useful.

Below: A heat diffuser is for use on a gas or electric hob; it will protect the pan from scorching or burning.

How to Assemble and Use your Pressure Cooker

If you have recently purchased a pressure cooker or have not used yours for some time, read your manufacturer's instruction book carefully in conjunction with the general information below.

ASSEMBLING THE COOKER

The pressure cooker consists of a cooking pot, a lid, a sealing gasket or ring and valves. Depending on your model, these are assembled in slightly different ways, but all achieve the same end result.

Gasket In order for your pressure cooker to work, it is essential that the gasket or seal is fitted properly. This ring creates the seal between the body and the lid. The gasket must be inspected before use to make sure it has not cracked or stiffened, and cleaned after each use. Some gaskets need to be placed under flanges in the lid and others can only be fitted in one direction, so check your instruction manual on how best to fit this.

Pressure valve All pressure cookers have a pressure valve used to seal the pressure cooker. It may be called a 'pressure limit valve' or 'pressure regulator valve'. Along with other valves, this seals when the pressure cooker reaches pressure. Without it, the cooker cannot function. Most valves are detachable, so do not lose it. The pressure valve also acts as a steam release valve after cooking, and can be a pressure-setting regulator if your pressure cooker has two settings.

Condenser collector Electric pressure cookers have a condensation collector which collects moisture from the lid, and should be fitted before using the pressure cooker and cleaned after each use.

HOW TO USE

• Food is placed in the pot or body of the pressure cooker. You may wish to sauté or brown vegetables or meat first, in a little oil, as no browning occurs in the closed pressure cooker.

• Follow a recipe in your handbook, or here, on how best to prepare ingredients before bringing to pressure.

• All recipes in the pressure cooker need liquid to produce steam and raise the temperature. The longer the cooking time, the more liquid is needed. Unless your manufacturer states otherwise, it should not be less than 250–300ml/8–10fl oz/1–1¼ cups.

• The liquid can be water, stock, wine, milk, beer, soup, juice from tinned tomatoes, or any combination of these.

• Melted fat or oil should not be used as the cooking liquid, but a small amount of these can be used for browning ingredients in the initial cooking stages.

• The trivet, steam basket or separator is used occasionally, and should be specified in the recipe when required. It is mainly used for steaming.

• Before placing the lid on the pressure cooker, make sure the sealing ring or gasket is correctly fitted.

• Once all the ingredients are added, the lid is placed on top and closed. Most stovetop cookers with long handles have an arrow on the base and lid to align the lid. The top is then turned to align the handles. Some have a central handle that closes down or swivels, and jaws lock the lid on to the base of the cooker. Electric pressure cookers have twist lids with open and closed indicators. Most lids will click when properly closed.

Below: A gasket fitted to a stovetop pressure cooker creates a good seal.

Below: For an electric cooker, a gasket may be fitted under a flange in the lid.

Below: Food is placed in the pot of an electric pressure cooker.

Above: All pressure cooker recipes need liquid to produce steam and increase the internal temperature.

Above: Place a steam rack in an electric pressure cooker to raise a cake tin or bowl off the base.

Above: Once all the ingredients have been added, fit the lid. This shows a stovetop cooker with a jaw lock system.

• After the lid is fitted, the pressure cooker can be brought to pressure. If your pressure cooker has more than one pressure level, select the desired one. This is usually done over a high heat. Make sure the electric ring is no bigger than the pressure cooker and that the gas flames do not lick up the sides of the pan. Steam will build up and create pressure and a visual indicator will appear. At this point, the heat can be turned down and the timing commenced. An electric pressure cooker automatically carries out this operation after you have programmed it to cook.

• On completion of cooking, the heat source can be switched off. Pressure cookers on electric hobs need to be moved away from the heat source. Electric pressure cookers can be switched off, otherwise the 'keep warm' mode will operate.

• Reduce the pressure, whether by the quick-release method recommended by your manufacturer or by natural or slow release over time.

• Do not attempt to open the cooker until all the steam is released. The visual indicator must drop naturally before you remove the lid.

SAFETY FEATURES

Whether stovetop or electric, all pressure cookers are fitted with several devices, each designed to release pressure if the pressure cooker overheats, a vent becomes blocked or the pressure cooker is allowed to boil dry.

The pressure limiter or regulator will release steam if the pressure exceeds the maximum safe working pressure. Pressure cookers will not reach pressure if the lid is not fitted correctly; the pressure indicator cannot rise, so pressure cannot build.

Pressure cookers always have an open safety device and the lid cannot be opened while under pressure. Never try to force the lid open. You must wait for the pressure valve to drop.

Stovetop pressure cookers Excess pressure safety devices are fitted on to these; a portion of the gasket or seal is pushed out and therefore allows the pressure to be released between the lid and the body through small holes. In addition, stovetop pressure cookers have a safety valve which is released to allow steam to escape.

Electric pressure cookers These include a temperature limiter which automatically cuts off when the unit reaches its maximum temperature limit. This also happens if the machine is accidentally switched on with the inner pot empty or without an inner pot.

In addition to the pressure limiter releasing steam, a safety pressure regulator will allow pressure to be released around the lid. If for any reason the limiter should fail and maximum pressure is reached, this feature will still work.

If you are buying a new electric pressure cooker, make sure features such as these are included.

Getting the Best from your Pressure Cooker

All pressure cookers work on the same principle, but each manufacturer will have instructions specific to their model, so always read your instruction manual before you start cooking. If you wish to adapt your favourite recipe to cook it in the pressure cooker, look for a similar recipe in your handbook or in this book. Make sure you use the correct amount of liquid, and do not overfill your pressure cooker. If your pressure cooker does not have an integrated timer, use a separate kitchen timer to ensure accurate cooking times.

TIMINGS

• As pressure cookers cook quickly, it is important to follow timings given in the charts and recipes and then make notes if you wish to make minor adjustments for next time.
• Use a timer, as 1 minute can make all the difference between perfectly cooked and overcooked. Electric cookers have programmable timers.
• The recipes in this book have been tested at the High setting of 11.5–12psi with 7–8psi in brackets, or at the Low setting of 7–8psi with 5.8psi in brackets. If your pressure cooker operates at different pressure to these, look for a similar recipe in your manufacturer's recipe book as a guide. Also use the ingredient with the longest cooking time as a guide.
• If you have a pressure cooker which operates at 15psi, 10psi and 5psi, you can either reduce the time given for 11.5–12psi by about a quarter, or select a time between the two given and cook at 10psi.
• Named programme functions for timing have been suggested in the recipes for the electric pressure cooker. Often more than one is given to accommodate different models. You may choose whichever function gives the time required on your cooker, checking first that it is at the suggested pressure.

Left: Exact timings are important due to the speed of pressure cooking, so make sure you have a timer that shows both seconds and minutes.

PRESSURE CONVERSIONS

Depending on the country of manufacture, the way in which the pressure levels are described can vary. The pressure setting is usually described as 'psi' or 'pounds per square inch'. Occasionally you will just see 'lbs' – this is the same as 'pounds per square inch'. Some European cookers refer to 'kPa' or 'kilopascal'. Also the term 'bar' is used. This refers to atmospheric pressure given in millibars, where standard sea level pressure is defined as 1000mbar or 100kPa or 1 bar. It is important to establish what pressure setting your pressure cooker cooks at, so that you can follow the correct timings.

FILL LEVELS

It is important to follow your manufacturer's guidelines for correct minimum and maximum fill levels for your pressure cooker. Here are some general guidelines.
• All pressure cookers have a minimum and maximum fill level. As a guide, for most pressure cookers the minimum fill is 250–300ml/ 8–10fl oz/1–1¼ cups for the first 15 minutes, then a further 150ml/5fl oz/⅔ cup for each extra 15 minutes.
• For steam cooking, use at least 750ml/ 1¼ pints/3 cups water.
• When cooking pulses, you need to add 500ml/17fl oz/generous 2 cups water for every 225g/8oz/1¼ cups pulses.
• Rice, pasta and cereals also need sufficient water to rehydrate them. Follow the instructions in the cooking charts that follow in this chapter and in your instruction manual.
• Foods that foam or contain starch need a larger headspace in the pressure cooker.

Type of food	Max. fill level, including liquid
Cereals, pulses and lentils	⅓ full
Rice and pasta	½ full
Stewed fruit	½ full
Liquid foods – soups/stews	½ full
Solid foods/joints/ one pot meals	⅔ full

Below: When cooking large joints of meat such as this beef pot roast, timing is calculated by weight.

Below: Strong herbs such as rosemary should be added at the beginning of cooking. Add tender herbs at the end.

Below: Rice can foam up and block the pressure cooker vents. It can help to drizzle oil over the cooking liquid.

ADAPTING RECIPES FOR THE PRESSURE COOKER

If you wish to adapt a recipe, select a similar recipe in your handbook or in this book. Use ingredients of a similar size so that they cook in the same length of time. Note that if vegetables are cut into different sizes, they will take different amounts of time to cook. Check the time for the main ingredient or the ingredient that will take the longest to cook in the pressure cooker, and use this as a guide for the cooking time. The quantity of food does not alter the timing; this is determined by the size of an individual ingredient. For example, 225g/8oz new potatoes takes the same time as 900g/2lb. It is only when cooking large joints of meat that the timing is by weight, and this is also true for steamed puddings.

Stronger herbs, such as thyme and rosemary, can be added at the beginning of cooking, while tender herbs need to be added at the end. Most manufacturers suggest adding salt as the end of cooking. The pressure cooker can intensify flavours, so only add a little salt or salty stock at the start, and adjust it once cooked.

As little or none of the liquid will evaporate, if you are adapting a recipe to cook in the pressure cooker you should reduce the liquid slightly, making sure you are within the minimum limits.

Foods such as pulses and rice can foam up and may block the vents. A drizzle of oil over the cooking liquid before bringing to pressure can help. Check your instruction manual on how best to cook these foods, and whether your manufacturer recommends it.

THICKENING AND BROWNING

Thickening As a result of less evaporation in the sealed pressure cooker, some gravies, sauces and liquids for stews, casseroles and soups may need thickening after cooking. They may be thickened slightly before cooking, but a thick sauce will result in insufficient steam and proper functioning of the pressure cooker. In many cases, the sauce can be thickened slightly by reducing the liquid in the uncovered pressure cooker at the end of cooking. Other options include thickening with a combination of cornflour (cornstarch) and water, or a beurre manié – a mixture of butter and plain (all-purpose) flour gradually added and stirred in at the end of cooking. This method is used for French Onion Soup (page 54) and Beef Bourguignon (page 92).

Browning Many foods – vegetables and meats in particular – benefit from browning first to develop flavour. You may do this in the open cooker before placing under pressure. Several electric pressure cookers have a separate sauté/brown control for this purpose. If not, you can just start one of the programmes, then reset for the correct pressure cooking time as you close the lid. Heat the fat or oil slightly before adding the ingredients, as you would in a pan or frying pan. After adding the liquid to the pressure cooker, scrape the base to ensure that no sediment remains attached.

Above: A fruit sponge is well suited to cooking in the pressure cooker when placed on a trivet or rack.

TECHNIQUES SUITED TO PRESSURE COOKING

Recipes that would conventionally be poached, braised, stewed, steamed or boiled are best for cooking in a pressure cooker. Poaching is perfect for delicate foods such as fish and young vegetables. Braising and stewing is ideal for cooking tough cuts of meat, as the pressure tenderizes the meat more quickly. Steaming in a pressure cooker is achieved by adding a rack or basket above the water level to produce tender–crisp vegetables. It is also used to cook steamed puddings, first steaming the pudding before finishing it under pressure. Boiling is perfect for dried beans and other pulses, which only need minimal soaking, and cook in a fraction of the time.

TROUBLESHOOTING

Some of the common problems are listed here, with suggested solutions.

- **It is difficult to close the lid** Check the sealing ring/gasket and re-fit. Try lubricating the rubber gaskets with a little oil.
- **It is difficult to open the lid** Check that the pressure indicator is down. There may still be pressure in the cooker. If necessary, depressurize.
- **The visual pressure indicator or float valve does not rise** The indicator may be sticking or dirty. The pressure regulator/limiter valve may be incorrectly positioned. The valve silicone ring on an electric pressure cooker may be worn out.
- **The visual pressure indicator or float valve does not rise and no steam emits from the pressure regulator/valve** This is normal until the contents boil. Check that the quantity of liquid in the pressure cooker is sufficient to produce steam. Check that the lid is properly closed. Check that the gasket/sealing ring is not damaged.

- **The visual pressure indicator falls after rising** This is possible with stovetop models if the heat is reduced too quickly.
- **Steam leaks from the side of the lid** Check that the sealing ring/gasket is installed. Check that the sealing ring is not caught between the lid and the body. Check that there is no food debris in the groove of the lid or attached to the ring. Check that the lid is properly closed.
- **Steam emits from the steam release exhaust valve on an electric pressure cooker** Check that the steam release handle is in the sealing position. The pressure control may have failed.
- **Electric pressure cooker flashes lid** The lid is not closed properly or is attached when sautéing.
- **Electric pressure cooker display remains blank** The power may not be switched on. The power cord may not be properly connected. Electric pressure cookers also display fault codes; you need to refer to your individual handbook for more information.

Care and Cleaning

Always look after your pressure cooker to prolong its life. It is important to clean it after use, and follow any specific manufacturer's instructions to keep it in good working order.

STOVETOP PRESSURE COOKERS
• After use, wash all parts in soapy water, rinse and dry immediately. Avoid leaving foodstuffs in the base of the cooker for long periods of time.
• The interior of aluminium cookers may become discoloured during use. This is normal and does not affect operation. To minimize discoloration when steaming, add a little lemon juice to the water.
• Never use bleach or caustic materials to clean a pressure cooker.
• Should the cooker ever boil dry, which hopefully will never happen, check that the base has not distorted. If it has, you can no longer use it. You can soak the inside of the pot overnight with hot soapy water, but do not leave it immersed in water.
• Check your instruction manual, as some parts may not be suitable for immersion in water.
• Always remove the gasket from the lid after cooking. Wash with a sponge and washing-up (dishwashing) liquid and allow to dry. Inspect periodically to make sure it has not stiffened, cracked or dried out. Most manufacturers recommend replacing the gasket every 12 months or so. Check what your instruction manual recommends.
• The lid seal and flanges should be cleaned carefully to make sure no food debris is present, as this could prevent the pan from sealing correctly when in use.
• If the lid is difficult to close and the pressure cooker is fitted with a rubber gasket, apply a light film of vegetable oil to the gasket.
• When storing, invert the lid and place it on top of the pan so that the gasket does not become deformed and remains well ventilated.
• Some cooker bases may be washed in the dishwasher, but check to see what your manufacturer recommends.

ELECTRIC PRESSURE COOKERS
• Ensure the cooker has cooled down and is unplugged from the power supply before you begin cleaning it.
• The main unit must not be immersed in water but should be wiped with a soft, damp cloth and dried thoroughly. Wipe the inner housing rim and slot dry.

• The inner pot and any accessories such as racks can be washed in warm, soapy water and then dried thoroughly. Never re-use while still damp.
• The lid can be cleaned with water, as can the pressure limiter valve and anti-block shield, if fitted.
• The lid has a silicone seal ring that is detachable; this should be cleaned after each use and checked to make sure it is not damaged in any way.
• Electric pressure cookers cannot be cleaned in a dishwasher. Some inner pots are dishwasher-safe – check your handbook.
• Do not use scouring pads, wire (steel) wool or strong solvents when cleaning.
• The dew pot or condensation collector should be emptied, cleaned and dried after each use.
• Some electric pressure cookers have a perforated sealing plate to which the sealing ring is attached. This can be removed and rinsed in warm, soapy water. The sealing ring can be detached for cleaning.

Right: Always wash the pressure cooker basket immediately after use and dry thoroughly, to keep it in good condition.

Using a Microwave Pressure Cooker

The microwave pressure cooker is a useful addition to your microwave oven. It will enable you to cook food such as casseroles faster, as it will reach a higher temperature than if cooked in the microwave in a conventional microwave container. It will also make and keep the food succulent.

HOW TO USE

• You can cook several foods together in the one container, if you wish, as you would in your pressure cooker.

• The microwave pressure cooker needs a certain size of microwave oven to cook in safely. Check with your manufacturer's instruction book, but a guide is at least 23 litres/5 gallons/6 US gallons or more internal capacity, with an internal cavity measurement of 16cm/6¼in above the tray and 30cm/12in width and depth.

• It can only be used with the microwave setting, not with any browning features that your microwave oven may have.

• Foods can be browned conventionally on the hob before adding to the microwave pressure cooker, but should not be cooked in oil in the microwave pressure cooker.

• The microwave pressure cooker may get warm from the hot food within, so handle with oven gloves after cooking in the microwave oven.

• As with a traditional pressure cooker, the microwave pressure cooker must contain an adequate amount of water to produce steam. Follow the instructions in your manufacturer's handbook for quantities.

Above: Microwave pressure cookers allow you to prepare food quickly while keeping it succulent. They come in a variety of colours to suit the style of your kitchen.

• The cooking times will vary in the microwave pressure cooker. Unlike the traditional pressure cooker, where most foods (apart from large meats and puddings) cook in a certain time, the microwave pressure cooker is influenced by the amount of food, as with a microwave oven, i.e. one chicken breast will cook more quickly than four.

• As with traditional pressure cookers, ingredients that tend to splutter or foam may clog the safety devices. These include foods such as cereals, pearl barley, pasta, cranberries and split peas. Check your manufacturer's advice regarding cooking these foods. Whole apples and potatoes should be pricked, as for microwave cooking, to protect them from bursting open as the pressure of the steam within builds up.

• The microwave pressure cooker has several safety devices to ensure the cooker will not build up pressure unless properly locked, and if it goes above the normal pressure, excess steam will escape. If clogged, the safety device is pushed out to diffuse the steam and pressure quickly.

Left: When pressure cooking in a microwave, the oven needs a minimum capacity of 23 litres/5 gallons/6 US gallons.

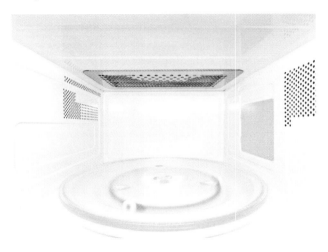

The three recipes that follow were tested using a 900 watt microwave oven. Add around 20 per cent more time for a 700 watt oven and subtract around 20 per cent for a 1000 watt oven. These recipe timings are just guidelines, and you may need to adjust them to suit your microwave pressure cooker, microwave oven and personal taste.

MICROWAVE LEEK AND POTATO SOUP

This is a quick and easy warming winter soup, perfect for your microwave pressure cooker.

Serves 4

1 small onion, chopped
225g/8oz potato, cubed
approximately 2 leeks, around 300g/11oz, sliced
800ml/27fl oz/3¼ cups hot vegetable stock
60ml/4 tbsp double (heavy) cream, plus extra
   to garnish (optional)
chopped fresh chives, to garnish
salt and ground black pepper

1 Place the onion, potato and leeks in the microwave pressure cooker. Add the stock until it reaches the half-fill level. If necessary, add the remaining stock at the end of cooking time.

2 Place the lid on the top and seal. Put in the microwave oven and cook on Full power for 15 minutes.

3 Carefully remove the cooker from the microwave oven and place on a heatproof surface. Once the visual pressure indicator has dropped, open the lid and cool slightly.

4 Transfer the soup to a food processor or blender and process to a purée. Add the remaining stock, if any. Stir in the cream and season to taste.

5 If necessary, reheat in the microwave oven in the open pressure cooker for 1–2 minutes. Serve in warmed bowls, sprinkled with chives and extra cream, if you like.

MICROWAVE SWEET AND SOUR PORK

A complete main course can made in under
30 minutes using your microwave pressure cooker.

Serves 4

75ml/3fl oz/⅓ cup grapefruit juice
30ml/2 tbsp soy sauce
50ml/3fl oz/¼ cup cider vinegar
225g can pineapple pieces or slices in syrup, drained,
  syrup reserved
375g/12oz pork tenderloin, cut into thin strips
5cm/2in piece fresh root ginger
½ red (bell) pepper, cut into strips
½ green (bell) pepper, cut into strips
1 small carrot, cut into thin sticks
1 garlic clove, thinly sliced
1 fresh red chilli, halved, seeded and chopped
15ml/1 tbsp cornflour (cornstarch)
shredded spring onions (scallions), to garnish
cooked long grain rice, to serve
salt and ground black pepper

1 Place the grapefruit juice, soy sauce, cider vinegar and drained pineapple syrup in a jug or pitcher, and make up to 250ml/8fl oz/1 cup with water.

2 Put the pork, ginger, peppers, carrot, garlic and chilli in the microwave pressure cooker. Add the liquid and stir well.

3 Close the lid, place in the microwave oven and cook on Full power for 18 minutes. Remove from the microwave oven and place on a heatproof surface. Allow the pressure to drop.

4 Meanwhile, mix the cornflour with 15ml/1 tbsp water to form a paste. Remove the lid and stir in the cornflour. Add the pineapple, cutting the slices, if using, into pieces.

5 Return the open pressure cooker to the microwave oven and cook on Full power for 1–2 minutes, until thickened, stirring once. Season to taste.

6 Transfer to a warmed serving dish and sprinkle with shredded spring onion. Serve with rice, if you wish.

MICROWAVE STEAMED MARMALADE PUDDINGS

Sponge puddings are perfect for the microwave pressure cooker. You can make two individual puddings at the same time. Use marmalade as shown here, or jam or golden syrup.

Serves 2

30ml/2 tbsp marmalade
40g/1½oz/3 tbsp caster (superfine) sugar
40g/1½oz/3 tbsp butter, at room temperature
1 egg
65g/2½oz/9 tbsp self-raising (self-rising) flour
a few drops of vanilla extract
custard, single (light) cream or crème fraîche,
  to serve

1 Lightly grease 2 x 175ml/6fl oz/¾ cup, 8cm/3¼in diameter ramekin dishes or individual pudding basins. Do not use metal basins. Place 15ml/1 tbsp marmalade in the base of each ramekin.

2 Place 200ml/7fl oz/scant 1 cup water in the base of the microwave pressure cooker.

3 Cream the sugar and butter together in a bowl, then gradually beat in the egg. Fold in the flour and vanilla extract. Divide the mixture between the two ramekin dishes.

4 Cover with clear film or plastic wrap and press firmly to the top edges of the dishes to seal. Tie with string, if necessary. Prick two holes in the top with a skewer, to allow steam to escape. Place in the microwave pressure cooker and close the lid.

5 Microwave on Full power for 3 minutes. Carefully lift the microwave pressure cooker from the microwave and leave to stand on a heatproof surface until the lid is released.

6 Remove the puddings from the microwave pressure cooker and leave to stand for a couple of minutes. Remove the clear film and run a knife around the side of each pudding. Place a serving plate on top and invert the pudding. Repeat with the second pudding. Serve warm with custard, cream or crème fraîche.

Cook's Tip
To make four puddings, double the quantities and cook the remaining two while the first two are standing and being transferred to warmed serving plates.

Making Stocks

Although ready-made stock cubes are available, they can never compete with freshly made stock. A good stock will always add to the flavour of any savoury dish, whether it is a soup, risotto, casserole or pot roast. Making stock without a pressure cooker can be a lengthy process, taking hours. However, the pressure cooker will reduce this to under an hour.

GENERAL GUIDELINES
• Use fresh vegetables, or vegetable peelings, providing they have been thoroughly cleaned first. Celery leaves are perfect for adding to a stock, as are the stalks of fresh herbs such as parsley.
• Use whole peppercorns, as ground pepper can add a bitter taste.
• Avoid adding salt if you are using your stock with salty foods, and adjust the seasoning in the finished recipe.
• Avoid large quantities of strongly flavoured vegetables such as parsnips and turnips, as they may overpower the flavour.
• Do not use starchy foods such as potatoes, green vegetables such as cabbage, or milk and milk products for stocks, as they will produce a cloudy stock. A good stock should be clear.
• When making fish stock, make it on the day you wish to use it. Meat stock will keep in the refrigerator for up to 3 days.

• Use white fish bones and shellfish for fish stock. Oily fish bones are unsuitable. You may include heads and shells, but the gills and eyes should be removed to prevent a bitter taste.
• When making a stock with meat or poultry bones, you will achieve a more intense flavour if the bones are small, so when asking your butcher for bones, request that they are cut into small sections.
• Once you have added all the ingredients for the stock, including the liquid, the pressure cooker should not be more than half full. The ingredients need room in the pressure cooker to rise once boiling and under pressure.
• When you have finished cooking a stock, always release the pressure slowly. Some pressure cookers call this method 'natural release'. If using an electric pressure cooker, most automatically switch to a 'keep warm' mode, so make sure this is switched off.
• Remove any fat that forms on the top of the stock before using, storing or freezing it.
• You can freeze stock. It is a good idea to make a batch so that it is ready for use when needed. Make stocks with slightly less liquid than usual, as they will take up less space. Freeze in small quantities of about 300ml/½ pint/1¼ cups.
• To freeze, place a freezer bag in a rigid container and pour the stock into the bag, leaving space for expansion. Freeze, then seal and remove from the container and label.

Below: Use both the leaves and stalks of green vegetables such as celery.

Below: Whole peppercorns give the best flavour to home-made stocks.

Below: Before using or storing a stock, scoop off any fat from the surface.

VEGETABLE STOCK

Use fresh vegetables or cleaned peelings to make this stock in your pressure cooker.

Pressure: High
Time under Pressure: 18 minutes (25 minutes)
Release: Natural/Slow
Makes about 1.5 litres/2½ pints/6¼ cups

30ml/2 tbsp vegetable oil
2 onions, roughly chopped, skins reserved
1 leek, roughly chopped
2 celery sticks, with leaves, roughly chopped
3 carrots, sliced
2 garlic cloves, halved
115g/4oz/1½ cups chopped mushrooms
2 tomatoes, chopped
1 bay leaf
6 parsley stalks
1 fresh thyme sprig
10 black peppercorns
salt

1 Heat the oil in the open pressure cooker. Add the onions, leek, celery, carrots and garlic and sauté for 4–5 minutes. Use the Sauté or Soup setting for the electric pressure cooker.

2 Add the mushrooms and sauté for 2 minutes. Stir in the tomatoes, bay leaf, parsley stalks, thyme, peppercorns and reserved onion skins.

3 Add 1.5 litres/2½ pints/6¼ cups water and mix together.

Electric: Close the lid and bring to High pressure using the Manual or Soup setting. Cook for 18 minutes (25 minutes). Release the pressure using natural release, making sure the 'keep warm' mode is switched off.
Stovetop: Close the lid and bring to High pressure. Cook for 18 minutes (25 minutes). Release the pressure slowly.

4 Carefully remove the lid and leave to cool slightly. Strain the stock through a fine sieve or strainer into a large bowl. Season with salt, if you wish. Leave to cool. Store in the refrigerator or freezer.

Cook's Tip
Adding the onion skins to the stock will add colour to the stock, but you do not have to add them for flavour.

CHICKEN STOCK

Home-made chicken stock is so much better than a stock cube, and with your pressure cooker it is very quick and easy to make.

Pressure: High
Time under Pressure: 30 minutes (40 minutes)
Release: Natural/Slow
Makes about 1 litre/1¾ pints/4 cups

1 chicken carcass, cooked or raw
30ml/2 tbsp sunflower oil
1 litre/1¾ pints/4 cups water
1 onion, unpeeled, root removed
  and quartered
2 carrots, thickly sliced
1 leek, roughly chopped
1 celery stick, with leaves, roughly chopped
1 tomato, halved
2 bay leaves
4 fresh parsley sprigs
2 fresh thyme sprigs
6 black peppercorns
salt

1 Cut the carcass into pieces, using poultry shears. Heat the oil in the open pressure cooker and brown the bones for 4–5 minutes. Use the Sauté or Soup setting for the electric pressure cooker.

2 Add the water and bring to the boil in the open cooker. Use the Sauté or Soup setting for the electric pressure cooker. Using a spoon, remove any scum from the surface.

3 Add the onion, carrots, leek, celery, tomato, bay leaves, parsley, thyme and peppercorns. Stir together.

Electric: Close the lid and bring to High pressure using the Manual or Soup setting. Cook for 30 minutes (40 minutes). You may need to reset the timer. Release the pressure using natural release, making sure the 'keep warm' mode is switched off.
Stovetop: Close the lid and bring to High pressure. Cook for 30 minutes (40 minutes). Release the pressure slowly.

4 Carefully remove the lid and leave to cool slightly. Strain the stock through a fine sieve or strainer into a large bowl. Taste and season with salt, if you wish. Leave to cool. When cold, place in the refrigerator, then remove the fat. Chill and use within 3 days, or freeze for up to 3 months.

MEAT STOCK

Follow the recipe for chicken stock, replacing the chicken carcass with 700–900g/1½–2lb beef or veal bones, cut into pieces. Use small bones or bones cut into pieces for a more intense flavour.

Brown the onion with the bones, to increase the depth of flavour and colour. Make sure you do not over-caramelize them, as this will affect the final flavour and add a bitter taste. If browning the onions, remove the onion skins and add with the remaining vegetables. Make sure your pressure cooker is at maximum half full before closing and bringing it to pressure. You should remove any fat from the top of the meat stock after cooling, before using or storing it.

FISH STOCK

To make fish stock, you can add the bones of any white fish such as cod, haddock or swordfish. Include mild-flavoured white fish such as flounder, sea bass (shown here) or whiting. Cut the fish into large chunks and removed any eyes or gills, because these give a bitter taste. You can also include shellfish such as prawn, crab or lobster shells, if you have these freshly to hand. Avoid adding too much shellfish, as this will become the predominant flavour.

Pressure: High
Time under Pressure: 18 minutes (25 minutes)
Release: Natural/Slow
Makes about 1 litre/1¾ pints/4 cups

900g/2lb fish and shellfish bones, heads, shells and trimmings – you can include inexpensive, mild-flavoured, whole white fish
1 celery stalk, including leaves, cut into chunks
1 onion, peeled and sliced
1 carrot, thickly sliced
1 bay leaf
3 fresh parsley sprigs
1 fresh thyme sprig
8 white peppercorns
1 litre/1¾ pints/4 cups water
salt

1 Rinse the fish bones, heads, trimmings and whole fish, if using, and cut into chunks.

2 Place the celery, onion, carrot, bay leaf, parsley, thyme and peppercorns in the pressure cooker. Add the fish and bones, and the water. Stir together.

Electric: Close the lid and bring to High pressure using the Manual or Soup setting. Cook for 18 minutes (25 minutes). Release the pressure using natural release, making sure the 'keep warm' mode is switched off.
Stovetop: Close the lid and bring to High pressure. Cook for 18 minutes (25 minutes). Release the pressure slowly.

3 Carefully remove the lid and leave to cool slightly. Strain the stock through a fine sieve or strainer into a large bowl. Taste and season with salt, if you wish.

4 Cool quickly, cover and refrigerate or freeze. Use on the same day, or freeze for up to 1 month.

Cooking Soups

The pressure cooker is ideal for making soups. It greatly reduces the long simmering time often associated with soup made in a pan. This book contains a selection of tasty soups made with vegetables, fish or meat. However, if you wish to use your favourite soup recipes and experiment with making them in the pressure cooker, there are some general guidelines worth noting before you start.

GENERAL GUIDELINES

• You can make soups in the main body of the pressure cooker. You do not need a trivet or basket.
• If making a large quantity of soup, make sure your pressure cooker is not more than half full when all the ingredients and liquid are added, as you need to leave room for boiling. You can always add more liquid after pressure cooking and just reheat it in the open cooker.
• Do not use more than around 750ml/1½ pints/ 3 cups liquid unless you are using dried beans or vegetables, in which case you can increase to 1 litre/1¾ pints/4 cups. You should always use at least the minimum amount of liquid recommended by your manufacturer. Refer to your instruction book. It will be around 250–300ml/8–10fl oz/1–1¼ cups.
• You will get less evaporation in a pressure cooker than in a pan, so add slightly less and top up at the end of cooking, if necessary.
• Do not release the pressure quickly after cooking when making soup that contains pasta, rice or beans. Use slow or natural release. Electric cookers often

take a long time to release the steam, so after 10 minutes, if still under pressure, you can slowly release any remaining pressure by carefully opening the vent release.
• If you wish to try a favourite recipe, look for a similar recipe in this book and use it as a guide for quantities of liquid and timings. Select the ingredient that is going to take the longest to cook and base your timings on this.
• The result of puréeing a soup usually means that no additional thickening, as above, is required.

THICKENING SOUPS

You may wish to thicken a soup. This is best done at the end of cooking. You can use cornflour blended with a little cold water to make a smooth paste. This can be stirred into the hot soup and boiled for a few minutes, to thicken and cook. You can also thicken soups using a beurre manié – this is a blend of softened butter and plain (all-purpose) flour which is gradually whisked into the finished soup.

Right: A beurre manié (butter and flour) can be used to thicken soups.

Below: Your cooker should be less than half full, to leave room for boiling.

Below: You can thicken French onion soup with a mixture of butter and flour.

Below: A soup made from puréed pumpkin should not need thickening.

Cooking Fish

The time required for fish to cook by any method is short, but the pressure cooker is still extremely useful. The cooking smell, which some people dislike, is greatly reduced, as it is contained within the pressure cooker. Steaming or poaching in the pressure cooker is ideal for delicate foods such as fish.

GENERAL GUIDELINES

• For steaming, place the fish on a trivet or in a steamer basket. Lightly grease the trivet or steamer basket first, to make sure the fish doesn't stick. If you wish, place the fish on a sheet of baking parchment, which makes lifting off the trivet or basket easier.

• Fish can be completely wrapped in foil or baking parchment and steamed in the steamer basket or on the trivet.

• For poaching, the cooking liquid may be water, fish stock, cider or a compatible wine. If using alcohol, bring to the boil first before adding the fish. Add 45ml/3 tbsp water to the wine or cider, then add the fish, close the lid and bring to pressure. There is no need to use a trivet or basket.

• When poaching or steaming, use the minimum amount of liquid suggested by your manufacturer's instruction book – around 250–300ml/ 8–10floz/ 1–1¼ cups.

• After cooking, you can use the fish stock for a sauce, if you wish.

• You may cook fish in milk, but you must release the pressure slowly, or use natural release for the electric pressure cooker. Take the time while the steam is slowly releasing into consideration, as the fish will still be cooking. As milk froths up, make sure it doesn't block the vent. With stovetop pressure cookers, keep the heat on medium to low.

• For a fish stew or casserole, cut the fish into chunks and add to sautéed vegetables with at least 250–300ml/8–10fl oz/1–1¼ cups wine, stock or a blend. Make sure the vegetables are cut into thin slices, as the cooking time will be short for the fish.

FISH COOKING TIMES		
Type	**Cooking time**	
	11.5–12psi	**7–8psi**
Cod, fillet	3–4 mins	4–5 mins
steak	4–5 mins	5–6 mins
Haddock, fillet	3–4 mins	4–5 mins
steak	4–5 mins	5–6 mins
Herrings, fillets	4 mins	5 mins
whole	6 mins	8 mins
Mackerel, fillets	4–5 mins	5–6 mins
whole	6–7 mins	8–9 mins
Mussels	2 mins	3 mins
Plaice, fillets	2–3 mins	2½–3½ mins
Prawns (shrimp)	1 min	1–2 mins
Salmon, steaks/cutlets	4–5 mins	5–6 mins
fillet pieces	4 mins	5 mins
Sea bass, fillets	4 mins	6 mins
Sole, fillets	1½–2 mins	2–2½ mins
Trout, steaks/cutlets	4–5 mins	5–6 mins

• Timings will vary depending on the thickness of the fish. The thicker the fillet or steak, the more time it will take. If your fish is not quite cooked, you can always increase the time by returning to High pressure for another minute. Release the pressure quickly, unless stated otherwise in a recipe, to avoid the fish overcooking. See earlier for fish cooked in milk.

Below: Put salmon on a trivet for steaming in the pressure cooker.

Below: Cut white fish into chunks, making sure they are a similar size.

Cooking Meat, Poultry and Game

Meat cooks perfectly in the pressure cooker. A pressure cooker is a great time-saver for cheaper cuts of meat, tenderizing them in a fraction of the time taken for conventional braising, casseroling and stewing. Poultry and game are tenderized by pressure cooking, and are very succulent. The pressure cooker is ideal for pot-roasting whole chickens or cheaper joints of meat such as brisket. Brown meat in a little oil in the open pressure cooker first, to add flavour.

GENERAL GUIDELINES

• There is no need to use a trivet or steamer basket, apart from some large joints, such as gammon, if stated in the recipe.
• Brown meat, poultry and game on all sides in a little oil in the base of the pressure cooker, selecting the sauté function on the electric pressure cooker, if you have this setting.
• Make sure any sediment is dissolved into the liquid before closing the pressure cooker, otherwise it may burn on to the base.
• Never fill the cooker more than half full with meat, vegetables and liquid when braising or stewing.
• The cooking time is determined by the size of the pieces of meat, not the overall amount.
• Small pieces of chicken cook in the least time, while chicken joints take slightly longer.
• Whole chickens are cooked by weight. You should include the stuffing in the weight, if using.
• Whole birds can be pot-roasted.

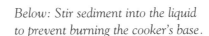

Above: When cooking a dish such as this beef goulash, a pressure cooker will tenderize the meat quickly.

• Use slightly less liquid than with conventional casseroles, as there is less evaporation.
• Use at least the minimum 300ml/½ pint/1¼ cups for the first 20 minutes, then at least 150ml/¼ pint/ ⅔ cup for each additional 15 minutes.
• Meat, poultry and game may be tossed in seasoned flour for a slightly thickened gravy, but for a thicker gravy this needs to be adjusted after cooking, otherwise it will reduce the amount of steam and may cause burning. Use a cornflour and water paste or a beurre manié after cooking (see page 34).
• In most cases, reduce the pressure quickly, unless the recipe states otherwise.

Below: You can brown small pieces of beef tossed in flour in a little oil.

Below: Stir sediment into the liquid to prevent burning the cooker's base.

Below: Sauté onions and garlic before adding pieces of poultry.

Above: A whole chicken can be pot-roasted with garlic and herbs.

Above: You can brown a pheasant with bacon before braising it in cider.

Above: Place ham on a trivet before cooking it in the pressure cooker.

• Salted smoked joints such as gammon should be soaked in cold water for 2–3 hours before cooking. Both smoked and unsmoked joints should be brought to the boil, drained to remove excess salt, and fresh cold water added.

• When cooking ham and gammon, use the trivet and place the rind uppermost. Add sufficient water to cover the thickest part, but do not fill more than half the pressure cooker with meat and liquid. Add around 750ml/1¼ pints/3 cups.

MEAT COOKING TIMES

Type	Cooking time 11.5–12psi	7–8psi
Beef, braising steak, cubed	25 mins	35 mins
topside/brisket, 900–1300g/2–3lb	16 mins per 500g/1lb	20–21 mins per 500g/1lb
Gammon/boneless ham	12 mins per 500g/1lb	14 mins per 500g/1lb
Lamb, shanks	25–30 mins	35–40 mins
stewing, cubed	25 mins	30 mins
chops	12–15 mins	15–20 mins
Pork, loin roast	14 mins per 500g/1lb	17 mins per 500g/1lb

POULTRY AND GAME COOKING TIMES

Type	Cooking time 11.5–12psi	7–8psi
Chicken, whole	8 mins per 500g/1lb	9 mins per 500g/1lb
breast fillets	6 mins	8 mins
thighs	8 mins	10 mins
drumsticks	8 mins	10 mins
Duck, pieces	10–12 mins	12–14 mins
Guinea fowl, pieces	10 mins	12 mins
Pheasant, whole	12–14 mins	15–18 mins
Rabbit, pieces	10 mins	12 mins
Turkey, mince	10 mins	12 mins
mini breast fillets	5–6 mins	7–8 mins
Venison, cubed	20 mins	25 mins

Cooking Vegetables

Vegetables cook quickly in the pressure cooker, so this helps to preserve both the flavour and nutrients. You can cook one type of vegetable or a selection, providing they all cook in the same amount of time. Most vegetables are cooked by steaming either on the trivet or in the steamer basket. Vegetables can be cooked straight in water or stock without the trivet or steamer basket, if you wish. Follow the guidelines below to get the best results.

GENERAL GUIDELINES

• Use a minimum of 250–300ml/8–10floz/1–1¼ cups water, unless your manufacturer's instructions state otherwise. Any vegetables that need longer cooking times, such as beetroot, will need more water.
• Place large vegetables on a trivet or a shallow rack – this keeps them just above the water, so they can steam.
• Place smaller vegetables in a perforated steamer basket or separator, for ease of handling.
• Always add green vegetables to boiling water in the open cooker, and then close. They will come to pressure more quickly and the green colour will be retained.
• Always cut vegetables into similar-sized pieces for even cooking. If you wish to cook a selection of vegetables, cut the vegetables that take the longest into small pieces.

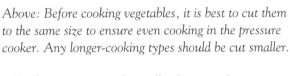

Above: Before cooking vegetables, it is best to cut them to the same size to ensure even cooking in the pressure cooker. Any longer-cooking types should be cut smaller.

• For beetroot, trim the stalks, leaving about 2.5cm/1in and leave the root attached. This will reduce the bleed from the beetroots during cooking.
• Release the pressure quickly after the cooking time, to prevent the vegetables from overcooking.
• Timings can vary according to the age and size of the vegetables. New-season vegetables will cook more quickly.

Below: Place larger vegetables such as corn on the cob on a trivet, shallow rack or in the basket.

Below: Cook smaller ingredients such as broccoli and cauliflower pieces in a perforated steamer basket.

Below: Onions, peppers and tomatoes can be fried in an electric pressure cooker using the sauté or soup setting.

Above: To make a ratatouille, first fry the vegetables in a little oil.

Above: Trim the stalks but leave the roots of beetroot attached.

Above: Pumpkin can be cooked and then mashed to make pumpkin pie.

The chart below gives a guide to cooking times. You may wish to cook for more or less time, depending on how crisp you like your vegetables. Use the chart the first time you cook a particular vegetable, then make a note of any personal adjustments you wish to make for future use. Try combining your favourite vegetables, checking first that they have similar cooking times.

VEGETABLE COOKING TIMES		
Type	Cooking time 11.5–12psi	7–8psi
Artichokes, globe, medium	12–14 mins	15–17 mins
Jerusalem, small whole	4–5 mins	6–7 mins
Asparagus	1–1½ mins	1½–2 mins
Beans, green, whole	1–2 mins	2–3 mins
Beetroot (beets), medium	23 mins	25 mins
use 900ml/1½ pints/3¾ cups water		
Broccoli, florets	2–3 mins	3–4 mins
Cabbage, green, shredded	2 mins	3 mins
red, shredded	4–5 mins	6–7 mins
Carrots, 1cm/½in slices	4 mins	5 mins
young whole	4–5 mins	5–6 mins
Cauliflower, florets	2–3 mins	3–4 mins
Corn on the cob	3 mins	4 mins
Courgettes (zucchini), 2.5cm/1in slices	1½–2 mins	2–3 mins
Leeks, 5cm/2in slices	4–5 mins	5–6 mins
Marrow (large zucchini), 2.5cm/1in slices	4 mins	5 mins
Parsnips, small halved	5 mins	6–7 mins
Potatoes, new baby	5–7 mins	7–8 mins
old, 40g/1½oz pieces	6–7 mins	8–9 mins
Pumpkin, 2.5cm/1in cubes	4–5 mins	5–6 mins
Swede, 2.5cm/1in cubes	7 mins	9 mins
Sweet potato, 2cm/¾in slices	5–6 mins	7–8 mins

Cooking Grains and Pasta

Rice, other grains and pasta can be successfully cooked, with care, in the pressure cooker. They can be cooked in the base of the cooker, or in a solid container such as a metal bowl or perforated container. You can also line the perforated separator or steamer basket with foil. Some manufacturers prefer you not to cook grains and pasta in your pressure cooker, so make sure you check your handbook before cooking these foods or any of the recipes in this book that contain ingredients such as rice, semolina, quinoa, pasta or noodles.

GENERAL GUIDELINES
• To cook savoury rice and pasta in the body of the cooker, there is no need for a trivet or basket. Do not more than half-fill. If using a stovetop pressure cooker, cook on a medium to low heat to prevent the contents from boiling up and blocking the vents.
• To cook rice and cereals with milk, do not cook more than 600ml/1 pint/2½ cups at a time. Do not use the trivet or basket, and cook on a medium to low heat if using a stovetop cooker. It is important to release the pressure slowly, using natural release for the electric pressure cooker. Milk can foam up and block the pressure release valve.
• To cook rice or pasta in a container, add 300ml/ ½ pint/1¼ cups water to the pressure cooker and place the trivet or a shallow rack in the cooker. Put 225g/8oz/generous1 cup long grain rice or pasta in the bowl and add 450ml/¾ pint/2 cups boiling water. Cover with baking parchment and tie down securely with string. Make sure the bowl is large enough to

Above: A risotto can be made with pearl barley instead of rice. Together with asparagus and porcini mushrooms, this dish will cook in around half the time in a pressure cooker.

allow for expansion of the pasta or rice. It should not rise more than two-thirds of the way up the sides of the cooker.
• To cook porridge, pearl barley or quinoa, make sure the pressure cooker is not more than one-third full. Use the amounts of liquid given in the chart for quinoa and pearl barley. Again, cook over a low to medium heat if using a stovetop pressure cooker. You can put the quinoa or porridge in a bowl, as with rice, above, following the same guideline for the bowl size. For porridge (oatmeal), see panel opposite.

GRAINS AND PASTA COOKING TIMES				
Type	Quantity	Water	Cooking time 11.5–12psi	7–8psi
Egg noodles	200g/7oz/1¾ cups	1½ litres/3 pints/7 cups	4 mins	5 mins
Pasta shapes: bows, shells, spirals etc	200g/7oz/1¾ cups	1½ litres/3 pints/7 cups	2–2½ mins	4 mins
Pearl barley	200g/7oz/generous 1 cup	900ml/1½ pints/3¾ cups	18–20 mins	22–24 mins
Quinoa	175g/6oz/1 cup	475ml/16fl oz/2 cups	1–1½ mins	1½–2 mins
Rice, basmati	200g/7oz/1 cup	450ml/¾ pint/2 cups	4–5 mins	5–6 mins
brown	200g/7oz/1 cup	550ml/18fl oz/2½ cups	18–20 mins	22–24 mins
long grain	200g/7oz/1 cup	450ml/¾ pint/2 cups	4–5 mins	5–6 mins
short grain	75g/3oz/scant ½ cup	600ml/1 pint/2½ cups	11–12 mins	14 mins
Semolina	40g/1½oz/¼ cup	600ml/1 pint/2½ cups	7 mins	8 mins

- When cooking grains and pasta, release the pressure slowly, using natural release if using an electric pressure cooker. If still under pressure after 10 minutes, you can release the remaining pressure slowly using the quick release method.
- Add a teaspoon of oil to the cooking water to help prevent the rice or pasta from sticking to the cooker.
- The pressure cooker is only suitable for small pasta shapes. Spaghetti and cannelloni are best cooked in an open pan.

Right: Small pasta shapes such as fusilli or penne cook quickly in a pressure cooker. The pasta becomes infused with the flavours of ingredients such as tomatoes and chilli.

MAKING PORRIDGE

For stovetop and electric pressure cookers, you can cook porridge (oatmeal) in a bowl on a trivet, which ensures that it does not stick to the base of the cooker.

1 Place 300ml/½ pint/1¼ cups water in the base of the cooker, then put the trivet, rack or steamer basket in the pressure cooker.

2 Place 100g/3¾oz/1 cup rolled oats into a stainless steel bowl and add 300ml/½ pint/1¼ cups water plus 150–175ml/5–6fl oz/⅔–¾ cup milk, depending on how thick you like your porridge. Stir together. You can use water only if you wish. Add a small knob of butter, if you like.

3 Cover the stainless steel bowl with pleated baking parchment and tie to seal. Place in the pressure cooker. Close the lid and bring to

Above: The finished porridge can be topped with sliced bananas, pecan nuts and a drizzle of honey.

High pressure for 5 minutes (6 minutes). Use the Soup, Rice or Manual setting for the electric pressure cooker. Release the steam slowly, using natural release for the electric pressure cooker, making sure the 'keep warm' mode is switched off. For electric cookers with porridge programmes, it is best to follow the instructions given by your manufacturer, as these vary greatly between models.

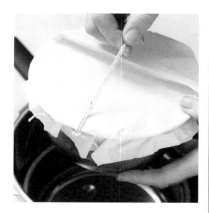

Cooking Pulses

This is certainly one area where the pressure cooker comes into its own. The cooking times are greatly reduced with the pressure cooker. In addition, pulses do not require soaking overnight; they can just be soaked for an hour before cooking.

GENERAL GUIDELINES

• Pulses are cooked in the main body of the pressure cooker. No trivet or basket is required.
• The pressure cooker should not be more than one-third full after adding the pulses and water.
• Place pulses in a heatproof bowl and cover with boiling water and soak for 1 hour before cooking. Drain and use fresh liquid to cook them. Use a minimum of 600ml/1 pint/2½ cups water to every 225g/8oz/1¼ cups pre-soaked beans.
• Season after cooking. Salt can toughen pulses if added before cooking.
• Lentils do not need to be soaked before cooking.
• The timings will vary according to the age of the pulses, so the chart is a guide only.
• Release the pressure slowly, using natural release for the electric pressure cooker, making sure the 'keep warm' mode is switched off.
• If you are short on time, pulses do not have to be soaked in advance, but are far better and less inclined to split if soaked in boiling water for 1 hour before

cooking. It is essential that kidney beans are soaked first. You may need to slightly increase the cooking time.
• Cook beans over a gentle heat if using a stovetop cooker. Pulses tend to froth and rise up, so keep a watchful eye over your pressure cooker while cooking pulses to make sure the vents do not become blocked. One electric pressure cooker manufacturer does not recommend cooking pulses, so check your instruction manual before you begin.

PULSES COOKING TIMES		
Type	**Cooking time**	
	11.5–12psi	**7–8psi**
Beans, black-eyed	12 mins	15 mins
black turtle	14–15 mins	18 mins
borlotti	12–15 mins	18–20 mins
butter	18–20 mins	22–25 mins
cannellini	20 mins	25 mins
haricot	18 mins	22 mins
pinto	14–15 mins	18–20 mins
red kidney	15–18 mins	18–20 mins
Lentils, green	5–8 mins	6–9 mins
Puy	9 mins	11 mins
red	2 mins	3 mins
Peas, chick	25 mins	35 mins
yellow split	4–5 mins	7–8 mins

Below: When making a cassoulet, you can add soaked cannellini beans to lardons in the bottom of the cooker.

Below: Red lentils can be cooked in water in the pressure cooker; they do not need soaking beforehand.

Below: Add fresh water to soaked and drained chickpeas. Release the pressure slowly after cooking.

Cooking Fruit

You can use your pressure cooker to cook both dried and fresh fruit. A dried fruit compote can be prepared quickly, without soaking the fruits overnight.

DRIED FRUIT
• Place the dried fruit in a bowl and cover with boiling water, using 280–300ml/½ pint/1¼ cups for each 225g/8oz/1 cup fruit. Leave to soak for 10 minutes.
• Place directly in the pressure cooker with the soaking liquid, adding 15g/½oz/1 tbsp sugar, if you wish.
• You can add lemon rind, cloves or a cinnamon stick, if you wish.
• Release the pressure slowly, using natural release for the electric pressure cooker. Release any remaining steam quickly after 10 minutes, if still under pressure.
• The timings are for dried fruits, not softened or ready-to-eat varieties.

FRESH FRUIT
• Place the fruit directly in the pressure cooker with 280–300ml/½ pint/1¼ cups water or syrup, or in a bowl on top of the trivet with 280–300ml/½ pint/ 1¼ cups water in the base as well. A glass dish will take longer than a metal one.
• If the fruit is cooked in a bowl, you can release the pressure quickly; if in the body, release slowly, using natural release for the electric pressure cooker, gradually releasing any remaining pressure quickly after 5 minutes.
• Timings in the chart are for fruits cooked in a container.

DRIED FRUIT COOKING TIMES		
Type	Cooking time	
	11.5–12psi	7–8psi
Apple rings	3 mins	4–5 mins
Apricots	3 mins	4 mins
Figs	4–5 mins	6–7 mins
Pears	4 mins	5–6 mins
Prunes	4–5 mins	5–6 mins

FRESH FRUIT COOKING TIMES		
Type	Cooking time	
	11.5–12psi	7–8psi
Apple, thick slices	3–4 mins	4–5 mins
layered with sugar	6 mins	7–8 mins
in a dish on trivet		
Peaches, stoned	2–3 mins	3–4 mins
and halved		
Pears, whole	5–6 mins	7–8 mins
halves in syrup	4–5 mins	6–7 mins
in a dish on trivet		

• Timings for fresh fruits vary greatly, depending on the ripeness of the fruit and also the size of whole fruits. Always err on the side of caution, as you can always return the cooker to High pressure and cook for a little longer.
• Choose fruits of a similar size and ripeness.
• For fruit purées, cook in syrup in the main body of the pressure cooker.

Far left: When preparing whole dried fruits such as these dried apricots, place them in a bowl and pour boiling water over the top to cover them completely. Leave them to soak as directed in the recipe, then drain off the soaking liquid before cooking them in the pressure cooker.

Left: Apples can be cooked either whole or cut into thick slices. This picture shows stuffed baked apples filled with pecans, sultanas (golden raisins) and cranberries, flavoured with cinnamon and stem ginger.

Cooking Puddings

A wide variety of puddings can be cooked successfully in the pressure cooker, from hearty steamed sponge puddings and Christmas puddings to lighter milk puddings, custards and creams.

SPONGE PUDDINGS

• Steamed sponge puddings can be cooked more quickly than with conventional steaming alone. To make a light pudding, the pudding must be steamed first for around 15–20 minutes to allow the raising agents to work correctly, before cooking under pressure. Without pre-steaming, the pudding will be close-textured and heavy.

• Use a heat-resistant container, such as ovenproof glass or china or boilable plastic. It must be watertight, not cracked, and able to withstand 130°C/262°F.

• Recipes in this book are tested in ovenproof glass and china basins; plastic bowls will be slightly quicker.

• Check that the basin will fit comfortably inside your pressure cooker.

• Grease the basin well before adding the sponge mix, and do not fill more than two-thirds, to allow room for the mixture to rise.

• Cover with a double thickness of baking parchment or foil and tie securely with string. Pleat the paper or foil first to allow for expansion while cooking. Avoid fitted lids, as they may come off during the cooking process and block the vent.

Above: A sponge pudding can be cooked rapidly in a pressure cooker. It could be flavoured with golden (light corn) syrup, marmalade, coconut and cherry, or chocolate.

• Either make a handle with string for easier lifting or place the pudding in the separator or steamer basket. Another option is to place a long, triple-thickness strip of foil under the basin.

• Add a minimum of 900ml/1½ pints/3¾ cups hot water to the pressure cooker to allow for loss during pre-steaming. Add a little lemon juice to aluminium pressure cookers to lessen discoloration.

• Pre-steam the pudding according to the time in the recipe. Check the manufacturer's operating instructions on how best to do this, as every model varies. For

Below: To make a sponge pudding, fill the bowl no more than two-thirds full, because the mixture will rise.

Below: When covering a steamed pudding bowl, pleat the baking parchment to allow for expansion.

Below: Create a handle using a piece of string, making sure the string catches under the lip of the bowl.

Above: A Christmas pudding should be covered with baking parchment and foil, and pre-steamed before cooking.

Above: When making a suet roly poly, make sure the width of the pastry will fit inside your pressure cooker.

Above: Cover the tops of crème caramels with baking parchment to catch any condensation that forms.

electric pressure cookers you may substitute the pressure lid for a glass lid, supplied with some cookers. Alternatively, use the pressure lid, but do not lock down, and leave the steam vent open. See which programme your manufacturer recommends. There is a tendency for electric models to cook more vigorously when steaming, so make sure there is plenty of water in the pressure cooker before you begin. Add a little extra to the amount given in the recipe, as long as it does not reach the top of the basin. A very quick check after steaming is worthwhile, but uncover for the shortest length of time possible to prevent the part-cooked pudding from sinking. With stovetop models, reduce the heat to a minimum so that the water just simmers.

• Release the pressure slowly. Use natural release for the electric pressure cooker.

• If you wish to adapt your favourite steamed pudding recipe to cook in the pressure cooker, use the following as a guide: normal cooking time of 1½ hours steaming time – pre-steam for 20 minutes, then cook at High pressure for 25 minutes (35 minutes).

CHRISTMAS AND SUET PUDDINGS

Both Christmas puddings and puddings made with suet pastry are pre-steamed and cooked in a similar way to sponge puddings. Avoid using an aluminium or foil basin, as the acid from the fruit may attack the surface of the basin during storage. Suet puddings, including jam roly poly, need pre-steaming as for sponge puddings, so follow the instructions above.

MILK PUDDINGS

• Egg custards cook quickly in a pressure cooker, with perfect results in a fraction of the time it would take in a bain marie in the oven.

• Use china, glass or boilable plastic containers. Soufflé dishes are ideal.

• Cover the tops with foil or baking parchment to prevent condensation collecting on the top of the custard when the steam is released.

• For rice and cereal milk puddings, follow the guidelines on page 40.

Below: Christmas pudding is a quintessential pressure cooker classic that can be made in a fraction of the time that is otherwise required for this type of recipe.

Cooking Preserves and Chutneys

When making jams, jellies, marmalades, chutneys and relishes, the pressure cooker will speed up the softening of the ingredients – fruit rind in the case of marmalade, and fruit and vegetables for chutneys. There is a wonderful selection of recipes in this book that are perfect for using seasonal fruits and vegetables, and you will find that your home-made versions will have a much more intense flavour than any shop-bought varieties.

JAM

• Choose fruit that is fresh and firm; over-ripe fruit will not produce a good set.
• Add lemon juice or use pectin-enriched jam sugar for fruits that are low in pectin to ensure a good set.
• Do not fill the pressure cooker more than half full with fruit and water. There is no need to use the trivet.
• Reduce the quantity of liquid recommended in an ordinary jam recipe by about a third to a half, as there will be less evaporation during softening.
• If you have a stovetop cooker with a High pressure of 15psi, use the Medium setting of 10psi to avoid adversely affecting the pectin.
• Use the open pressure cooker for boiling the cooked fruit and sugar.
• Release the pressure slowly, using natural release for the electric pressure cooker.

Above: All sorts of wonderful jams can be made in the pressure cooker, using fruits that are in season at the time.

MARMALADE

• Follow the guidelines for jam. You will not need to add pectin-enriched preserving sugar, as Seville oranges are rich in pectin.
• Make sure you add the pith and pips or seeds tied in a muslin or cheesecloth bag to the pressure cooker when cooking the rind, as these contain pectin.
• Cook the fruit rind in half the quantity of liquid in the recipe and add the remainder with the sugar. This will allow more fruit rind to be softened without it blocking the steam vent while cooking under pressure.

Below: You can make a smooth jelly by straining out the fruit pulp after cooking in the pressure cooker.

Below: When cooking orange rind to make marmalade, add the pith and pips (seeds) tied in a bag.

Below: A relish can be thickened by adding cornflour (cornstarch) and vinegar at the end of cooking.

Above: Using a pressure cooker to make marmalade is an ideal method because it quickly tenderizes the citrus rind.

CHUTNEYS AND RELISHES

• Vinegar is the preservative with chutneys and relishes. You can use almost any fruit or vegetable that is in plentiful supply, even if misshapen, as long as it is of good quality.

• As with preserves, do not fill more than half full.

• Use High pressure to soften the fruits and vegetables. Release the pressure slowly or using natural release. With electric pressure cookers this often takes longer than stovetop models, so follow the recipe instructions for releasing the remaining steam quickly, after 5 or 10 minutes.

Below: Green tomato chutney can be made from leftover green tomatoes which will be tenderized in the pressure cooker. It is perfect served with cheese and crackers.

TESTING FOR A SET

Jam, jellies and marmalade need to be cooked in the open pressure cooker with sugar, until setting point is reached. Overcooking will darken the preserve. There are various tests, and the quickest and most accurate is as follows:

Temperature test Use a sugar thermometer. It should read 105°C/221°F.

Other tests are:

Flake test Using a wooden spoon, lift a little preserve out of the cooker. Let it cool slightly, then tip the spoon so that the preserve drips back into the cooker. If the drips run together and slightly set, falling from the spoon as a 'flake' rather than as drips, it is ready.

Saucer test Spoon a little preserve on to a cold saucer and push a finger over the surface. If it wrinkles, it is ready to set. This is best done with the pressure cooker off the heat, so is not ideal for the electric pressure cooker.

There is no accurate test for chutneys and relishes; these are more about the consistency than the cooking time guide. They are ready when the mixture is thick and little or no excess liquid remains.

Right: Test your jam by pushing a finger over the surface – if it wrinkles, it is ready to set.

POTTING

• Use warm, dry, sterilized jars. Wash in hot soapy water, rinse thoroughly, then dry in a warm oven. Stand upside down on a clean dish towel until ready to use.

• Pour into warmed jars, to reduce the chance of the glass cracking.

• Cover with a waxed disc while still hot. Cover with dampened clear film or plastic wrap and a rubber band when hot or cold. If you seal when warm, mould is likely to grow on the surface.

• If using metal covers for relishes and chutneys, they should be vinegar-proof.

• Chutneys often benefit from storing for 1–2 weeks minimum to mature before opening. They are best stored in a cool, dark place.

Pressure Cooking for One

Pressure cookers are not just for large quantities of food for the family – they can be equally useful when cooking for one or two. You can cook a main course and vegetables or dessert at the same time, as the pressure cooker distributes only heat, not flavours. As well as economy of fuel, it also makes it extremely useful for where there is limited space for cooking.

The main point to consider is choosing foods with the same cooking time, or to cut foods to cook in the same time. You can also open the pressure cooker part of the way through cooking to add an item with a shorter cooking time. Meat often takes the longest time to cook, so you need to choose vegetables such as carrots and other root vegetables that take longer to cook. In contrast, fish requires less time, so more tender vegetables can be cooked alongside it. The following is a suggestion of a meal for one.

TWO-COURSE SUPPER FOR ONE

This meal for one consists of salmon and asparagus served with new potatoes tossed in melted butter and parsley, followed by a cranberry bread and butter pudding. Both of these courses are cooked in the pressure cooker at the same time.

Pressure: High
Time under Pressure: 5 minutes (6 minutes)
Release: Natural/Slow
Serves 1

2 slices bread
15g/½oz/1 tbsp butter, at room temperature,
    plus extra for greasing
15ml/1 tbsp dried cranberries
150ml/¼ pint/⅔ cup milk
1 egg
10ml/2 tsp caster (superfine) sugar
a pinch of grated nutmeg
2 asparagus spears, cut in half
1 salmon fillet, about 175g/6oz
2 slices lemon
2 fresh dill sprigs
15ml/1 tbsp lemon juice or dry white wine
100g/4oz/4–5 baby new potatoes
5ml/1 tsp soft light brown sugar
black pepper
melted butter and chopped fresh parsley,
    to garnish the potatoes, optional

1 Butter the bread and cut into triangles. Layer into a lightly buttered 250–300ml/8–10fl oz/1–1¼ cup ovenproof dish, scattering with cranberries.

2 In a small pan, warm the milk until lukewarm. Whisk the egg and caster sugar together in a small bowl, then whisk in the milk. Pour over the pudding and sprinkle with grated nutmeg. Cover with pleated, lightly greased greaseproof paper and tie with string to seal.

3 Cut a square of foil and lightly butter. Put the asparagus spears on the foil, place the salmon fillet top and finish with the lemon slices and dill. Sprinkle over the lemon juice or wine. Seal the foil to enclose the fish.

4 Put 300ml/½ pint/1¼ cups water in the base of the pressure cooker. Add the trivet, steamer basket or a round cooling rack. Place the fish parcel and bread and butter pudding on the trivet with the potatoes in the remaining space.

Electric: Close the lid and bring to High pressure using the Manual, Poultry or Fish setting. Cook for 5 minutes (6 minutes). Release the pressure using natural release, making sure the 'keep warm' mode is switched off.
Stovetop: Close the lid and bring to High pressure. Cook for 5 minutes (6 minutes). Release the pressure slowly.

5 Remove the bread and butter pudding, discard the greaseproof paper and string, and sprinkle with the brown sugar. Place under a preheated grill or broiler to brown. Set aside to cool.

6 Remove the fish from the foil parcel and serve on a warmed plate with the asparagus and potatoes. Sprinkle with black pepper. Drizzle a little melted butter over the potatoes, and sprinkle with parsley, if you wish.

Below: A two-course meal of salmon and asparagus with new potatoes followed by cranberry bread and butter pudding can be made together in the pressure cooker.

COOKING FOR YOUR BABY OR TODDLER

You can use the pressure cooker to cook for infants. Choose fairly bland meat, such as chicken, and place on a small heatproof plate with 30ml/2 tbsp water. Place on top of the trivet in the pressure cooker, having first added 300ml/½ pint/1¼ cups water in the base.

Another option is to use fish such as cod, haddock or plaice, without any skin and bones, with 30ml/2 tbsp milk. You can place a small bowl, ramekin dish or teacup with chopped fresh fruit alongside. Also add a ramekin with diced vegetables such as potatoes and carrots or peas. These will cook at High pressure in 3 minutes (4 minutes). You can then mash or purée the cooked fruit and vegetables as required.

Whatever method of cooking you use for preparing baby food, sugar is always best kept to a minimum. The same care and caution applies to adding salt to any savoury foods. No extra salt should be added.

SOUPS, STARTERS AND SNACKS

What could be better than a warming soup on a cold winter's day? Whether it's a vegetable soup such as carrot and coriander, pumpkin, French onion, tasty Italian vegetable or a Mediterranean fish soup, your pressure cooker will help speed up the preparation. Also in this chapter are recipes suitable for starters and snacks, such as baked eggs, pâté, nut loaf and a fresh chickpea-based hummus dip. Don't forget that each recipe provides two timings, which vary according to the particular model of pressure cooker you are using. Where recipes are cooked on High, the first timing is for pressure cookers that cook at 11.5–12psi/80–82kPa, and the second timing in brackets is for pressure cookers that cook at 7–8psi/50–55kPa. Where recipes are cooked on Low, the first timing is for 7–8psi/50–55kPa, and the timing in brackets is for 5.8psi/40kPa. Check your manufacturer's handbook to establish the pressure for your cooker before using the recipes.

Carrot and Coriander Soup

Root vegetables such as carrots are perfect for soups. Their earthy flavour becomes rich and sweet within minutes when cooked in your pressure cooker, and their texture becomes beautifully smooth when puréed.

1 Trim and peel the carrots and cut into 2.5cm/1in chunks. Heat the oil and butter in the pressure cooker. Use the Sauté or Soup setting for the electric pressure cooker.

2 Fry the onion for 4–5 minutes, stirring occasionally, until softened. Meanwhile, slice the celery and chop the potatoes. Add the carrot, celery and potatoes to the cooker and cook for 2 minutes. Stir in the ground coriander and stock.

Electric: Close the lid and bring to High pressure using the Manual or Soup setting. Cook for 5 minutes (6 minutes). Release the pressure using natural release, making sure the 'keep warm' mode is switched off. After 10 minutes, quickly release the remaining pressure, if any.
Stovetop: Close the lid and bring to High pressure. Cook for 5 minutes (6 minutes). Release the pressure slowly. After 10 minutes, quickly release the remaining pressure, if any.

3 Stir in the chopped fresh coriander, ladle the soup into a food processor or blender and process until smooth.

4 Return to the open pressure cooker, check the seasoning and reheat, if necessary. Serve garnished with celery leaves and coriander leaves.

Pressure: High
Time under Pressure: 5 minutes (6 minutes)
Release: Natural/Slow
Serves 4

450g/1lb carrots
15ml/1 tbsp sunflower oil
25g/1oz/2 tbsp butter
1 onion, chopped
1 celery stick, plus 2–3 pale leafy tops
2 small potatoes, peeled
10ml/2 tsp ground coriander
900ml/1½ pints/3¾ cups hot vegetable stock
15ml/1 tbsp chopped fresh coriander (cilantro), plus a few sprigs
30ml/2 tbsp single (light) cream
salt and ground black pepper

Energy 174kcal/725kJ; Protein 2.3g; Carbohydrate 20.2g, of which sugars 11.4g; Fat 9.9g, of which saturates 4.7g; Cholesterol 34mg; Calcium 52mg; Fibre 5.1g; Sodium 79mg.

Spicy Pumpkin Soup

This stunning golden-orange soup has a smooth velvety texture and a delicious taste, which is subtly spiced with cumin and garlic. It is a classic soup for autumn, and the pressure cooker makes light work of this recipe.

Pressure: High

Time under Pressure: 7 minutes (9 minutes)

Release: Natural/Slow

Serves 4

900g/2lb pumpkin

30ml/2 tbsp sunflower oil

2 leeks, trimmed and sliced

1 garlic clove, crushed

5ml/1 tsp ground ginger

5ml/1 tsp ground cumin

750ml/1¼ pints/3 cups hot chicken stock

salt and ground black pepper

60ml/4 tbsp natural (plain) yogurt, to serve

fresh coriander (cilantro) leaves, to garnish

1 Using a sharp knife, peel the pumpkin and remove the seeds. Cut the flesh into even-sized 4cm/1½in chunks.

2 Heat the oil in the pressure cooker. Add the leeks and cook until softened. Use the Sauté or Soup setting for the electric pressure cooker. Add the garlic, ginger and cumin and cook for 1 minute. Add the pumpkin and stock.

Electric: Close the lid and bring to High pressure using the Manual or Soup setting. Cook for 7 minutes (9 minutes). Release the pressure using natural release, making sure the 'keep warm' mode is switched off. After 10 minutes, quickly release the remaining pressure, if any.

Stovetop: Close the lid and bring to High pressure. Cook for 7 minutes (9 minutes). Release the pressure slowly. After 10 minutes, quickly release the remaining pressure, if any.

3 Open the pressure cooker and ladle the soup into a food processor or blender and process until smooth.

4 Return to the open pressure cooker, check the seasoning and reheat if necessary. Use the Sauté or Soup setting for the electric pressure cooker. Serve in warmed individual bowls, with a swirl of yogurt and a few coriander leaves.

Energy 97kcal/404kJ; Protein 2.8g; Carbohydrate 7.3g, of which sugars 4.9g; Fat 6.5g, of which saturates 1g; Cholesterol 0mg; Calcium 82mg; Fibre 4.5g; Sodium 2mg.

French Onion Soup

This is probably the most famous of all onion soups. Use large, yellow Spanish onions for the best results. It is important to sauté the onions slowly to develop the flavour. If using an electric pressure cooker, you may need to stir more often in step 1.

1 Heat 25g/1oz butter and the oil in the pressure cooker. Use the Sauté or Soup setting for the electric pressure cooker. Add the onions and cook for 10–15 minutes, stirring occasionally, until well coloured, but taking care not to burn.

2 Add the vinegar, brandy and wine, stirring well to remove any sediment from the base of the cooker. Bring to the boil and boil for 1 minute. Stir in the stock and thyme.

Electric: Close the lid and bring to High pressure using the Manual or Soup setting. Cook for 6 minutes (8 minutes). While the soup is cooking, blend the remaining butter and flour together. Release the pressure using natural release, making sure the 'keep warm' mode is switched off.
Stovetop: Close the lid and bring to High pressure. Cook for 6 minutes (8 minutes). While the soup is cooking, blend the remaining butter and flour together. Release the pressure slowly.

3 Meanwhile, prepare the croûtes. Place the bread slices under the grill (broiler) and cook until dry and lightly browned. Rub the bread with the cut surface of the garlic and spread with mustard, then sprinkle the grated cheese over the slices. Turn the grill to high and cook the croûtes for 2–3 minutes, until the cheese melts.

4 Open the pressure cooker and return the soup to the boil. Add teaspoonfuls of the flour and butter to the soup, stirring constantly to thicken the soup. Use the Sauté or Soup setting for the electric pressure cooker.

5 Ladle the soup into warmed bowls and float a Gruyère croûte on top of each bowl. Serve straight away.

Pressure: High
Time under Pressure: 6 minutes
  (8 minutes)
Release: Natural/Slow
Serves 4

40g/1½oz/3 tbsp butter
30ml/2 tbsp sunflower oil
900g/2lb onions, peeled and
  thinly sliced
15ml/1 tbsp sherry vinegar
30ml/2 tbsp brandy
120ml/4fl oz/½ cup dry white wine
1 litre/1¾ pints/4 cups hot beef or
  chicken stock
5ml/1 tsp chopped fresh thyme
15ml/1 tbsp plain (all-purpose) flour
salt and ground black pepper

For the croûtes
4 slices day-old French stick or
  baguette, about 2.5cm/1in thick
1 garlic clove, halved
5ml/1 tsp French mustard
50g/2oz/1/2 cup grated
  Gruyère cheese

Energy 412kcal/1720kJ; Protein 10.2g;
Carbohydrate 43.5g, of which sugars 14.1g; Fat
19.3g, of which saturates 8.6g; Cholesterol 34mg;
Calcium 234mg; Fibre 5.7g; Sodium 436mg.

Thai Chicken Noodle Soup

This dish is a refreshing, aromatic chicken noodle soup. The soft noodles contrast beautifully with the crunchiness of the spring onion. Do not be tempted to quickly release the pressure, as this may cause the coconut milk to split.

Pressure: High
Time under Pressure: 4 minutes (5 minutes)
Release: Natural/Slow
Serves 4

225g/8oz chicken breast fillet
¼ Savoy cabbage or 1 pak choi (bok choi), shredded
25g/1oz piece fresh root ginger, peeled and grated
1 lemon grass stalk, finely chopped
5ml/1 tsp green curry paste
1 fresh red chilli, seeded and thinly sliced
900ml/1½ pints/3¾ cups chicken stock
200ml/7fl oz/scant 1 cup coconut milk
100g/4oz rice noodles
juice of 1 lime
15ml/1 tbsp soy sauce
4 spring onions (scallions), thinly sliced
salt and ground black pepper
coriander (cilantro) leaves, to finish

1 Cut the chicken into strips. Place in the pressure cooker with the cabbage or pak choi, ginger, lemon grass, curry paste, chilli, stock and coconut milk.

Electric: Close the lid and bring to High pressure using the Manual, Soup or Vegetable setting. Cook for 4 minutes (5 minutes). Release the pressure using natural release, making sure the 'keep warm' mode is switched off. After 10 minutes, quickly release the remaining pressure, if any.
Stovetop: Close the lid and bring to High pressure. Cook for 4 minutes (5 minutes). Release the pressure slowly. After 10 minutes, quickly release the remaining pressure, if any.

2 Meanwhile, place the noodles in a bowl. Pour over boiling water and leave to stand for 2 minutes. Drain.

3 Remove the lid. Add the noodles to the open cooker and cook for 2 minutes. Use the Sauté or Soup setting for the electric pressure cooker. Stir in the lime juice, soy sauce and spring onions, and season with salt and ground black pepper.

4 Ladle into warmed soup bowls and scatter with coriander leaves.

Energy 176kcal/741kJ; Protein 15.9g; Carbohydrate 24.7g, of which sugars 4.2g; Fat 1.3g, of which saturates 0.3g; Cholesterol 39mg; Calcium 43mg; Fibre 1.5g; Sodium 380mg.

Italian Vegetable Soup

This soup is packed full of tasty vegetables – leeks, carrots, celery, cabbage and tomatoes. Release the pressure quickly once the soup is cooked, to make sure the vegetables do not overcook. Serve with crusty bread chunks and Parmesan cheese.

1 Heat the oil in the pressure cooker. Add the bacon and cook for 3–4 minutes. Add the leek, celery and carrots and cook for 5 minutes. Use the Sauté or Soup setting for the electric pressure cooker.

2 Add the cabbage, garlic, sugar, thyme, chopped tomatoes and tomato purée and mix together. Stir in the stock and pasta.

Electric: Close the lid and bring to High pressure using the Manual or Soup setting. Cook for 5 minutes (6 minutes). Release the pressure quickly, making sure the 'keep warm' mode is switched off.
Stovetop: Close the lid and bring to High pressure. Cook for 5 minutes (6 minutes). Release the pressure quickly.

3 Taste and adjust the seasoning. Stir in the basil and serve immediately in warmed soup bowls. Serve sprinkled with grated Parmesan cheese.

Pressure: High
Time under Pressure: 5 minutes (6 minutes)
Release: Quick
Serves 4–6

15ml/1 tbsp sunflower oil
3 streaky bacon rashers (strips), chopped
1 leek, sliced
2 celery sticks, diced
2 carrots, diced
¼ Savoy cabbage, shredded
2 garlic cloves, crushed
5ml/1 tsp caster (superfine) sugar
3–4 small fresh thyme sprigs
400g/14oz can chopped tomatoes
30ml/2 tbsp tomato purée (paste)
1 litre/1¾ pints/4 cups hot vegetable stock
50g/2oz small pasta shapes
30ml/2 tbsp shredded fresh basil leaves
salt and ground black pepper
finely grated Parmesan cheese, to serve

Energy 104kcal/435kJ; Protein 4.4g; Carbohydrate 10.5g, of which sugars 6.5g; Fat 5.2g, of which saturates 1.3g; Cholesterol 8mg; Calcium 37mg; Fibre 3.3g; Sodium 209mg.

Mediterranean Fish Soup with Garlic Rouille

This dish is perfect for making in your pressure cooker, which quickly cooks the fish stock and greatly reduces any fishy cooking odours. Serve it with plenty of crusty bread. In France, they prefer to serve the fish separately on a plate with the bowl of fish broth.

1 Remove the heads, tails, fins and skins from the fish. Place in the pressure cooker with the chopped onion, 1 sliced celery stick, parsley sprigs, bouquet garni and 5ml/1 tsp salt. Add 900ml/1½ pints/3¾ cups water.

Electric: Close the lid and bring to High pressure using the Manual or Soup setting. Cook for 15 minutes (20 minutes). Release the pressure using natural release, making sure the 'keep warm' mode is switched off.
Stovetop: Close the lid and bring to High pressure. Cook for 15 minutes (20 minutes). Release the pressure slowly.

2 Meanwhile, place the saffron in a small bowl with 60ml/4 tbsp boiling water and leave to soak. Cut the fish into 5cm/2in chunks and shell the prawns, leaving the tails intact. Cover and chill.

3 Make the rouille. Place the pepper, garlic, bread, mustard, egg yolk, lemon and seasoning in a food processor and process until smooth. With the machine running, slowly drizzle in the olive oil. Transfer to a bowl.

4 Open the pressure cooker, strain the fish stock and set aside. In the cleaned pressure cooker, heat the oil, add the sliced onion, leek, fennel and remaining sliced celery and fry for 4–5 minutes, stirring occasionally, until softened. Use the Manual or Soup setting for the electric pressure cooker. Add the tomatoes, garlic and orange rind and stir together. Add the fish, except the prawns, reserved fish stock, wine and saffron liquid.

Electric: Close the lid and bring to High pressure using the Manual, Fish or Soup setting. Cook for 5 minutes (6 minutes). Release the pressure quickly, making sure the 'keep warm' mode is switched off.
Stovetop: Close the lid and bring to High pressure. Cook for 5 minutes (6 minutes). Release the pressure quickly.

5 Add the prawns and cook in the open cooker for 2–3 minutes. Use the Sauté or Soup setting for the electric pressure cooker. Remove the orange rind. Using a slotted spoon, transfer the fish to warmed soup bowls. Stir the tomato purée into the broth, adjust the seasoning and pour over the fish. Sprinkle with chopped parsley, if you wish, and serve with the rouille.

Pressure: High
Time under Pressure: 20 minutes
    (26 minutes)
Releases: Natural/Slow and Quick
Serves 4

900g/2lb mixed fish and shellfish, such as red mullet, monkfish, bass and large prawns (shrimp)
1 onion, chopped
2 celery sticks, sliced
a few parsley sprigs
bouquet garni
a few saffron threads
15ml/1 tbsp sunflower oil
1 onion, sliced
1 leek, sliced
½ fennel bulb, chopped
225g/8oz tomatoes, peeled and chopped
2 garlic cloves, crushed
a strip of orange rind
150ml/¼ pint/⅔ cup dry white wine
30ml/2 tbsp tomato purée (paste)
salt and ground black pepper
chopped fresh parsley, to serve (optional)

For the rouille

1 red (bell) pepper, roasted and peeled
3 garlic cloves, chopped
1 slice white bread, crust removed and torn into pieces
15ml/1 tbsp Dijon mustard
1 egg yolk
15ml/1 tbsp lemon juice
100ml/3½fl oz/½ cup olive oil
salt and ground black pepper

Energy 498kcal/2080kJ; Protein 47.8g; Carbohydrate 16.3g, of which sugars 11.5g; Fat 24.6g, of which saturates 3.8g; Cholesterol 230mg; Calcium 363mg; Fibre 5.3g; Sodium 338mg.

Hummus Dip

This classic dip can be varied widely to taste – some enjoy it spiked with cumin or chilli; others like it light and lemony. Whichever you prefer, the flavour and texture of freshly cooked chickpeas is worth the effort, and with the pressure cooker it takes very little time.

1 Place the chickpeas in a bowl. Cover with boiling water and leave to stand for 1 hour.

2 Drain the chickpeas and place in the pressure cooker. Add 1 litre/ 1¾ pints/4 cups hot water.

Electric: Close the lid and bring to High pressure using the Manual, Bean or Pulse setting. Cook for 25 minutes (35 minutes). Release the pressure using natural release, making sure the 'keep warm' mode is switched off. **Stovetop**: Close the lid and bring to High pressure. Cook for 25 minutes (35 minutes). Release the pressure slowly.

3 Drain the chickpeas, reserving a few spoonfuls of the cooking liquid. Leave to cool.

4 Put the chickpeas into a food processor or blender with the olive oil, garlic, lemon juice, orange juice and tahini and process to a purée. Add the reserved cooking liquid if too thick. Season with salt and pepper to taste.

5 Spoon the hummus into a serving bowl and drizzle over the olive oil. Sprinkle over the paprika and chopped coriander, if you wish. Serve with warm pitta bread or crudités such as carrot, celery and (bell) pepper sticks.

Pressure: High
Time under Pressure: 25 minutes
   (35 minutes)
Release: Natural/Slow
Serve 4–6
225g/8oz dried chickpeas
45–60ml/3–4 tbsp olive oil
2 cloves garlic, crushed
juice of 1 lemon
juice of 1 small orange
45–60ml/3–4 tbsp tahini
salt and ground black pepper
pitta breads or crudités, to serve

To garnish
15ml/1 tbsp olive oil
5ml/1 tsp paprika
small bunch of fresh coriander
   (cilantro), finely chopped (optional)

Energy 217kcal/907kJ; Protein 9.5g; Carbohydrate 19g, of which sugars 1.1g; Fat 12g, of which saturates 1.6g; Cholesterol 0mg; Calcium 112mg; Fibre 6.3g; Sodium 16mg.

Electric: Close the lid and bring to High pressure using the Manual or Soup setting. Cook for 12 minutes (15 minutes). Release the pressure using natural release, making sure the 'keep warm' mode is switched off. After 10 minutes, quickly release the remaining pressure, if any.
Stovetop: Close the lid and bring to High pressure. Cook for 12 minutes (15 minutes). Release the pressure slowly. After 10 minutes, quickly release the remaining pressure, if any.

8 Leave the loaf to cool in the tin for about 15 minutes, then turn out on to a serving plate. Serve the loaf hot or cold, cut into thick slices and garnished with fresh chives and sprigs of flat leaf parsley.

Fine Chicken Liver and Porcini Pâté

Check that your dish will fit inside your pressure cooker before making this pâté. It is perfect eaten with Melba toast or slices of French bread. If you wish, serve it in individual pots, or serve scoops of pâté with a tomato and onion salad.

Pressure: High
Time under Pressure: 25 minutes
**   (28 minutes)**
Release: Natural/Slow
Serves 6–8

50g/2oz/4 tbsp butter
15g/½oz dried porcini mushrooms, soaked in hot water for 15 minutes
1 onion, finely chopped
2 garlic cloves, crushed
400g/14oz chicken livers, trimmed
5ml/1 tsp fresh thyme leaves
30ml/2 tbsp single (light) cream
30ml/2 tbsp brandy or sherry
50g/2oz melted butter
fresh bay leaves or herbs and peppercorns, to garnish
salt and ground black pepper

1 Melt half the butter in a frying pan. Drain the mushrooms and cook with the butter for 1 minute. Remove and set aside.

2 Add the remaining butter and onion to the pan and cook until the onions are softened. Add the garlic and livers and cook for 2–3 minutes to sear the livers.

3 Transfer to a food processor or blender with the thyme leaves, cream and brandy or sherry. Add half the mushrooms and blend until smooth.

4 Season well with salt and pepper. Chop the remaining mushrooms and stir into the pâté. Transfer to a 600ml/1 pint/2½ cup heatproof soufflé dish and cover securely with foil.

5 Place in the pressure cooker inside the steamer basket, on the rack or trivet. Add 450ml/¾ pint/scant 2 cups water.

Electric: Close the lid and bring to High pressure using the Manual, Soup or Meat setting. Cook for 25 minutes (28 minutes). Release the pressure using natural release, making sure the 'keep warm' mode is switched off.
Stovetop: Close the lid and bring to High pressure. Cook for 25 minutes (28 minutes). Release the pressure slowly.

6 Open the lid and remove from the cooker. Leave to cool.

7 Spoon the yellow liquid from the melted butter over the top of the pâté, leaving the sediment behind. Decorate with bay leaves or herbs and black peppercorns, and chill until ready to serve.

Energy 164kcal/680kJ; Protein 9.7g; Carbohydrate 1.7g, of which sugars 1.3g; Fat 12.3g, of which saturates 7.3g; Cholesterol 219mg; Calcium 16mg; Fibre 0.7g; Sodium 117mg.

Globe Artichokes with Lemon and Tarragon Sauce

Elegant globe artichokes are a welcome summer treat. The pressure cooker reduces their cooking time, so they make a quick and tasty snack or appetizer, served here with a tangy lemon dipping sauce flavoured with shallot, tarragon and parsley.

1 Trim the artichoke stalks close to the base. Pull the toughest outer leaves off. Cut the tips off the remaining leaves. Rub the cut surface with lemon juice.

2 Place the artichokes on the trivet or in the steamer basket, base down. Add 450ml/¾ pint/scant 2 cups hot water. Add the crushed garlic.

Electric: Close the lid and bring to High pressure using the Manual, Soup or Meat setting. Cook for 13 minutes (16 minutes). Release the pressure quickly, making sure the 'keep warm' mode is switched off.
Stovetop: Close the lid and bring to High pressure. Cook for 13 minutes (16 minutes). Release the pressure quickly.

3 While the artichokes are cooking, mix together the mayonnaise and lemon juice for the sauce. Fold in the shallot, tarragon and parsley.

4 After quickly releasing the pressure, check to make sure the artichokes are cooked. As artichokes vary in size, they may need a couple of minutes more. When ready, you should easily be able to pull out a leaf. You can also put a skewer down the centre of the artichoke.

5 Remove the artichokes from the pressure cooker and place upside down for a few seconds to drain. Place the lemon and tarragon sauce in small dishes and serve with the artichoke, for dipping.

Pressure: High
Time under Pressure: 13 minutes (16 minutes)
Release: Quick
Serves 2

2 medium artichokes
1 lemon
1 garlic clove, crushed

For the sauce
45ml/3 tbsp mayonnaise
juice of 1 lemon
1 shallot, finely chopped
15ml/1 tbsp chopped fresh tarragon
15ml/1 tbsp chopped fresh parsley

Energy 229kcal/948kJ; Protein 8.1g; Carbohydrate 7.4g, of which sugars 3.9g; Fat 20.2g, of which saturates 3.2g; Cholesterol 31mg; Calcium 139mg; Fibre 1.2g; Sodium 152mg.

FISH AND SEAFOOD

In general, fish requires very little cooking as its delicious flavour and texture can be easily spoilt. However, the pressure cooker is extremely helpful in reducing the cooking smells, as they are mostly contained within the cooker. Fish dishes made in the pressure cooker also remain succulent, as this is a moist method of cooking. The recipes in this section feature both white and oily fish, including curry, fish stews and haddock fillets with lentils, as well as stuffed mackerel, trout and salmon. You can also make kedgeree, cooking the egg, rice and haddock in the pressure cooker at the same time, making for easy preparation and clean-up afterwards.

Green Fish Curry

Fresh-tasting spicy curries made with coconut milk are a classic of Thai cuisine. This pressure-cooked version of green curry uses desiccated coconut and cream to create a rich flavour and texture, which is offset by the generous use of spices, chilli and fragrant herbs.

1 Place the onion, chilli, garlic, cashew nuts, fennel seeds and coconut in a food processor with 45ml/3 tbsp water and blend to make a smooth paste. Alternatively, work the dry ingredients to a paste, with a mortar in a pestle, then stir in the 45ml/3 tbsp water.

2 Cut the fish into 5cm/2in chunks and place in a glass bowl. Combine the turmeric, lime juice and a pinch of salt in a separate bowl and pour over the fish. Use your hands to rub it into the fish.

3 Heat the oil in the pressure cooker. Add the cumin seeds and cook for 30 seconds. Stir in the coconut paste and fry for 4–5 minutes, stirring. Use the Sauté or Soup setting for the electric pressure cooker.

4 Stir in the ground coriander and cumin. Add the remaining water and half the cream. Stir the fish into the sauce.

Electric: Close the lid and bring to High pressure using the Manual or Soup setting. Cook for 3 minutes (4 minutes). Release the pressure quickly, making sure the 'keep warm' mode is switched off.
Stovetop: Close the lid and bring to High pressure. Cook for 3 minutes (4 minutes). Release the pressure quickly.

5 Stir in the remaining cream and coriander. Spoon the curry into warmed bowls. Garnish with chopped coriander and sliced green chilli, and serve with rice, if you wish.

Pressure: High
Time under Pressure: 3 minutes (4 minutes)
Release: Quick
Serves 4

1 onion, chopped
1 large fresh green chilli, halved, seeded and chopped, plus extra slices, to garnish
1 garlic clove, crushed
50g/2oz/½ cup cashew nuts
2.5ml/½ tsp fennel seeds
30ml/2 tbsp desiccated (dry unsweetened shredded) coconut
300ml/½ pint/1¼ cups water
4 white fish fillets, such as cod or haddock, skinned
1.5ml/¼ tsp ground turmeric
30ml/2 tbsp lime juice
30ml/2 tbsp sunflower oil
1.5ml/¼ tsp cumin seeds
1.5ml/¼ tsp ground coriander
2.5ml/½ tsp ground cumin
150ml/¼ pint/⅔ cup double (heavy) cream
salt
45ml/3 tbsp chopped fresh coriander (cilantro), plus extra to garnish
boiled rice, to serve (optional)

Cook's Tip
Some electric pressure cookers will not let you set less than 5 minutes, so you will have to set the minimum and turn the machine off after the given time.

Energy 447kcal/1854kJ; Protein 23.4g; Carbohydrate 6.4g, of which sugars 3.8g; Fat 37.7g, of which saturates 18.5g; Cholesterol 87mg; Calcium 84mg; Fibre 2.6g; Sodium 86mg.

Haddock and Puy Lentils

Dark green Puy lentils have a delicate taste and texture and hold their shape during cooking, which makes them particularly good for pressure-cooked dishes. Red chilli pepper and ground cumin add a hint of heat and spice without overpowering the flavour of the fish.

Pressure: High
Time under Pressure: 9 minutes
 (11 minutes)
Release: Natural/Slow
Serves 4

175g/6oz/¾ cup Puy lentils
4 thick 150g/5oz pieces of
 haddock fillet
25g/1oz/2 tbsp butter, softened
10ml/2 tsp lemon juice
5ml/1 tsp finely grated lemon rind
30ml/2 tbsp olive oil
1 onion, finely chopped
2 celery sticks, finely chopped
1 fresh red chilli, halved, seeded
 and finely chopped
2.5ml/½ tsp ground cumin
600ml/1 pint/2½ cups hot
 vegetable stock
salt and ground black pepper
lemon wedges, to garnish

Cook's Tip
Any firm white fish can be cooked in this way. Cod and swordfish give particularly good results.

Energy 362kcal/1526kJ; Protein 39.7g;
Carbohydrate 24.5g, of which sugars 2.8g; Fat
12.5g, of which saturates 4.3g; Cholesterol 67mg;
Calcium 69mg; Fibre 6.1g; Sodium 154mg.

1 Place the lentils in a sieve or strainer and rinse under cold running water, then drain.

2 Place each haddock fillet on a square of foil. Mix the butter, lemon juice and rind together and dot over the fish. Season with salt and ground black pepper. Wrap the foil over the top of each piece of fish to make a parcel.

3 Put the oil in the pressure cooker, add the onion and sauté for 3–4 minutes, or until the onion is softened. Add the celery, chilli and cumin and cook for 2 minutes, stirring. Use the Sauté or Soup setting for the electric pressure cooker.

4 Add the drained lentils and stock and mix thoroughly. Place the fish parcels on top.

Electric: Close the lid and bring to High pressure using the Manual, Soup or Fish setting. Cook for 9 minutes (11 minutes). Release the pressure using natural release, making sure the 'keep warm' mode is switched off.
Stovetop: Close the lid and bring to High pressure. Cook for 9 minutes (11 minutes). Release the pressure slowly.

5 Open the lid and carefully remove the fish parcels. Check the lentils; if they need a little longer, simmer for a few minutes, uncovered.

6 To serve, divide the lentils between four plates. Unseal the fish parcels and carefully place on top on the lentils. Serve garnished with lemon wedges.

Fish Stew with Lemon Grass

Lemon grass and ginger give this delicate stew of fish, prawns, new potatoes and broccoli an appetizing, aromatic flavour. It is easy to release the pressure part way through cooking, and add extra ingredients that take less time to cook, before returning to pressure again.

Pressure: High
Time under Pressure: 6 minutes (8 minutes)
Release: Quick
Serves 4

25g/1oz/2 tbsp butter
1 large onion, chopped
2.5cm/1in piece fresh root ginger
2 lemon grass stalks, trimmed and finely chopped
15ml/1 tbsp plain (all-purpose) flour
150ml/¼ pint/⅔ cup dry white wine
400ml/14fl oz/1⅔ cup light fish stock
450g/1lb baby new potatoes, scrubbed
225g/8oz small broccoli florets
450g/1lb chunky white fish fillets, skinned and cut into large chunks
175g/6oz large, cooked, peeled prawns (shrimp)
150ml/¼ pint/⅔ cup double (heavy) cream
60ml/4 tbsp chopped fresh garlic chives
salt and ground black pepper
crusty bread, to serve

1 Melt the butter in the open pressure cooker. Add the onion and sauté for 3–4 minutes, until softened. Add the ginger and lemon grass and cook for 1 minute. Stir in the flour, wine and stock and bring to the boil, stirring continuously. Use the Sauté or Soup setting for the electric pressure cooker. Stir in the potatoes.

Electric: Close the lid and bring to High pressure using the Manual, Soup or Fish setting. Cook for 3 minutes (4 minutes). Release the pressure quickly, making sure the 'keep warm' mode is switched off.
Stovetop: Close the lid and bring to High pressure. Cook for 3 minutes (4 minutes). Release the pressure quickly.

2 Add the broccoli and fish fillets and stir to combine.

Electric: Close the lid and return to High pressure using the Manual, Soup or Fish setting. Cook for 3 minutes (4 minutes). Release the pressure quickly, making sure the 'keep warm' mode is switched off.
Stovetop: Close the lid and return to High pressure. Cook for 3 minutes (4 minutes). Release the pressure quickly.

3 Remove the lid carefully and stir in the prawns and cream. Simmer for 1 minute, to heat through. Use the Sauté or Soup setting for the electric pressure cooker. Adjust the seasoning. Transfer to a warmed serving dish and sprinkle in the chives. Serve with plenty of crusty bread.

Energy 509kcal/2122kJ; Protein 34.3g; Carbohydrate 26.9g, of which sugars 6.1g; Fat 27.3g, of which saturates 16.2g; Cholesterol 239mg; Calcium 124mg; Fibre 4.6g; Sodium 217mg.

Salmon Provençale

As well as being a quick and easy way to prepare salmon, using the pressure cooker also helps to reduce the fishy smell while cooking. The depth of the salmon can vary, so increase the timings by 1 minute if the fish is quite thick. Serve with new potatoes and a green salad.

Pressure: High

Time under Pressure: 4 minutes (5 minutes)

Release: Quick

Serves 4

15ml/1 tbsp sunflower oil

1 large onion, chopped

1 garlic clove, crushed

1 yellow (bell) pepper, halved, seeded and sliced

1 red (bell) pepper, halved, seeded and sliced

400g/14oz can chopped tomatoes

75ml/2½fl oz/⅓ cup vegetable stock or water

10ml/2 tsp fresh thyme leaves

1 bay leaf

4 salmon fillets, about 175g/6oz each

30ml/2 tbsp tomato purée (paste)

salt and ground black pepper

fresh thyme sprigs, to garnish

1 Heat the oil in the open pressure cooker. Add the onion and sauté for 4–5 minutes, until softened. Use the Sauté or Soup setting for the electric pressure cooker.

2 Add the garlic and peppers and cook, stirring frequently for 3–4 minutes, or until softened. Stir in the chopped tomatoes, stock or water, thyme and bay leaf. Place the salmon on top, skin side down.

Electric: Close the lid and bring to High pressure using the Manual, Soup or Fish setting. Cook for 4 minutes (5 minutes). Release the pressure quickly, making sure the 'keep warm' mode is switched off.
Stovetop: Close the lid and bring to High pressure. Cook for 4 minutes (5 minutes). Release the pressure quickly.

3 Transfer the salmon fillets to warmed serving plates.

4 Stir the tomato purée into the sauce, adjust the seasoning and remove the bay leaf. Heat for 1 minute. Use the Sauté or Soup setting for the electric pressure cooker. Divide the sauce between the salmon fillets. Garnish with thyme sprigs and serve.

Energy 403kcal/1681kJ; Protein 38.1g; Carbohydrate 12.6g, of which sugars 11.3g; Fat 22.6g, of which saturates 3.8g; Cholesterol 88mg; Calcium 68mg; Fibre 3.8g; Sodium 141mg.

Kedgeree

You can cook all the ingredients at the same time in your pressure cooker by layering the fish, eggs and rice on top of each other, then combining them once cooked. Kedgeree is perfect for brunch or as a light supper dish, served with coriander-flavoured natural yogurt.

Pressure: High

**Time under Pressure: 7 minutes
(9 minutes)**

Release: Natural/Slow

Serves 4

350g/12oz smoked haddock fillet

3 eggs

200g/7oz/1 cup long grain rice

25g/1oz/2 tbsp butter

15ml/1 tbsp sunflower oil

1 onion, chopped

2.5cm/1 in piece fresh root ginger, peeled and grated

10ml/2 tsp curry powder

115g/4oz/1 cup frozen peas

45ml/3 tbsp single (light) cream

45ml/3 tbsp chopped fresh parsley

salt and ground black pepper

coriander (cilantro) yogurt, to serve (optional)

Energy 458kcal/1913kJ; Protein 29.4g;
Carbohydrate 47.4g, of which sugars 3.3g;
Fat 16.8g, of which saturates 6.6g; Cholesterol
224mg; Calcium 120mg; Fibre 4g; Sodium 786mg.

1 Place a trivet or rack in the base of the pressure cooker. Add 300ml/½ pint/1¼ cups water. Enclose the haddock in foil, skin side down, to make a parcel. Lay the fish and eggs on top of the trivet.

2 Line the separator or steamer basket with foil and add the rice. You can use a metal bowl, which will fit inside the pressure cooker, if you prefer. Make sure the bowl is large enough to allow the rice to expand. Place in the pressure cooker on top of the fish and eggs. Add 450ml/15fl oz/scant 2 cups boiling water.

Electric: Close the lid and bring to High pressure using the Manual, Soup or Fish setting. Cook for 7 minutes (9 minutes). Release the pressure for 5 minutes using natural release, making sure the 'keep warm' mode is switched off, then quickly release the remaining steam, if any.
Stovetop: Close the lid and bring to High pressure. Cook for 7 minutes (9 minutes). Release the pressure slowly for 5 minutes, then quickly release the remaining steam, if any.

3 Remove the rice container and set aside. Using a slotted spoon, remove the eggs and place in a bowl of cold water. Remove the fish.

4 In the cleaned pan, heat the butter and oil. Add the onion and sauté for 3–4 minutes. Add the ginger and curry powder and cook for 1 minute. Meanwhile, flake the fish, removing any skin or bones.

5 Add the rice to the pressure cooker with the peas, cream and seasoning. Heat for a couple of minutes. Peel the eggs and cut into quarters. Stir the fish into the rice and heat for 1 minute.

6 Stir in half the parsley and egg quarters. Transfer to a warmed serving dish. Sprinkle with the remaining parsley and serve with coriander yogurt, if you wish.

Orange and Thyme Stuffed Mackerel

This recipe shows the versatility of your pressure cooker, as the new potatoes are cooked with the mackerel, saving on both time and washing-up. The horseradish sauce is the perfect foil for this oily fish. The fragrant stuffing can be used with herring, if you prefer.

Pressure: High
**Time under Pressure: 10 minutes
  (13 minutes)**
Release: Quick
Serves 4

4 medium fresh mackerel, cleaned,
  gutted and heads removed
50g/2oz/1 cup fresh breadcrumbs
30ml/2 tbsp chopped fresh
  thyme leaves
45ml/3 tbsp chopped fresh chives
30ml/2 tbsp chopped walnuts
grated rind and juice of 1 orange
450g/1lb baby new potatoes,
  or small halved, scrubbed
25g/1oz/2 tbsp butter
salt and ground black pepper
orange wedges, to garnish
mangetouts (snow peas), to serve
  (optional)

For the horseradish sauce
30ml/2 tbsp light mayonnaise
30ml/2 tbsp light crème fraîche
15ml/1 tbsp hot horseradish sauce
10ml/2 tsp lemon juice
5ml/1 tsp Dijon mustard
15ml/1 tbsp chopped fresh dill
15ml/1 tbsp chopped chives

1 Wash the mackerel in cold water, remove any scales and dry on kitchen paper. Open out the cavity and place skin side down on a chopping board and remove the backbone.

2 Mix together the breadcrumbs, thyme, 30ml/2 tbsp chives, walnuts and orange rind and juice. Season with salt and pepper. Divide the stuffing between the cavities and close the fish, securing with wooden cocktail sticks or toothpicks. Place each mackerel on a buttered square of foil, large enough to enclose it completely. Fold over and seal.

3 In a small bowl, mix together the mayonnaise, crème fraîche, horseradish, lemon juice and mustard for the sauce. Stir through the dill and chives. Place in a small serving dish and set aside.

4 Pour 275ml/9fl oz/generous 1 cup water into the base of the pressure cooker and place the trivet, rim side down, in the cooker. Use a round cooling rack if you do not have a trivet. Lay the fish on top.

Electric: Close the lid and bring to High pressure using the Manual, Soup or Fish setting. Cook for 3 minutes (4 minutes). Release the pressure quickly, making sure the 'keep warm' mode is switched off.
Stovetop: Close the lid and bring to High pressure. Cook for 3 minutes (4 minutes). Release the pressure quickly.

5 Meanwhile, place the potatoes in the separator or steamer basket. Carefully remove the lid and place the potatoes on top of the fish.

Electric: Close the lid and return to High pressure using the Manual, Soup or Fish setting. Cook for 7 minutes (9 minutes). Release the pressure quickly, making sure the 'keep warm' mode is switched off.
Stovetop: Close the lid and return to High pressure. Cook for 7 minutes (9 minutes). Release the pressure quickly.

6 Carefully remove the lid and lift out the potatoes. Place in a warmed bowl and toss with the butter.

7 Lift the fish out, open the parcels and remove the cocktail sticks or toothpicks. Garnish with orange wedges and serve with the potatoes, horseradish sauce, and mangetouts, if you wish. Sprinkle over the remaining chives.

Cook's Tip
You can cook the mackerel without the new potatoes. Just cook at High pressure for 8–10 minutes.

Energy 760kcal/3168kJ; Protein 52.4g; Carbohydrate 32.3g, of which sugars 5.6g; Fat 47.5g, of which saturates 11.9g; Cholesterol 186mg; Calcium 83mg; Fibre 3.3g; Sodium 496mg.

Far Eastern Fish

Sea bass fillets steamed in parchment with Eastern flavours of ginger, chilli and lime served on a bed of cabbage make a healthy yet delicious supper dish. Use your pressure cooker basket or separator to keep the cabbage contained, for easier removal at the end of cooking.

Pressure: High

Time under Pressure: 4 minutes (6 minutes)

Release: Natural/Slow

Serves 4

4 sea bass fillets

1 lime, thinly sliced

2.5cm/1in piece fresh root ginger, peeled and cut into thin strips

1 fresh red chilli, halved, seeded and sliced

30ml/2 tbsp sweet chilli sauce

350g/12oz green cabbage

15ml/1 tbsp light soy sauce

15ml/1 tbsp toasted sesame seeds

2 spring onions (scallions), cut into strips, to garnish

lime wedges, to garnish

1 Cut four squares of baking parchment large enough to wrap and enclose each fillet. Place a fillet on each sheet and top with lime slices, ginger and chilli.

2 Sprinkle over the sweet chilli sauce and enclose each piece of fish in the parchment to make a parcel.

3 Shred the cabbage and place in the separator or steamer basket. Place the four fish parcels on top.

4 Add 275ml/9fl oz/generous 1 cup water to the pressure cooker. Place the separator or steamer basket in the pressure cooker.

Electric: Close the lid and bring to High pressure using the Manual, Soup or Fish setting. Cook for 4 minutes (6 minutes). Reduce the pressure for 5 minutes using natural release, making sure the 'keep warm' mode is switched off, then quickly release the remaining steam, if any.
Stovetop: Close the lid and bring to High pressure. Cook for 4 minutes (6 minutes). Reduce the pressure slowly for 5 minutes, then quickly release the remaining steam, if any.

5 Remove the fish fillets from the basket. Drain the cabbage and place in a warm bowl. Toss with the soy sauce and sesame seeds. Divide between four serving plates. Unwrap the fish and place on top of the cabbage. Sprinkle with spring onions and garnish with lime wedges.

Energy 203kcal/852kJ; Protein 31.3g; Carbohydrate 5.3g, of which sugars 5.1g; Fat 6.3g, of which saturates 1.1g; Cholesterol 120mg; Calcium 268mg; Fibre 3.3g; Sodium 572mg.

Trout en Papillote

This method of cooking fish in a foil parcel in the pressure cooker ensures the fish remains succulent. It is equally delicious with salmon fillets, if you prefer. Serve with new potatoes, or a jacket potato if new potatoes are out of season, and a green salad or vegetable.

 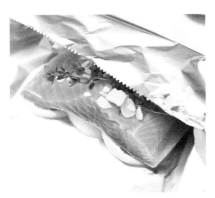 

1 Cut four squares of foil, large enough to enclose the fish, about 20cm/8in. Lightly butter each square.

2 Place one slice of onion and two slices of lemon on each piece of foil and then place the trout on top. Place a thyme sprig on top of each piece of fish and sprinkle with almonds and ground black pepper.

3 Spoon over the white wine. Fold the foil over the fish and seal the edges to make parcels.

4 Place the trivet or rack in the pressure cooker and add 250ml/8fl oz/1 cup water. Place the parcels on the trivet or rack.

Electric: Close the lid and bring to High pressure using the Manual, Soup or Fish setting. Cook for 4 minutes (5 minutes). Release the pressure using natural release, making sure the 'keep warm' mode is switched off. After 5 minutes, release any remaining pressure quickly.
Stovetop: Close the lid and bring to High pressure. Cook for 4 minutes (5 minutes). Release the pressure slowly. After 5 minutes, release any remaining pressure quickly.

5 Remove the parcels, open and sprinkle with parsley. Serve the parcels on warmed serving plates, accompanied by potatoes and a green salad or vegetable.

Pressure: High
Time under Pressure: 4 minutes
  (5 minutes)
Release: Natural/Slow
Serves 4

25g/1oz/2 tbsp butter
1 onion, cut into 4 slices
8 lemon slices
4 trout fillets, about 2.5cm/1in thick
4 thyme sprigs
30ml/2 tbsp toasted flaked almonds
60ml/4 tbsp dry white wine
30ml/2 tbsp chopped fresh parsley
salt and ground black pepper
potatoes and a green salad or
  vegetable, to serve

Energy 273kcal/1138kJ; Protein 31g; Carbohydrate 0.9g, of which sugars 0.6g; Fat 15.1g, of which saturates 3.6g; Cholesterol 13mg; Calcium 49mg; Fibre 0.5g; Sodium 126mg.

Jamaican Fish Stew

This Caribbean fish is cooked in coconut milk flavoured with tomatoes, peppers and coriander, spiced up with a little fresh chilli. If using an electric pressure cooker, make sure the 'keep warm' mode is switched off when reducing the pressure quickly.

Pressure: High
Time under Pressure: 4 minutes
   (6 minutes)
Release: Quick
Serves 4

15ml/1 tbsp lime juice
1 jalapeño, halved, seeded and
   chopped
500g/1¼lb red snapper fillets,
   or cod, halibut or salmon,
   cut into chunks
15ml/1 tbsp butter
15ml/1 tbsp sunflower oil
1 onion, chopped
1 garlic clove, finely chopped
1 red (bell) pepper, seeded and sliced
1 green (bell) pepper, seeded
   and sliced
400g/14oz can chopped tomatoes
250ml/8fl oz/1 cup coconut milk
225g/8oz raw peeled king prawns
   (jumbo shrimp)
30ml/2 tbsp chopped fresh coriander
   (cilantro)
salt and ground black pepper
rice or crusty bread, to serve

1 Mix the lime juice and jalapeño together in a bowl. Add the fish chunks and toss together.

2 Heat the butter and oil in the open pressure cooker. Add the onion and sauté for 3–4 minutes. Add the garlic and cook for 30 seconds. Use the Sauté or Soup setting for the electric pressure cooker.

3 Add the peppers, chopped tomatoes and coconut milk and stir to combine.

Electric: Close the lid and bring to High pressure using the Manual, Soup or Fish setting. Cook for 4 minutes (6 minutes). Release the pressure quickly, making sure the 'keep warm' mode is switched off.
Stovetop: Close the lid and bring to High pressure. Cook for 4 minutes (6 minutes). Release the pressure quickly.

4 Carefully remove the lid and stir through the fish chunks and marinade with the prawns.

5 Cook in the open pressure cooker for 3–4 minutes, until the fish chunks and prawns are just cooked through, stirring occasionally. Use the Sauté or Soup setting for the electric pressure cooker. Adjust the seasoning and transfer to a warmed serving dish. Sprinkle with chopped coriander and serve with rice or crusty bread.

Energy 266kcal/1119kJ; Protein 36.5g;
Carbohydrate 11.7g, of which sugars 11.2g; Fat
8.4g, of which saturates 2.9g; Cholesterol 164mg;
Calcium 132mg; Fibre 2.8g; Sodium 337mg.

Prawn Jambalaya

You can vary the ingredients in this Creole-inspired pressure cooker recipe. It is traditionally made with a mixture of seafood, chicken and rice. You can replace the sausage with ham, or just use fish and chicken. Here, the emphasis is on the deliciously juicy prawns.

1 Heat the oil in the open pressure cooker. Add the chicken then chorizo and sauté for 3–4 minutes. Remove with a slotted spoon on to a plate and set aside. Use the Sauté or Soup setting for the electric pressure cooker.

2 Add the onion and sauté for 3–4 minutes, then add the garlic, jalapeño and peppers and sauté for 2–3 minutes.

3 Stir in the rice and cook for 30 seconds. Return the chicken and chorizo to the cooker. Add the tomatoes and stock and stir thoroughly to remove any sediment from the base of the cooker.

Electric: Close the lid and bring to High pressure. Cook for 5 minutes (7 minutes). Release the pressure using natural release, making sure the 'keep warm' mode is switched off. After 5 minutes, quickly release any remaining pressure, if any.

Stovetop: Close the lid and bring to High pressure. Cook for 5 minutes (7 minutes). Release the pressure slowly. After 5 minutes, quickly release any remaining pressure, if any.

4 Carefully remove the lid and stir in the prawns. Cook in the open pressure cooker for 3–4 minutes, until the prawns are just cooked through, stirring occasionally. Use the Sauté or Soup setting for the electric pressure cooker. Adjust the seasoning and transfer to a warmed serving dish. Garnish with flat leaf parsley and serve.

Cook's Tip
If the rice is quite dry at the end of step 4, add a little extra stock with the prawns in step 5, to prevent the rice from sticking while cooking the prawns.

Pressure: High
Time under Pressure: 5 minutes (7 minutes)
Release: Natural/Slow
Serves 4

30ml/2 tbsp sunflower oil
1 chicken breast fillet, cut into 2.5cm/1in chunks
50g/2oz chorizo, cut into 1.2cm/½in slices
1 onion, chopped
2 garlic cloves, finely chopped
1 green jalapeño, halved, seeded and finely chopped
1 yellow (bell) pepper, seeded and sliced
1 red (bell) pepper, seeded and sliced
175g/6oz/scant 1 cup basmati rice
400g/14oz can chopped tomatoes
300ml/½ pint/1¼ cups chicken or vegetable stock
16 raw king prawns (jumbo shrimp), peeled and deveined
fresh flat leaf parsley sprig, to garnish
salt and ground black pepper

Energy 349kcal/1460kJ; Protein 24.9g; Carbohydrate 46.5g, of which sugars 10.2g; Fat 7g, of which saturates 0.9g; Cholesterol 128mg; Calcium 79mg; Fibre 3.5g; Sodium 165mg.

Calamari with Tomato Sauce

A spicy tomato sauce is used to braise these calamari or squid rings. By using the pressure cooker, you can quickly achieve the same results as a long, slow cook. Serve with pasta, creamy polenta, rice or crusty bread to mop up the delicious sauce.

1 In a bowl, mix the chillies, garlic and olive oil together with a pinch of salt. Add the squid and mix well. Leave to marinate for 30 minutes.

2 Heat the sunflower oil in the open pressure cooker. Add the onion and sauté for 3–4 minutes. Add the squid and marinade and sauté for 2–3 minutes. Use the Sauté or Soup setting for the electric pressure cooker.

3 Add the white wine and bring to the boil. Stir in the chopped tomatoes.

Electric: Close the lid and bring to High pressure using the Manual, Soup or Meat setting. Cook for 20 minutes (25 minutes). Release the pressure quickly, making sure the 'keep warm' mode is switched off.
Stovetop: Close the lid and bring to High pressure. Cook for 20 minutes (25 minutes). Release the pressure quickly.

4 Remove the lid and stir in the tomato purée and black olives. Season to taste. Leave to stand for 5 minutes. Stir in the chopped parsley and transfer to a warmed serving dish. Serve with pasta, polenta, rice or crusty bread, if you wish.

Pressure: High
Time under Pressure: 20 minutes (25 minutes)
Release: Quick
Serves 4

2 fresh red chillies, seeded and chopped
2 garlic cloves, crushed
15ml/2 tbsp olive oil
675g/1½lb squid, cleaned and cut into rings, tentacles left whole
15ml/1 tbsp sunflower oil
1 red onion, finely chopped
200ml/7fl oz/scant 1 cup dry white wine
400g/14oz can chopped tomatoes
30ml/2 tbsp tomato purée (paste)
50g/2oz black olives, pitted
30ml/2 tbsp chopped fresh flat leaf parsley
salt and ground black pepper
pasta, polenta, rice or crusty bread, to serve (optional)

Cook's Tip
To prepare the calamari or squid, hold the body in one hand and firmly pull the tentacles with the other. This should also remove the soft contents of the body pouch. Cut the tentacle just in front of the eyes and discard the body cavity, but keep the tentacles. Rinse the body in cold running water and dry.

Energy 294kcal/1234kJ; Protein 28.7g; Carbohydrate 8.7g, of which sugars 6.4g; Fat 12.9g, of which saturates 2g; Cholesterol 380mg; Calcium 72mg; Fibre 2.2g; Sodium 534mg.

Saffron Mussels

Mussels are very quick and easy to cook in a pressure cooker. The saffron adds a lovely pungent flavour, as well as its characteristic yellow colour, to the creamy parsley sauce. Serve with French bread, to soak up the tasty liquid.

Pressure: High
Time under Pressure: 2 minutes (3 minutes)
Release: Quick
Serves 4

a few saffron threads
1kg/2¼lb mussels, in their shells
25g/1oz/2 tbsp butter
2 shallots, finely chopped
2 garlic cloves, finely chopped
250ml/8fl oz/1 cup dry white wine
60ml/4 tbsp double (heavy) cream
30ml/2 tbsp chopped fresh parsley
salt and ground black pepper
French bread, to serve

Cook's Tip

Saffron is the stigma of a type of crocus. It is an expensive spice, and is sold as thin, wiry threads. It has a mild aroma and adds a slightly pungent flavour to both sweet and savoury dishes, and also to buns, cakes and breads. However, the main characteristic of saffron is the distinctive yellow colour it imparts once it is diluted in water.

Energy 246kcal/1023kJ; Protein 12.1g; Carbohydrate 5.9g, of which sugars 2.8g; Fat 15g, of which saturates 8.5g; Cholesterol 74mg; Calcium 59mg; Fibre 0.7g; Sodium 285mg.

1 Put the saffron in a small bowl. Add 15ml/1 tbsp boiling water and leave to soak.

2 Scrub the mussels, pull off all the beards and discard any open mussels that do not close when tapped.

3 Melt the butter in the pressure cooker, add the shallots and garlic and cook for 4–5 minutes, to soften. Use the Sauté or Soup setting for the electric pressure cooker. Stir in the wine and bring to the boil. Add all the closed mussels.

Electric: Close the lid and bring to High pressure using the Manual or Soup setting. Cook for 2 minutes (3 minutes). Release the pressure quickly, making sure the 'keep warm' mode is switched off.
Stovetop: Close the lid and bring to High pressure. Cook for 2 minutes (3 minutes). Release the pressure quickly.

4 Open the lid carefully. All the mussels should have opened. Discard any that have not.

5 Using a slotted spoon, transfer the mussels to four warmed serving bowls. Stir the cream into the cooking liquid with the parsley. Season to taste. Pour the cooking liquid over the mussels and serve immediately with French bread, to soak up the sauce.

Braised Beef and Horseradish

This dark, rich beef with a spicy kick makes an ideal alternative to a meat roast. The meat tenderizes in the pressure cooker and all the flavours blend together beautifully. It is also a great dish for entertaining, because it can be made in advance.

Pressure: High
Time under Pressure: 30 minutes
   (41 minutes)
Release: Quick
Serves 4

15ml/1 tbsp plain (all-purpose) flour
4 x 175g/6oz braising steaks or
   feather steak
30ml/2 tbsp sunflower oil
1 garlic clove, crushed
1.5ml/¼ tsp ground ginger
5ml/1 tsp curry powder
15ml/1 tbsp Worcestershire sauce
30ml/2 tbsp creamed horseradish
1 bay leaf
450ml/¾ pint/scant 2 cups
   beef stock
25g/1oz/2 tbsp butter
12 small shallots
225g/8oz baby carrots
5ml/1 tsp soft light brown sugar
salt and ground black pepper
30ml/2 tbsp chopped fresh chives,
   to garnish
roasted potatoes and parsnips,
   to serve (optional)

Energy 379kcal/1586kJ; Protein 41g; Carbohydrate 12.7g, of which sugars 8.2g; Fat 18.6g, of which saturates 7g; Cholesterol 115mg; Calcium 62mg; Fibre 3.6g; Sodium 215mg.

1 Place the flour in a large, flat dish and season with salt and pepper. Toss the steaks in the flour to coat.

2 Heat the oil in the open pressure cooker. Add the meat and brown on both sides. Use the Sauté or Meat setting for the electric pressure cooker.

3 Add the garlic, ginger, curry powder, Worcestershire sauce, horseradish, bay leaf and beef stock. Stir thoroughly and scrape any sediment off the base of the cooker.

Electric: Close the lid and bring to High pressure using the Manual, Soup or Meat setting. Cook for 25 minutes (35 minutes). Release the pressure quickly, making sure the 'keep warm' mode is switched off.
Stovetop: Close the lid and bring to High pressure. Cook for 25 minutes (35 minutes). Release the pressure quickly.

4 Meanwhile, melt the butter in a heavy pan, add the shallots and sauté until lightly caramelized. Stir in the carrots and sugar and cook for 2 minutes.

5 Remove the lid carefully. Add the shallots and carrots.

Electric: Close the lid and return to High pressure using the Manual, Soup or Vegetable setting. Cook for 5 minutes (6 minutes). Release the pressure quickly, making sure the 'keep warm' mode is switched off.
Stovetop: Close the lid and return to High pressure. Cook for 5 minutes (6 minutes). Release the pressure quickly.

6 Uncover the stew and remove the bay leaf. Transfer to a warmed serving dish or serving plates and sprinkle with chopped chives. Serve with roasted potatoes and parsnips, if you wish.

Chilli con Carne

Always a favourite recipe, this spicy beef, tomato and red kidney bean dish can be cooked together with the rice in the pressure cooker, making it an easy-to-prepare meal. You could serve it with green salad and guacamole, or a bowl of sour cream.

1 Place the kidney beans in a bowl. Cover with boiling water and leave to stand for 1 hour.

2 Heat the oil in the open pressure cooker and add the onion. Fry for 4–5 minutes, until golden. Use the Sauté or Meat setting for the electric pressure cooker. Add the beef and garlic and fry until browned. Stir in the chilli or chilli powder, beef stock, chopped tomatoes and tomato purée. Drain the kidney beans and add to the cooker.

Electric: Close the lid and bring to High pressure using the Manual or Meat setting. Cook for 16 minutes (20 minutes). Release the pressure using natural release, making sure the 'keep warm' mode is switched off. After 10 minutes, quickly release the remaining pressure, if any.
Stovetop: Close the lid and bring to High pressure. Cook for 16 minutes (20 minutes). Release the pressure slowly. After 10 minutes, quickly release the remaining pressure, if any.

3 Meanwhile, place the rice in a metal bowl that will fit in the pressure cooker. Add 450ml/¾ pint/scant 2 cups water and salt. Cover with a double layer of baking parchment and tie securely with string.

4 Remove the lid carefully and season the chilli. Stand the bowl of rice on top of the chilli mix.

Electric: Close the lid and return to High pressure using the Manual or Meat setting. Cook for 9 minutes (10 minutes). Release the pressure using natural release, making sure the 'keep warm' mode is switched off.
Stovetop: Close the lid and bring to High pressure. Cook for 9 minutes (10 minutes). Release the pressure slowly.

5 Remove the rice, uncover and drain, if necessary. Serve with the chilli, garnished with chopped parsley and sour cream or guacamole and a green salad, if you wish.

Pressure: High
Time under Pressure: 25 minutes (30 minutes)
Release: Natural/Slow
Serves 4

125g/4¼oz/⅝ cup dried red kidney beans
30ml/2 tbsp sunflower oil
1 onion, chopped
400g/14oz lean minced (ground) beef
2 garlic cloves, crushed
1 fresh red chilli, chopped, or 5ml/1 tsp chilli powder
280ml/½ pint/1¼ cups beef stock
400g/14oz can chopped tomatoes
15ml/1 tbsp tomato purée (paste)
225g/8oz/generous 1 cup long grain white rice
salt and ground black pepper
chopped fresh parsley, to garnish
sour cream or guacamole and green salad, to serve (optional)

Energy 496kcal/2082kJ; Protein 35.2g; Carbohydrate 65.2g, of which sugars 6.2g; Fat 10.7g, of which saturates 2.5g; Cholesterol 58mg; Calcium 70mg; Fibre 8.3g; Sodium 118mg.

Beef Pot Roast

This pressure-cooked version of the classic pot roast greatly reduces the cooking time, without any loss of flavour. Cooked in red wine with herbs, the succulent joint is delicious served with crusty bread to soak up the juices, or is equally good with Dauphinois potatoes.

1 Heat the oil in the open pressure cooker. Add the beef and brown on all sides, turning frequently. Transfer to a plate. Use the Sauté or Meat setting for the electric pressure cooker. Add the onion slices and bacon lardons and cook for 3–4 minutes, until browned. Add the wine, stir thoroughly, and scrape any sediment off the base of the cooker. Bring to the boil. Mix in the tomato purée and stock. Add the herb sprigs and potato chunks. Nestle the meat into the vegetables.

Electric: Close the lid and bring to High pressure using the Manual, Soup or Meat setting. Cook for 40 minutes (50 minutes).
Stovetop: Close the lid and bring to High pressure. Cook for 40 minutes (50 minutes).

2 Meanwhile, prepare the carrots and parsnips. Peel the carrots and cut in half, then into four lengthwise. Peel the parsnips and cut in half. Cut the chunkier end into four lengthwise and the thinner end into two, so they are a similar size to the carrots.

3 Release the pressure quickly, making sure the 'keep warm' mode is switched off for the electric pressure cooker. Remove the lid carefully and transfer the meat to a warmed serving plate. Cover with foil and leave to rest. Transfer the sauce to a bowl.

4 Place the prepared vegetables in the pressure cooker with 250ml/8fl oz/ 1 cup hot water.

Electric: Close the lid and bring to High pressure using the Manual, Meat or Vegetable setting. Cook for 5 minutes (6 minutes).
Stovetop: Close the lid and bring to High pressure. Cook for 5 minutes (6 minutes).

5 Meanwhile, remove the herb sprigs from the sauce and mash the potatoes into the sauce. They will be very soft and may have already broken down.

6 Release the pressure quickly, making sure the 'keep warm' mode is switched off for the electric pressure cooker. Remove the lid and drain the vegetables. Return the sauce to the cooker and reheat in the open cooker. Use the Manual, Sauté or Soup setting for the electric pressure cooker. Serve the meat with the vegetables and sauce, garnished with fresh herbs.

Cook's Tip
Some electric pressure cookers do not have a programme that will complete the full cooking time. If this is the case, note the maximum time and reset the cooker for the remaining time as soon as the initial time has finished.

Energy 485kcal/2034kJ; Protein 46.4g; Carbohydrate 30g, of which sugars 14.4g; Fat 18.4g, of which saturates 6g; Cholesterol 137mg; Calcium 79mg; Fibre 9g; Sodium 532mg.

Pressure: High
Time under Pressure: 45 minutes (56 minutes)
Release: Quick
Serves 4

15ml/1 tbsp sunflower oil
675g/1½lb beef silverside (pot roast) or brisket
1 onion, sliced
115g/4oz/⅔ cup smoked bacon lardons
125ml/4fl oz/½ cup red wine
45ml/3 tbsp tomato purée (paste)
350ml/12fl oz/1½ cups hot beef stock
2 fresh thyme sprigs, plus extra to garnish
2 fresh rosemary sprigs, plus extra to garnish
1 large potato, peeled and cut into chunks
3 carrots
3 parsnips
salt and ground black pepper

Steak and Kidney Pie

Use your pressure cooker to speed up the preparation of this tasty pie filling made with chunks of succulent beef and kidney in a mustard gravy. The pie is finished in the oven with a crispy puff pastry top. Serve with a selection of green vegetables.

Pressure: High

Time under Pressure: 25 minutes (35 minutes)

Release: Quick

Serves 4

675g/1½lb stewing beef

225g/8oz lamb's or ox kidney

30ml/2 tbsp plain (all-purpose) flour

15ml/1 tbsp sunflower oil

25g/1oz/2 tbsp butter

2 onions, chopped

350ml/12fl oz/1/1½ cups hot beef stock

2 bay leaves

15ml/1 tbsp tomato purée (paste)

10ml/2 tsp English (hot) mustard

225g/8oz puff pastry

beaten egg, to glaze

salt and ground black pepper

creamed potatoes and green
 vegetables, to serve

Variation

To make Steak and Kidney Pudding, use the filling for a suet crust pudding. Follow the instructions on pages 158–9, replacing the filling with the steak and kidney filling.

Energy 592kcal/2478kJ; Protein 52.9g;
Carbohydrate 33.1g, of which sugars 5.6g; Fat
28.5g, of which saturates 12.7g; Cholesterol
308mg; Calcium 79mg; Fibre 1.9g; Sodium 436mg.

1 Cut the meat into 2.5cm/1in pieces. Remove the white core from the kidney and cut into 2.5cm/1in pieces. Place in a bowl. Season the flour with salt and pepper, add to the meat and toss to coat the meat.

2 Heat the oil and butter in the open pressure cooker. Add the onions and fry for 3–4 minutes, until softened, stirring occasionally. Add the steak and kidney and any remaining flour and cook for 5 minutes, or until lightly browned. Use the Sauté or Meat setting for the electric pressure cooker.

3 Add the stock and stir to make sure all the sediment is removed from the base of the cooker. Bring to the boil, stirring. Add the bay leaves. Reduce the heat if using a stovetop pressure cooker.

Electric: Close the lid and bring to High pressure using the Manual, Meat or Soup setting. Sook for 25 minutes (35 minutes). Release the pressure quickly, making sure the 'keep warm' mode is switched off.
Stovetop: Close the lid and bring to High pressure. Cook for 25 minutes (35 minutes). Release the pressure quickly.

4 Carefully remove the lid and stir the tomato purée and mustard into the meat. Remove the bay leaves and check the seasoning. Transfer the meat to a bowl, cover and leave to cool.

5 Preheat the oven to 200°C/400°F/Gas 6. Roll the pastry out on a lightly floured surface. Using a 1.5 litre/2½ pint/6¼ cup pie dish, roll the pastry into an oval or round shape 5cm/2in larger than the dish. Cut off a 2.5cm/1in strip all around the pastry. Dampen the rim of the dish with water and place the pastry strip on to the rim of the dish, trimming the length to fit. Add the meat and sufficient gravy to cover the meat.

6 If you have a pie funnel, push it down into the middle of the filling, to support the pastry. Brush the pastry rim with beaten egg, then cover with the pastry lid. Make a slit in the middle to let steam escape, allowing the funnel, if using, to protrude through. Press the edges of the pastry together, to seal, then, using a sharp knife, knock up the edges.

7 Decorate the top with leaves cut from the pastry trimmings. Brush the pastry with beaten egg, to glaze, then bake for 25–30 minutes, until golden brown and well risen.

8 Leave to stand for 5 minutes, while warming the reserved gravy in a small pan. Serve the pie on warmed serving plates with creamed potatoes and green vegetables. Serve the remaining gravy separately.

Oxtail Casserole with Herb Dumplings

The pressure cooker is excellent for tenderizing this economical cut of meat. The casserole is delicious served with mashed sweet potato and a green vegetable.

Pressure: High

Time under Pressure: 40 minutes (50 minutes)

Release: Natural/Slow

Serves 4

1kg/2½lb oxtail, chopped into 4–5cm/1½–2in chunks

15ml/1 tbsp plain (all-purpose) flour

30ml/2 tbsp sunflower oil

2 onions, sliced

2 garlic cloves, finely chopped

2 large carrots, cut into 2.5cm/1in chunks

1 celery stick, cut into chunks

600ml/1 pint/2½ cups hot beef stock

a few fresh sprigs of rosemary, plus extra to garnish

a few sprigs of fresh thyme

15ml/1 tbsp redcurrant jelly

salt and ground black pepper

For the dumplings

150g/6oz/1½ cups self-raising (self-rising) flour

2.5ml/½ tsp salt

75g/3oz/6 tbsp butter, diced

15ml/1 tbsp chopped fresh mixed herbs, such as parsley, rosemary and sage

approximately 120ml/4fl oz/ ½ cup water

Cook's Tip

If using an electric pressure cooker, check the dumplings after 10 minutes to make sure there is still enough liquid in the cooker. You may need to add a little more boiling stock. An electric cooker releases more steam than a stovetop cooker.

Energy 630kcal/2638kJ; Protein 34.6g; Carbohydrate 48.4g, of which sugars 11.1g; Fat 34.6g, of which saturates 10.6g; Cholesterol 40mg; Calcium 209mg; Fibre 5.1g; Sodium 717mg.

1 Place the oxtail chunks in a bowl. Add the flour and toss to coat. Heat the oil in the open pressure cooker. Add the oxtail in batches and fry until brown on all sides. Remove with a slotted spoon and set aside. Use the Sauté or Meat setting for the electric pressure cooker.

2 Add the onions and sauté for 3–4 minutes. Add the garlic, carrots and celery and cook for 1 minute, stirring. Drain off any excess fat. Add the hot stock, stir thoroughly and scrape any sediment off the base of the cooker. Bring to the boil.

3 Return the oxtail to the pressure cooker. Add the rosemary and thyme.

Electric: Close the lid and bring to High pressure using the Manual, Soup or Meat setting. Cook for 40 minutes (50 minutes), or until the oxtail is tender. Reset the timer, if necessary, to complete the cooking time.
Stovetop: Close the lid and bring to High pressure. Cook for 40 minutes (50 minutes), or until the oxtail is tender.

4 Just before the meat is cooked, make the dumplings. Sift the flour and salt together. Add the butter and rub in until it resembles fine breadcrumbs. Stir in the herbs and sufficient cold water to make a soft but not sticky dough. Form into 12 balls on a floured surface.

5 Release the pressure slowly. Use natural release for the electric pressure cooker, making sure the 'keep warm' mode is switched off. After 5 minutes, quickly release the remaining pressure, if any. Remove the lid carefully and remove the rosemary and thyme sprigs. Check the seasoning.

6 Bring to the boil, then add the dumplings on top of the oxtail. Cover with the lid, but do not close. Leave the steam vent open. Simmer for 15 minutes. Use the Manual or Soup setting for the electric pressure cooker.

7 Transfer the oxtail and dumplings to warmed serving plates. Stir the redcurrant jelly into the sauce and pour over the top. Serve garnished with a sprig of rosemary.

Osso Buco with Gremolata

Shin of beef needs time to tenderize when cooked conventionally. Your pressure cooker helps speed up this process. Osso buco is a classic veal stew from Italy, usually served topped with a lemon and parsley dressing called gremolata.

1 In a bowl, mix the flour with a little salt and pepper, to season. Add the veal and toss to coat in flour.

2 Heat the oil and butter in the open pressure cooker and brown the meat on both sides. You may need to cook two at a time. Remove with a slotted spoon, put on a plate and set aside. Use the Sauté or Soup setting for the electric pressure cooker.

3 Add the onion and sauté for 3–4 minutes to soften, then add the celery and cook for 1 minute. Stir in the wine and bring to the boil, stirring and scraping the base of the cooker to remove any sediment.

4 Add the chicken stock and return the veal to the cooker. Add the chopped tomatoes and tomato purée.

Electric: Close the lid and bring to High pressure using the Manual, Soup or Meat setting. Cook for 25 minutes (30 minutes).
Stovetop: Close the lid and bring to High pressure. Cook for 25 minutes (30 minutes).

5 Meanwhile, mix the garlic, lemon rind and parsley together for the gremolata and set aside.

6 Release the pressure quickly, making sure the 'keep warm' mode is switched off if using an electric pressure cooker. Open carefully and transfer to warmed serving plates, topped with gremolata. Serve with saffron risotto and sugar snap peas.

Pressure: High
Time under Pressure: 25 minutes (30 minutes)
Release: Quick
Serves 4

30ml/2 tbsp plain (all-purpose) flour
4 thick slices veal shin
15ml/1 tbsp olive oil
15g/½oz//1 tbsp butter
1 large onion, chopped
1 celery stick, chopped
150ml/¼ pint/⅔ cup dry white wine
300ml/½ pint/1¼ cups chicken stock
400g/14oz can chopped tomatoes
15ml/1 tbsp tomato purée (paste)
salt and ground black pepper
saffron risotto and sugar snap peas, to serve

For the gremolata
1 garlic clove, crushed
grated rind of 1 lemon
45ml/3 tbsp chopped fresh flat leaf parsley

Energy 302kcal/1269kJ; Protein 36.6g; Carbohydrate 14.1g, of which sugars 7.3g; Fat 8.7g, of which saturates 3.3g; Cholesterol 86mg; Calcium 51mg; Fibre 2.8g; Sodium 171mg.

Beef Goulash

Goulash is a Hungarian meat stew with peppers, seasoned with paprika. Cooking it in the pressure cooker greatly reduces the time required to tenderize the meat. This dish is often served with noodles or mashed potato topped with a dollop of sour cream.

Pressure: High
Time under Pressure: 30 minutes (36 minutes)
Release: Quick
Serves 4

15ml/1 tbsp plain (all-purpose) flour
500g/1lb lean braising steak, cut into strips or cubes
30ml/2 tbsp sunflower oil
2 onions, cut into wedges
2 garlic cloves, crushed
30ml/2 tbsp paprika
300ml/½ pint/1¼ cups beef stock
400g/14oz can chopped tomatoes
30ml/2 tbsp tomato purée (paste)
½ green (bell) pepper, seeded and cut into chunks
1 red (bell) pepper, halved, seeded and sliced
100ml/3½fl oz/scant ½ cup sour cream
salt and ground black pepper
fresh flat leaf parsley, to garnish
noodles or mashed potato, to serve

1 In a bowl, mix the flour with a little salt and pepper, to season. Add the beef and toss to coat in flour. Heat the oil in the open pressure cooker and add the onions. Cook for 4–5 minutes, stirring occasionally, until browned. Use the Sauté or Meat setting for the electric pressure cooker. Remove with a slotted spoon and set aside.

2 Add the beef to the pressure cooker and cook for 3–4 minutes, until browned. Add the garlic and paprika and cook for 1 minute.

3 Add the stock, tomatoes, tomato purée and half the onions. Stir thoroughly and scrape the base of the cooker to remove any sediment.

Electric: Close the lid and bring to High pressure using the Manual, Soup or Meat setting. Cook for 25 minutes (30 minutes). Release the pressure quickly, making sure the 'keep warm' mode is switched off.
Stovetop: Close the lid and bring to High pressure. Cook for 25 minutes (30 minutes). Release the pressure quickly.

4 Open carefully and add the peppers and remaining onions. Stir to combine.

Electric: Reseal and return to High pressure using the Manual, Soup or Vegetable setting. Cook for 5 minutes (6 minutes). Release the pressure quickly, making sure the 'keep warm' mode is switched off.
Stovetop: Reseal and return to High pressure. Cook for 5 minutes (6 minutes). Release the pressure quickly.

5 Remove the lid carefully and serve on warmed serving plates, with noodles or mashed potato, topped with sour cream and flat leaf parsley.

Energy 349kcal/1458kJ; Protein 32.7g;
Carbohydrate 16.8g, of which sugars 10.1g;
Fat 17.3g, of which saturates 6.2g; Cholesterol
88mg; Calcium 77mg; Fibre 3.4g; Sodium 152mg.

Meat Loaf

This tasty meat loaf is made with a mixture of minced beef and sausage meat, but can just as easily be made with all minced beef. It can be served hot, but is also perfect served cold for a picnic or lunchbox. Be sure to select a loaf tin that will fit inside your pressure cooker.

1 Melt the butter in a frying pan and add the onion. Fry for 4–5 minutes, until golden. Add the celery, carrot and garlic and cook for 3–4 minutes, until softened. Set aside to cool.

2 In a large bowl, mix together the beef, sausage meat, parsley, sage and breadcrumbs. Mix in the cooked vegetables, Worcestershire sauce, tomato sauce and season with salt and pepper. Bind together with the beaten egg.

3 Grease a 450g/1lb loaf tin (pan) and line the base with baking parchment, first making sure it will fit inside your pressure cooker. Transfer the meat loaf mixture to the tin, pushing it down firmly with a spoon. Sprinkle over the grated cheese. Cover with greased foil.

4 Place a trivet, upturned rack or round cooling rack in the base of the pressure cooker. Add 450ml/¾ pint/scant 2 cups water. Stand the loaf tin on the trivet or rack. The water needs to cover the base of the loaf tin. Depending on the depth of your rack, you may need to turn the rack over to reduce the height, or add a little more water.

Electric: Close the lid and bring to High pressure using the Manual, Soup or Meat setting. Cook for 30 minutes (35 minutes). Reset the timer, if necessary, to complete the cooking time. Release the pressure using natural release, making sure the 'keep warm' mode is switched off. After 5 minutes, quickly release the remaining pressure, if any.
Stovetop: Close the lid and bring to High pressure. Cook for 30 minutes (35 minutes). Release the pressure slowly. After 5 minutes, quickly release the remaining pressure, if any.

5 Leave to stand for 10 minutes, then carefully remove from the pressure cooker, using oven gloves. Remove the foil and turn out on to a warmed serving dish, if serving hot, or leave in the tin to cool. Serve the meat loaf sliced, either hot or cold.

Pressure: High
Time under Pressure: 30 minutes (35 minutes)
Release: Natural/Slow
Serves 4

25g/1oz/2 tbsp butter
1 onion, finely chopped
1 small celery stick, finely chopped
1 small carrot, finely chopped
2 garlic cloves, finely chopped
225g/8oz/1 cup lean minced (ground) beef
225g/8oz sausage meat
30ml/2 tbsp chopped fresh parsley
10ml/2 tsp chopped fresh sage
40g/1½oz/¾ cup fresh white breadcrumbs
5ml/1 tsp Worcestershire sauce
30ml/2 tbsp tomato sauce
1 egg, lightly beaten
25g/1oz/¼ cup mature (sharp) Cheddar cheese, grated
salt and ground black pepper

Energy 419kcal/1745kJ; Protein 23.8g; Carbohydrate 18.8g, of which sugars 5.9g; Fat 28.2g, of which saturates 12.8g; Cholesterol 133mg; Calcium 147mg; Fibre 2.6g; Sodium 895mg.

Spicy Meatballs in Tomato Sauce

These meatballs are equally delicious made with beef or lamb mince. They are flavoured with spices and chilli, and finished in a red pepper and passata sauce. It is important to release the pressure slowly after cooking, to make sure the meatballs do not break up.

Pressure: High

Time under Pressure: 7 minutes (10 minutes)

Release: Natural/Slow

Serves 4

450g/1lb minced (ground) beef or lamb
1 onion, grated
2 garlic cloves, chopped
5ml/1 tsp ground cumin
1 fresh green chilli, halved, seeded and chopped
50g/2oz fresh white breadcrumbs
1 egg yolk
grated rind of 1 lemon
fresh flat leaf parsley, to garnish
salt and ground black pepper
noodles, spaghetti or crusty bread, to serve (optional)

For the sauce

15ml/1 tbsp sunflower oil
1 onion, sliced
1 red (bell) pepper, sliced
125ml/4fl oz/½ cup red wine or beef stock
700g passata (bottled strained tomatoes)
5ml/1 tsp fresh thyme leaves
salt and ground black pepper

1 Place the beef or lamb in a large bowl. Add the onion, garlic, cumin, chilli, breadcrumbs, egg yolk and lemon rind and mix thoroughly. Shape into 20 balls.

2 Place the meatballs on a tray, cover and refrigerate while preparing the sauce.

3 Heat the oil in the open pressure cooker. Add the onion and sauté for 3–4 minutes, to soften. Add the pepper and cook for 3–4 minutes, to soften. Use the Sauté, Soup or Meat setting for the electric pressure cooker.

4 Stir in the wine or stock and bring to the boil. Stir well to remove any sediment from the base of the cooker. Add the passata, thyme and seasoning and mix thoroughly. Place the meatballs one at a time into the sauce, coating with the sauce.

Electric: Close the lid and bring to High pressure using the Manual, Soup or Meat setting. Cook for 7 minutes (10 minutes). Release the pressure using natural release, making sure the 'keep warm' mode is switched off. After 10 minutes, quickly release the remaining pressure, if any.
Stovetop: Close the lid and bring to High pressure. Cook for 7 minutes (10 minutes). Release the pressure slowly. After 10 minutes, quickly release the remaining pressure, if any.

5 Carefully remove the lid and spoon on to warmed serving plates. Garnish with flat leaf parsley. Serve with noodles, spaghetti or crusty bread, if you wish.

Energy 428kcal/1784kJ; Protein 27.5g; Carbohydrate 23.7g, of which sugars 12.2g; Fat 23.1g, of which saturates 8.6g; Cholesterol 118mg; Calcium 78mg; Fibre 4.3g; Sodium 262mg.

Lamb and Carrot Casserole

Barley and carrots make natural partners for lamb and mutton. Rinse the barley before adding to your pressure cooker to minimize any frothing. Set your stovetop pressure cooker on the lowest heat setting to maintain pressure once it is reached.

1 Trim the lamb and cut into bitesize pieces. Heat the oil in the open pressure cooker and brown the lamb. Use the Sauté or Meat setting for the electric pressure cooker. Remove with a slotted spoon.

2 Add the onions and cook for 4–5 minutes, to soften. Add the carrots and celery and cook for 1 minute.

3 Add the pearl barley and the stock. Stir thoroughly.

Electric: Close the lid and bring to High pressure using the Manual, Soup or Meat setting. Cook for 25 minutes (30 minutes). Release the pressure using natural release, making sure the 'keep warm' mode is switched off. After 5 minutes, quickly release the remaining pressure, if any.
Stovetop: Close the lid and bring to High pressure. Cook for 25 minutes (30 minutes). Release the pressure slowly. After 5 minutes, quickly release the remaining pressure, if any.

4 Remove the lid carefully and check the seasoning. Serve with spring cabbage and baked potatoes.

Pressure: High
Time under Pressure: 25 minutes (30 minutes)
Release: Natural/Slow
Serves 6

675g/1½lb stewing lamb, such as neck
15ml/1 tbsp sunflower oil
2 onions, sliced
675g/1½lb carrots, cut into chunks
4–6 celery sticks, cut into chunks
45ml/3 tbsp pearl barley, rinsed
450ml/¾ pint/scant 2 cups lamb or vegetable stock
salt and ground black pepper
chopped fresh parsley, to garnish
spring cabbage and baked potatoes, to serve

Energy 274kcal/1147kJ; Protein 24.7g; Carbohydrate 19.3g, of which sugars 11.3g; Fat 11.4g, of which saturates 4.3g; Cholesterol 83mg; Calcium 64mg; Fibre 4.8g; Sodium 121mg.

Irish Stew

Simple and delicious, this is the quintessential Irish main course. Traditionally mutton chops are used, but as they are harder to find these days, you can use lamb instead. This heartwarming stew is a perfect recipe to try in your pressure cooker.

Pressure: High

Time under Pressure: 20 minutes (26 minutes)

Release: Quick

Serves 4

900g/2lb boneless lamb chops

15ml/1 tbsp sunflower oil

3 onions

4 large carrots

600ml/1 pint/2½ cups
  vegetable stock

4 large potatoes, cut into
  large chunks

15g/½oz/1 tbsp butter

salt and ground black pepper

15ml/1 tbsp chopped fresh parsley,
  to garnish

1 Trim any fat from the lamb chops and cut into chunks. Dust with salt and pepper. Heat the oil in the open pressure cooker and brown the lamb on all sides. Use the Sauté or Meat setting for the electric pressure cooker. Remove with a slotted spoon and set aside.

2 Meanwhile, cut the onions into quarters and the carrots into chunks. Add the onions to the pressure cooker and cook for 3–4 minutes.

3 Return the meat to the cooker. Add the carrots and pour over the stock. Stir thoroughly and scrape the base of the cooker to remove any sediment.

Electric: Close the lid and bring to High pressure using the Manual or Meat setting. Cook for 15 minutes (20 minutes). Release the pressure quickly, making sure the 'keep warm' mode is switched off.
Stovetop: Close the lid and bring to High pressure. Cook for 15 minutes (20 minutes). Release the pressure quickly.

4 Open carefully and add the potatoes.

Electric: Reseal and return to High pressure using the Manual, Soup or Vegetable setting. Cook for 5 minutes (6 minutes). Release the pressure quickly, making sure the 'keep warm' mode is switched off.
Stovetop: Reseal and return to High pressure. Cook for 5 minutes (6 minutes). Release the pressure quickly.

5 Remove the lid. Discard any excess fat from the liquid using a spoon and serve in bowls. Dot the potatoes with butter and sprinkle with parsley.

Energy 813kcal/3387kJ; Protein 44.4g;
Carbohydrate 43g, of which sugars 14.1g; Fat
52.7g, of which saturates 24.6g; Cholesterol
236mg; Calcium 87mg; Fibre 6.8g; Sodium 183mg.

Lamb Curry

The pressure cooker is ideal for making a curry. Gone are the hours of cooking that are traditionally needed to make this type of spicy and aromatic recipe. This dish can be served with flatbreads such as naan or chapati, or with rice – or both – and a cucumber raita.

1 Mix the yogurt, garlic, ginger and turmeric together in a large bowl. Add the lamb and stir to coat. Cover and leave to marinate in the refrigerator for 2 hours, or longer, if time allows.

2 Place the onions, 1 red pepper and 2 chillies in the food processor with 30ml/2 tbsp water and process to finely chop.

3 Heat the oil in the open pressure cooker, add the onion, pepper and chilli mix and cook for 2–3 minutes, stirring. Stir in the coriander, cumin, cinnamon and cardamom seeds. Cook for 1 minute, stirring constantly. Use the Sauté or Meat setting for the electric pressure cooker.

4 Gradually add the meat and marinade to the cooker, stirring well between each addition. Add the remaining sliced pepper, chilli and the chopped tomatoes. Add 250ml/8fl oz/1 cup water and season with salt and pepper. Stir thoroughly and scrape the base of the cooker to remove any sediment.

Electric: Close the lid and bring to High pressure using the Manual or Meat setting. Cook for 12 minutes (15 minutes). Release the pressure using natural release, making sure the 'keep warm' mode is switched off.
Stovetop: Close the lid and bring to High pressure. Cook for 12 minutes (15 minutes). Release the pressure slowly.

5 Open carefully and transfer to a warmed serving dish. Garnish with fresh coriander sprigs. Serve with naan, basmati rice and a cucumber raita, if you wish.

Cook's Tip
If the sauce is too thin, you can boil it in the open cooker for 3–4 minutes, to reduce it. Use the Sauté or Meat setting for the electric pressure cooker.

Pressure: High
Time under Pressure: 12 minutes (15 minutes)
Release: Natural/Slow
Serves 4

60ml4 tbsp natural (plain) yogurt
2 garlic cloves, crushed
2.5cm/1in piece fresh root ginger, peeled and grated
5ml/1 tsp ground turmeric
675g/1½lb boneless leg or shoulder of lamb, cut into chunks
2 onions, peeled and quartered
2 red (bell) peppers, halved, seeded and sliced
3 fresh red chillies, halved, seeded and sliced
30ml/2 tbsp sunflower oil
10ml2 tsp ground coriander
5ml/1 tsp ground cumin
1 cinnamon stick, broken into three pieces
4 cardamom pods, split open
400g/14oz can chopped tomatoes
salt and ground black pepper
fresh coriander sprigs, to garnish
naan, basmati rice and cucumber raita, to serve (optional)

Energy 409kcal/1707kJ; Protein 38.7g; Carbohydrate 18.3g, of which sugars 13.5g; Fat 20.7g, of which saturates 6.8g; Cholesterol 125mg; Calcium 96mg; Fibre 4.2g; Sodium 175mg.

Lamb Shanks with Cannellini Beans

Brown your lamb shanks thoroughly in the open pressure cooker before adding the other ingredients in this recipe. This is an important part of the flavouring process, which is completed by braising in a rich tomato and herb sauce with onions, carrots and celery.

Pressure: High

Time under Pressure: 30 minutes (40 minutes)

Release: Natural/Slow

Serves 4

175g/6oz/1 cup dried cannellini beans

4 lamb shanks, about 225g/8oz each

30ml/2 tbsp olive oil

1 onion, finely chopped

3 carrots, cut into thick chunks

2 celery sticks, finely diced

900ml/1½ pints/3¾ cups hot vegetable stock

450g/1lb tomatoes, peeled if you wish, and quartered

4 fresh rosemary sprigs

2 bay leaves

30ml/2 tbsp tomato purée (paste)

salt and ground black pepper

Energy 584kcal/2442kJ; Protein 45.8g; Carbohydrate 31.3g, of which sugars 11.7g; Fat 31.5g, of which saturates 9.3g; Cholesterol 131mg; Calcium 96mg; Fibre 13.2g; Sodium 193mg.

1 Put the beans in a bowl, cover with boiling water and leave to stand for 1 hour.

2 Season the lamb shanks with salt and ground black pepper. Heat the oil in the open pressure cooker and cook the lamb shanks for about 5 minutes, until evenly browned. It may be easier to cook two at a time. Remove to a plate and set aside. Use the Sauté or Meat setting for the electric pressure cooker.

3 Add the onion and sauté for 3–4 minutes, until softened, stirring occasionally. Add the carrots and celery and cook for 2 minutes.

4 Add the stock and stir well to remove any sediment from the base of the cooker. Stir in the tomatoes and herbs. Drain the beans and add to the pressure cooker. Return the lamb shanks to the pressure cooker.

Electric: Close the lid and bring to High pressure using the Manual, Soup or Beans setting. Cook for 30 minutes (40 minutes). Reset the timer, if necessary, to complete the cooking time. Release the pressure using natural release, making sure the 'keep warm' mode is switched off. After 10 minutes, quickly release the remaining pressure, if any.
Stovetop: Close the lid and bring to High pressure. Cook for 30 minutes (40 minutes). Release the pressure slowly. After 10 minutes, quickly release the remaining pressure, if any.

5 Carefully remove the lid and, using tongs, remove the shanks to a warmed plate. Remove the rosemary sprigs and stir in the tomato purée. Boil for 3–4 minutes to thicken the sauce, if necessary. Use the Sauté or Meat setting for the electric pressure cooker.

6 Check the seasoning and serve on warmed plates, placing each lamb shank on a bed of beans and vegetables.

Italian Pork Sausage Stew

This hearty casserole, made with spicy sausages and haricot beans, is flavoured with fragrant fresh herbs and dry Italian wine. Serve with Italian bread for mopping up the delicious juice. The pressure cooker is perfect for cooking dried pulses.

Pressure: High
Time under Pressure: 15 minutes (20 minutes)
Release: Natural/Slow
Serves 4

225g/8oz/1¼ cups dried haricot (navy) beans
30ml/2 tbsp sunflower oil
450g/1lb fresh Italian pork sausages
1 onion, finely chopped
2 celery sticks, finely diced
10ml/2 tsp fresh thyme leaves
200ml/7fl oz/scant 1 cup dry red or white wine, preferably Italian
1 fresh rosemary sprig
1 bay leaf
300ml/½ pint/1¼ cups vegetable stock
200g/7oz can chopped tomatoes
¼ head Savoy cabbage, finely shredded
30ml/2 tbsp tomato purée (paste)
salt and ground black pepper
chopped fresh thyme, to garnish
crusty Italian bread, to serve

1 Put the beans in a bowl and cover with boiling water. Leave to stand for 1 hour.

2 Heat the oil in the open pressure cooker and fry the sausages, until browned. Remove to a plate. Add the onion and celery and cook for 5 minutes, until softened. Use the Sauté or Meat setting for the electric pressure cooker.

3 Drain the beans and add to the cooker with the thyme leaves, wine, rosemary and bay leaf. Stir well to remove any sediment from the base of the cooker.

4 Return the sausages to the cooker and bring to the boil. Add the stock.

Electric: Close the lid and bring to High pressure using the Manual, Meat or Beans setting. Cook for 15 minutes (20 minutes). Release the pressure using natural release, making sure the 'keep warm' mode is switched off. After 10 minutes, quickly release the remaining pressure, if any.
Stovetop: Close the lid and bring to High pressure. Cook for 15 minutes (20 minutes). Release the pressure slowly. After 10 minutes, quickly release the remaining pressure, if any.

5 Remove the lid carefully and stir in the chopped tomatoes, cabbage and tomato purée. Simmer for 3–4 minutes. Season with salt and pepper. Use the Sauté or Meat setting for the electric pressure cooker. Divide between warmed plates and garnish with a little chopped fresh thyme. Serve with crusty Italian bread.

Energy 618kcal/2580kJ; Protein 27.9g; Carbohydrate 42.6g, of which sugars 10.5g; Fat 34.8g, of which saturates 11.1g; Cholesterol 68mg; Calcium 216mg; Fibre 14.7g; Sodium 1030mg.

Pot Roast Loin of Pork with Apple

This pork loin filled with a lightly spiced apple and raisin stuffing makes a wonderful Sunday-lunch main course. Make sure that when you roll your pork loin in step 4, it will fit in your pressure cooker. Rest the cooked meat for 15 minutes before serving.

Pressure: High

Time under Pressure: 40 minutes (50 minutes)

Release: Natural/Slow

Serves 4

1.5kg/3lb boneless loin or
  leg of pork
200ml/7fl oz/scant 1 cup dry
  (hard) cider
250ml/8fl oz/1 cup apple juice
30ml/2 tbsp sunflower oil

For the stuffing

25g/1oz/2 tbsp butter
1 small onion, chopped
25g/1oz fresh white breadcrumbs
1 apple, cored, peeled and chopped
50g/2oz/scant ½ cup raisins
grated rind of 1 orange
15ml/1 tbsp fresh chopped sage
salt and ground black pepper

1 Melt the butter for the stuffing in the pressure cooker, add the onion and sauté for 3–4 minutes, or until soft. Use the Sauté or Meat setting for the electric pressure cooker. Remove from the heat, or remove the inner pot of the electric pressure cooker and stir in the breadcrumbs, apple, raisins, grated orange rind and sage. Season with salt and pepper.

2 Put the pork, rind side down, on a board and make a horizontal cut between the meat and outer layer of fat. Cut to within 2.5cm/1in of the edges to make a pocket. Push the prepared stuffing into the pocket.

3 Roll up the pork lengthwise and tie firmly with string. Score the rind at 2cm/¾in intervals with a sharp knife. Heat the oil in the open pressure cooker. Add the pork and brown on all sides. Use the Sauté or Meat setting for the electric pressure cooker. Pour on the cider and bring to the boil. Add the apple juice.

Electric: Close the lid and bring to High pressure using the Manual, Soup or Meat setting. Cook for 40 minutes (50 minutes). Reset the timer, if necessary, to complete the cooking time. Release the pressure using natural release, making sure the 'keep warm' mode is switched off.
Stovetop: Close the lid and bring to High pressure. Cook for 40 minutes (50 minutes). Release the pressure slowly.

4 Remove the meat from the pressure cooker and, if you wish, transfer to the oven to crisp the fat. Sprinkle with a little salt and roast at 200°C/400°F/Gas 6 for 15–20 minutes. Leave to stand for 15 minutes before carving.

Energy 764kcal/3214kJ; Protein 104.3g; Carbohydrate 26g, of which sugars 20.4g; Fat 26.3g, of which saturates 10.4g; Cholesterol 257mg; Calcium 79mg; Fibre 1.6g; Sodium 314mg.

Pulled Pork with Barbecue Sauce and Salsa

Although often made with pork shoulder, pulled pork is quite fatty. This recipe uses pork fillet, which keeps moist even though it is lean, because it is cooked in the pressure cooker. Serve hot or cold with tortillas or rolls alongside the tomato salsa and coleslaw, if you wish.

Pressure: High
Time under Pressure: 50 minutes (60 minutes)
Release: Natural/Slow
Serves 4

30ml/2 tbsp sunflower oil
500g/1¼lb pork fillet, cut in half
1 onion, sliced
2 garlic cloves, chopped
400ml/14fl oz/1⅔ cups ginger beer
200ml/7 fl oz/scant 1 cup water
115g/4oz tomato ketchup
30ml/2 tbsp Worcestershire sauce
15ml/1 tbsp brown sugar
2.5ml/½ tsp mustard powder
1.2ml/¼ tsp chilli powder
15ml/1 tbsp malt vinegar

For the salsa

½ red onion, finely chopped
12 cherry tomatoes, quartered
1 fresh red chilli, halved, seeded and chopped
1 avocado
juice of 1 lime
15ml/1 tbsp white wine vinegar
15ml/1 tbsp olive oil
30ml/2 tbsp chopped fresh coriander (cilantro)
tortillas or rolls, to serve (optional)

Cook's Tip

If you wish to use pork shoulder, increase the cooking time by 10–20 minutes and check to see if the meat is tender; if not, cook for a little longer.

Energy 368kcal/1539kJ; Protein 29.2g; Carbohydrate 22.9g, of which sugars 20.9g; Fat 18.4g, of which saturates 3.9g; Cholesterol 79mg; Calcium 47mg; Fibre 2.9g; Sodium 643mg.

1 Heat the oil in the open pressure cooker. Add the pork and cook for about 5 minutes, until evenly browned on all sides. Remove and set aside. Add the onion and garlic and sauté for 4–5 minutes, until softened. Use the Sauté or Meat setting for the electric pressure cooker.

2 Return the meat to the pressure cooker. Add the ginger beer and water and stir well to remove any sediment from the base of the cooker.

Electric: Close the lid and bring to High pressure using the Manual, Soup or Meat setting. Cook for 50 minutes (60 minutes). Reset the timer, if necessary, to complete the cooking time.
Stovetop: Close the lid and bring to High pressure. Cook for 50 minutes (60 minutes).

3 Meanwhile, in a small pan, mix together the tomato ketchup, Worcestershire sauce, brown sugar, mustard powder, chilli powder and malt vinegar. Wrap the tortillas, if using, in foil. Preheat the oven to 190°C/375°F/Gas 5.

4 Just before the pork is cooked, mix together the salsa. Place the onion, tomatoes and chilli in a bowl and mix together. Halve, stone and peel the avocado. Chop and toss in the lime juice. Add to the tomato and onion mix. Add the vinegar, olive oil and coriander and gently toss together. Warm the tortillas or rolls in the preheated oven for 5 minutes.

5 Release the pressure slowly. Use natural release for the electric pressure cooker, making sure the 'keep warm' mode is switched off. Test the meat by pulling it apart with two forks. Heat the barbecue sauce.

6 Remove the pork from the pressure cooker and shred. Mix with a little barbecue sauce. Serve with a pile of warmed tortillas or rolls, a bowl of the remaining barbecue sauce and the salsa, or assemble first, if you wish.

Barbecued Pork Ribs

A marinade of passata flavoured with ginger, shallots, Worcestershire sauce, mustard and honey coats these tasty pork ribs. By cooking in the pressure cooker, the ribs quickly become tender and succulent. Leave to marinade for up to 2 hours if time allows.

1 Peel and grate the ginger. Place in a large bowl with the shallots, Worcestershire sauce, honey, mustard powder, crushed garlic and passata. Mix together thoroughly.

2 Add the pork ribs and mix together to coat in the marinade. Cover and leave in the refrigerator for 30 minutes to marinate.

3 Place the ribs and marinade in the pressure cooker. Stir in the water or beer.

Electric: Close the lid and bring to High pressure using the Manual, Soup or Meat setting. Cook for 20 minutes (25 minutes). Release the pressure using natural release, making sure the 'keep warm' mode is switched off.
Stovetop: Close the lid and bring to High pressure. Cook for 20 minutes (25 minutes). Release the pressure slowly.

4 Carefully remove the lid and remove the ribs using a slotted spoon. Either place on a warmed serving plate, or for a stickier finish, place on a baking tray and cook under a preheated grill for 2–3 minutes per side to brown and crisp slightly.

5 Bring the remaining sauce to the boil, and boil for 4–5 minutes, to reduce, stirring 3–4 times to prevent it sticking. Use the Sauté or Soup setting for the electric pressure cooker. Serve separately or pour over the ribs. Garnish the ribs with shredded spring onions and serve.

Pressure: High
Time under Pressure: 20 minutes
   (25 minutes)
Release: Natural/Slow
Serves 4

2.5cm/1in piece fresh root ginger
2 shallots, finely chopped
15ml/1 tbsp Worcestershire sauce
30ml/2 tbsp clear honey
5ml/1 tsp mustard powder
2 garlic cloves, crushed
300g/11oz passata (bottled
   strained tomatoes)
1kg/2¼lb lean pork loin ribs
120ml/4fl oz/½ cup water or beer
salt and ground black pepper
shredded spring onions (scallions),
   to garnish

Energy 569kcal/2384kJ; Protein 77.1g;
Carbohydrate 8.6g, of which sugars 8.4g; Fat
25.3g, of which saturates 9g; Cholesterol 245mg;
Calcium 97mg; Fibre 0.7g; Sodium 223mg.

Swedish Meatballs

These Swedish-style pork meatballs are flavoured with dill, nutmeg and cardamom. The creamy sauce is flavoured with lingonberry jam, but if you can't find this, redcurrant jelly or cranberry sauce is a good alternative. A pressure cooker must!

1 Place the pork in a large bowl with the breadcrumbs, grated onion, egg, milk, parsley, dill, nutmeg and ground cardamom pods. Add a good pinch of salt and pepper. Using your hands, mix together thoroughly. Shape into a long sausage. Cut into 24 pieces and shape each piece into a ball. Place on an oiled tray, cover and chill for 1 hour, to firm.

2 Heat the oil in the open pressure cooker and fry the meatballs in batches, to brown. Transfer to a large plate. Use the Sauté or Meat setting for the electric pressure cooker.

3 Add the beef stock and lingonberry jam or redcurrant jelly to the pressure cooker and stir to dissolve the jam or jelly. Add the meatballs.

Electric: Close the lid and bring to High pressure using the Manual, Soup or Meat setting. Cook for 5 minutes (7 minutes). Release the pressure using natural release, making sure the 'keep warm' mode is switched off. After 5 minutes, quickly release the remaining pressure, if any.
Stovetop: Close the lid and bring to High pressure. Cook for 5 minutes (7 minutes). Release the pressure slowly. After 5 minutes, quickly release the remaining pressure, if any.

4 Carefully remove the lid and transfer the meatballs to a warmed serving dish. Mix the cream and flour together and gently whisk into the sauce. Bring to the boil, stirring until thickened. Use the Sauté or Soup setting for the electric pressure cooker. Return the meatballs to the sauce, and stir to coat.

5 Spoon into the warmed serving dish or on to warmed serving plates. Garnish with dill sprigs and serve with extra lingonberry jam or redcurrant jelly and mashed potato, if you wish.

Variation
Replace the double (heavy) cream with sour cream for a slightly more astringent flavour.

Pressure: High
Time under Pressure: 5 minutes (7 minutes)
Release: Natural/Slow
Serves 4

450g/1lb minced (ground) pork
50g/2oz fresh white breadcrumbs
1 onion, grated
1 egg
30ml/2 tbsp milk
15ml/1 tbsp chopped fresh flat leaf parsley
15ml/1 tbsp chopped fresh dill
5ml/1 tsp grated nutmeg
2.5ml/½ tsp ground cardamom pods
30ml/2 tbsp olive oil
300ml/½ pint/1¼ cups hot beef stock
15ml/1 tbsp lingonberry jam or redcurrant jelly
90ml/6 tbsp double (heavy) cream
15ml/1 tbsp plain (all-purpose) flour
salt and ground black pepper
fresh dill sprigs, to garnish
lingonberry jam or redcurrant jelly, and mashed potato (optional), to serve

Energy 451kcal/1879kJ; Protein 26.4g; Carbohydrate 18.7g, of which sugars 5.6g; Fat 30.7g, of which saturates 12.9g; Cholesterol 163mg; Calcium 67mg; Fibre 1.2g; Sodium 201mg.

Cider-glazed Gammon Joint

This classic buffet centrepiece can be served hot or cold with cranberry sauce or redcurrant jelly, if you wish. Soaking the gammon overnight helps to remove the excess salts before cooking in the pressure cooker. Finish in the oven to brown the glaze.

1 Drain the gammon joint, if soaked overnight. Add the trivet or cooling rack and place the gammon on top. Cover with water and bring to the boil. Use the Manual, Sauté or Soup setting for the electric pressure cooker.

2 Drain off the liquid. Add the onions, peppercorns, 6 cloves and bay leaves. Add 450ml/¾ pint/scant 2 cups cider and the stock. Make sure the liquid does not more than half-fill the pressure cooker.

Electric: Close the lid and bring to High pressure using the Manual, Soup or Meat setting. Cook for 55 minutes (65 minutes). Release the pressure using natural release, making sure the 'keep warm' mode is switched off.
Stovetop: Close the lid and bring to High pressure. Cook for 55 minutes (65 minutes). Release the pressure slowly.

3 Using large forks or slotted spoons, carefully lift the gammon joint out of the pressure cooker and place it in a roasting tin (pan), or ovenproof dish. Leave to stand for about 15 minutes, until cool enough to handle.

4 Meanwhile, make the glaze. Pour the remaining cider into a small pan, add the soft light brown sugar and heat gently, stirring until dissolved. Simmer for 5 minutes to make a sticky glaze, then remove from the heat and leave to cool for a few minutes so that it thickens slightly.

5 Preheat the oven to 220°C/425°F/Gas 7. Using a pair of scissors, cut the string off the gammon, then carefully slice off the rind, leaving a thin, even layer of fat over the meat.

6 Using a sharp knife, score the fat into neat diamond patterns. Press a clove into the centre of each diamond, then spoon over the glaze. Bake for about 25 minutes, or until the fat is brown, glistening and crisp. Remove from the oven and set aside until ready to serve. Serve the gammon with cranberry sauce or redcurrant jelly.

Pressure: High
Time under Pressure: 55 minutes (65 minutes)
Release: Natural/Slow
Serves 8

2kg/4½lb middle gammon joint, soaked overnight if smoked
2 onions, sliced
10 black peppercorns
about 30 whole cloves
3 bay leaves
600ml/1 pint/2½ cups medium dry (hard) cider
300ml/½ pint/1¼ cups hot vegetable stock
45ml/3 tbsp soft light brown sugar
cranberry sauce or redcurrant jelly, to serve

Cook's Tips
• Some electric pressure cookers will need to be reset as they cannot be programmed for 55/65 minutes. Make a note of the time set and then reset for the remaining time, as soon as it reaches zero.
• If serving hot, cover the gammon with foil and leave to rest for 15 minutes before carving.

Energy 394kcal/1646kJ; Protein 43.8g; Carbohydrate 7.8g, of which sugars 7.8g; Fat 18.8g, of which saturates 6.3g; Cholesterol 58mg; Calcium 25mg; Fibre 0g; Sodium 2206mg.

POULTRY AND GAME

Both poultry and game work really well in the pressure cooker – the lean meat associated with chicken, turkey, guinea fowl and pheasant remains moist and succulent. With dishes containing wine, cider or ale – such as coq au vin, tarragon chicken or pheasant with apples – make sure you bring the alcohol to the boil in the open cooker first, before closing the lid. If not, sometimes a bitter flavour may occur. Your pressure cooker is also perfect for making suet puddings. Try the venison, beef and ale version. Not only does the pressure cooker quickly tenderize the filling, but it cooks the pudding more quickly than just steaming. Make sure you use Low pressure to cook it. Last but not least, don't forget to try the magnificent duck cassoulet, Moroccan-inspired turkey and chickpea tagine, or the classic chicken korma.

Coq au Vin

This French country casserole was traditionally made with an old boiling bird, marinated overnight in red wine. Modern recipes use tender roasting birds, as they are more readily available. Prepare in advance using your pressure cooker, and reheat when needed.

Pressure: High

Time under Pressure: 8 minutes (10 minutes)

Release: Quick

Serves 4

15ml/1 tbsp olive oil
25g/1oz/2 tbsp butter
4 boneless chicken thighs
2 chicken breast fillets, halved
8 shallots
125g/4oz rindless streaky (fatty)
   bacon rashers (strips), chopped
150g/5oz small mushrooms, halved
2 garlic cloves, finely chopped
300ml/½ pint/1¼ cups red wine
150ml/¼ pint/⅔ cup chicken stock
salt and freshly ground black pepper
fresh flat leaf parsley sprigs,
   to garnish

For the bouquet garni

3 sprigs each parsley, thyme
   and sage
1 bay leaf
4 peppercorns
boiled potatoes, to serve (optional)

For the beurre manié

25g/1oz/2 tbsp butter, softened
25g/1oz/¼ cup plain (all-purpose)
   flour

1 Heat the oil and half the butter in the open pressure cooker, add the chicken portions and fry on each side for 4–5 minutes or until golden brown. Remove to a plate. Use the Sauté or Meat setting for the electric pressure cooker.

2 Add the remaining butter and cook the shallots for 2–3 minutes, add the bacon and cook for 3–4 minutes, or until the shallots are golden and the bacon is browned.

3 Add the mushrooms and garlic and cook for 1 minute. Stir in the wine and bring to the boil, stirring well to remove any sediment from the base of the cooker. Use the Sauté or Meat setting for the electric pressure cooker.

4 Add the chicken portions. Tie the ingredients for the bouquet garni in a small piece of muslin (cheesecloth) and add to the casserole, with the stock.

Electric: Close the lid and bring to High pressure using the Manual, Meat or Poultry setting. Cook for 8 minutes (10 minutes).
Stovetop: Close the lid and bring to High pressure. Cook for 8 minutes (10 minutes).

5 Meanwhile, make the beure manié. Using a small spoon, cream the butter and flour together in a small bowl, to make a smooth paste.

6 Reduce the pressure quickly, making sure the 'keep warm' mode is switched off, if using an electric pressure cooker. Carefully remove the lid and transfer the chicken pieces to a warmed serving dish and keep warm. Remove and discard the bouquet garni.

7 Reheat the sauce and add small lumps of the beurre manié to the sauce, stirring well until each piece has melted. Bring to the boil and cook for 2 minutes. Use the Manual, Sauté or Soup setting for the electric pressure cooker.

8 Season the casserole sauce and pour the sauce over the chicken pieces. Serve on individual warmed serving plates, garnished with flat leaf parsley and accompanied by boiled potatoes, if you wish.

Energy 480kcal/2003kJ; Protein 46g; Carbohydrate 6.9g, of which sugars 2.1g; Fat 24.4g, of which saturates 10.6g; Cholesterol 204mg; Calcium 43mg; Fibre 1.8g; Sodium 617mg.

Chicken Casserole with Bacon and Barley

This casserole of wonderfully tender chicken flavoured with bacon, celery and herbs has the addition of barley, which absorbs the sauce and becomes nutty in texture. When cooking pearl barley, reduce the pressure slowly to make sure it doesn't clog the vents.

Pressure: High

Time under Pressure: 20 minutes (25 minutes)

Release: Natural/Slow

Serves 4

15ml/1 tbsp plain (all-purpose) flour
500g/1¼lb skinless, boneless chicken breast fillets, cut into large pieces
30ml/2 tbsp sunflower oil
115g/4oz lean bacon rashers (strips), sliced
2 onions, halved and cut into thick slices
2 celery sticks, cut into chunks
45ml/3 tbsp pearl barley, rinsed
30ml/2 tbsp chopped fresh thyme
5ml/1 tsp chopped fresh rosemary
150ml/¼ pint/⅔ cup dry white wine
150ml/¼ pint/⅔ cup chicken stock
salt and freshly ground black pepper
chopped fresh parsley, to garnish
sugar snap peas, to serve

1 Season the flour with salt and pepper and toss the chicken pieces in the flour. Heat 15ml/1 tbsp oil in the open pressure cooker, add the chicken pieces and brown on both sides, cooking in batches, if necessary. Use the Sauté or Meat setting for the electric pressure cooker.

2 Remove the chicken and set aside. Add the remaining oil with the bacon and onions and cook for 4–5 minutes, stirring occasionally, until light golden.

3 Add the celery, pearl barley, thyme and rosemary and pour over the wine. Bring to the boil, stirring well to remove any sediment from the base of the cooker.

4 Return the chicken pieces to the casserole and add the stock. Stir to combine.

Electric: Close the lid and bring to High pressure using the Manual, Meat or Poultry setting. Cook for 20 minutes (25 minutes). Release the pressure using natural release, making sure the 'keep warm' mode is switched off. After 5 minutes, quickly release the remaining pressure, if any.
Stovetop: Close the lid and bring to High pressure. Cook for 20 minutes (25 minutes). Release the pressure slowly. After 5 minutes, quickly release the remaining pressure, if any.

5 Check the seasoning and transfer to a warmed serving dish. Sprinkle with chopped parsley and serve with sugar snap peas.

Energy 375kcal/1573kJ; Protein 36.6g; Carbohydrate 18.6g, of which sugars 4.6g; Fat 15.1g, of which saturates 3.4g; Cholesterol 104mg; Calcium 44mg; Fibre 1.8g; Sodium 514mg.

Tarragon Chicken in Cider

Aromatic tarragon has a distinctive flavour that goes wonderfully with both cream and chicken. This recipe is truly effortless in your pressure cooker, yet provides an elegant dish for entertaining or a special family meal. Serve with sautéed potatoes and a green vegetable.

1 Put the onions in a heatproof bowl and pour over enough boiling water to cover. Leave to stand for 10 minutes, then drain and peel. (They should come off very easily after soaking.)

2 Heat the oil in the open pressure cooker, add the onions and sauté for 6–8 minutes, until lightly browned, turning them frequently. Add the garlic and cook for 1 minute. Use the Sauté or Meat setting for the electric pressure cooker. Using a slotted spoon, remove the onions to a plate. Add the chicken portions to the pressure cooker and cook for 3–4 minutes, turning once or twice, until lightly browned on both sides. Add the cider and bring to the boil. Add the bay leaf and season with salt and pepper.

Electric: Close the lid and bring to High pressure using the Manual, Meat or Poultry setting. Cook for 7 minutes (9 minutes). Release the pressure quickly, making sure the 'keep warm' mode is switched off.
Stovetop: Close the lid and bring to High pressure. Cook for 7 minutes (9 minutes). Release the pressure quickly.

3 Remove the lid carefully and stir in the onions.

Electric: Return to High pressure using the Manual, Meat or Poultry setting. Cook for 2 minutes (3 minutes). Reduce the pressure quickly, making sure the 'keep warm' mode is switched off.
Stovetop: Return to High pressure. Cook for 2 minutes (3 minutes). Reduce the pressure quickly.

4 Meanwhile, in a small bowl, mix the cream into the flour.

5 Carefully remove the lid from the pressure cooker. Lift out the chicken breasts and transfer to warmed serving plates. Stir the cream and flour mixture into the cider sauce and bring to the boil, stirring continuously for 1–2 minutes. Use the Sauté or Meat setting for the electric pressure cooker. Stir in the tarragon and parsley and check the seasoning. Spoon the sauce over each chicken breast. Serve immediately with sautéed potatoes and a green vegetable such as cabbage, if you wish.

Pressure: High
Time under Pressure: 9 minutes (12 minutes)
Release: Quick
Serves 4

350g/12oz small baby (pearl) onions
30ml/2 tbsp sunflower oil
4 garlic cloves, chopped
4 boneless chicken breast portions, skin on
300ml/½ pint/1¼ cups dry (hard) cider
1 bay leaf
150ml/¼ pint/⅔ cup single (light) cream
15ml/1 tbsp plain (all-purpose) flour
30ml/2 tbsp chopped fresh tarragon
15ml/1 tbsp chopped fresh parsley
salt and freshly ground black pepper
sautéed potatoes and a green vegetable, to serve (optional)

Cook's Tip
In step 3, if using an electric pressure cooker, you may not be able to set such short times, so set the minimum time possible and switch off once the 2 or 3 minutes' cooking time is reached.

Variation
Try using 1 or 2 fresh thyme sprigs in place of the tarragon. It gives a very different flavour, but is equally as good. Serve with rice and roasted tomatoes.

Energy 326kcal/1364kJ; Protein 32.7g; Carbohydrate 12.6g, of which sugars 7.7g; Fat 14.3g, of which saturates 5.6g; Cholesterol 108mg; Calcium 73mg; Fibre 1.8g; Sodium 94mg.

Chicken Korma

The use of ground almonds to thicken the sauce gives this fragrant chicken curry a beautifully creamy texture. Its mild taste makes it particularly suitable for children, and the pressure cooker is very good for cooking curries.

 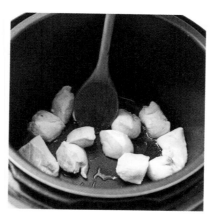 

1 Dry-fry the almonds in a frying pan until pale golden. Transfer two-thirds to a plate and continue to fry the remainder until they are a slightly deeper colour. Put these on a separate plate and set aside to use for the garnish. Leave the paler almonds to cool, then grind them until fine in a spice grinder or food processor.

2 Heat the ghee or butter in the open pressure cooker. Add the chicken and fry until browned. Use the Sauté or Manual setting for the electric pressure cooker. Transfer to a plate.

3 Add the sunflower oil and the onion and sauté for 4–5 minutes until the onion softens and starts to colour. Stir in the cardamom and garlic and cook for 1 minute.

4 Add the ground almonds, cumin, coriander, turmeric, cinnamon stick and chilli powder and cook for 1 minute. Add the coconut milk, chicken stock and garam masala. Stir well to remove any sediment from the base of the cooker. Add the chicken and season with salt and pepper and stir to combine.

Electric: Close the lid and bring to High pressure using the Manual, Meat or Poultry setting. Cook for 10 minutes (12 minutes). Release the pressure using natural release, making sure the 'keep warm' mode is switched off.
Stovetop: Close the lid and bring to High pressure. Cook for 10 minutes (12 minutes). Release the pressure slowly.

5 Open the cooker and stir in the cream, citrus juice and rind. Check the seasoning and serve in a warmed serving dish, garnished with the reserved almonds. If you wish, serve with saffron rice and poppadums.

Energy 377kcal/1572kJ; Protein 36g; Carbohydrate 9.1g, of which sugars 5.5g; Fat 22.2g, of which saturates 5.9g; Cholesterol 106mg; Calcium 99mg; Fibre 0.7g; Sodium 153mg.

Pressure: High
Time under Pressure: 10 minutes (12 minutes)
Release: Natural/Slow
Serves 4

75g/3oz/¾ cup flaked (sliced) almonds
15ml/1tbsp ghee or butter
500g/1¼lb skinless, boneless chicken breast portions, cut into bitesize pieces
15ml/1 tbsp sunflower oil
1 onion, chopped
4 green cardamom pods
2 garlic cloves, crushed
10ml/2 tsp ground cumin
5ml/1 tsp ground coriander
a pinch of ground turmeric
1 cinnamon stick
a good pinch of chilli powder
250ml/8fl oz/1 cup coconut milk
120ml/4fl oz/½ cup hot chicken stock
5ml/1 tsp garam masala
75ml/5 tbsp single (light) cream
15ml/1 tbsp fresh lime or lemon juice
10ml/2 tsp grated lime or lemon rind
salt and ground black pepper
saffron rice and poppadums, to serve (optional)

Chicken Pot Roast with Jerusalem Artichokes

Pot roast is the perfect way to cook a chicken in the pressure cooker. As chicken is low in natural fat, the pressure cooker makes it wonderfully succulent and tender. Make sure you use a chicken that will fit inside your pressure cooker.

Pressure: High
Time under Pressure: 29 minutes
  (35 minutes)
Release: Quick
Serves 4

1.3–1.5kg/3–3¼lb chicken
1 lemon, cut in half
15ml/1 tbsp sunflower oil
25g/1oz/2 tbsp butter
12 baby (pearl) onions or shallots
2 garlic cloves, crushed
5ml/1 tsp fresh thyme leaves
1 bay leaf
100ml/3½fl oz/scant ½ cup dry
  white wine
300ml/½ pint/1¼ cups chicken stock
2 carrots, peeled
350g/12oz Jerusalem artichokes
15ml/1 tbsp cornflour (cornstarch)
175g/6oz/1½ cups frozen peas
10ml/2 tsp wholegrain mustard
salt and freshly ground black pepper
fresh thyme sprigs, to garnish

1 Season the chicken all over with salt and pepper. Squeeze a teaspoonful of lemon juice from one lemon half into a bowl and set aside for later. Place the squeezed lemon half in the cavity of the chicken.

2 Heat the oil and butter in the open pressure cooker and brown the baby onions or shallots. Remove and set aside. Add the chicken and brown on all sides. Use the Sauté, Meat or Poultry setting for the electric pressure cooker.

3 Remove the pressure cooker from the heat, if stovetop. Remove the chicken and place a trivet or cooling rack in the base of the cooker. Return the chicken to the pressure cooker and add the garlic, thyme, bay leaf and wine. Cut the remaining lemon half into quarters and add. Bring to the boil. Use the Sauté, Meat or Poultry setting for the electric pressure cooker. Add the stock.

Electric: Close the lid and bring to High pressure using the Manual, Soup or Poultry setting. Cook for 25 minutes (30 minutes). Release the pressure quickly, making sure the 'keep warm' mode is switched off.
Stovetop: Close the lid and bring to High pressure. Cook for 25 minutes (30 minutes). Release the pressure quickly.

4 Cut the carrots into sticks and scrub the artichokes. Cut the artichokes into 2.5cm/1in pieces and place in the bowl with the lemon juice and cover with water. Mix the cornflour with 30ml/2 tbsp cold water.

5 Carefully remove the lid and transfer the chicken to a warmed serving dish and keep warm. Remove the trivet or rack and bay leaf. Add the carrots, drained artichokes and baby onions or shallots.

Electric: Close the lid and bring to High pressure. Cook for 4 minutes (5 minutes). Release the pressure quickly, making sure the 'keep warm' mode is switched off.
Stovetop: Close the lid and bring to High pressure. Cook for 4 minutes (5 minutes). Release the pressure quickly.

6 Open the lid carefully and stir in the peas and cornflour mixture. Bring to the boil, stirring until thickened. Use the Sauté, Meat or Poultry setting for the electric pressure cooker.

7 Stir in the mustard and check the seasoning. Arrange the vegetables around the chicken and spoon the sauce over. Serve immediately, garnished with fresh thyme sprigs.

Energy 578kcal/2429kJ; Protein 45.2g; Carbohydrate 17.5g, of which sugars 5.5g; Fat 35.5g, of which saturates 11.7g; Cholesterol 228mg; Calcium 64mg; Fibre 8.2g; Sodium 238mg.

Jerk-glazed Chicken Drumsticks

These Jamaican-style chicken drumsticks are hot and spicy. Brown them in the open pressure cooker thoroughly before pressurizing, to help develop the flavour. They are accompanied by a tangy corn and avocado salsa.

Pressure: High

Time under Pressure: 8 minutes (10 minutes)

Release: Quick

Serves 4

5cm/2in piece fresh root ginger, finely chopped

2 garlic cloves, finely crushed

20ml/4 tsp jerk seasoning

45ml/3 tbsp soy sauce

1 fresh red chilli, seeded and finely chopped

12 chicken drumsticks, skinned

45ml/3 tbsp sunflower oil

1 onion, finely chopped

250ml/8fl oz/1 cup chicken stock

30ml/2 tbsp clear honey

salt and freshly ground black pepper

shredded spring onions (scallions) and lime wedges, to garnish

For the salsa

1 avocado

rind and juice of 2 limes

225g/8oz frozen corn kernels, defrosted

1 tomato, peeled, seeded and chopped

½ small red onion, finely chopped

30ml/2 tbsp chopped fresh coriander (cilantro)

30ml/2 tbsp chopped fresh parsley

45ml/3 tbsp olive oil

a few drops of Tabasco sauce

salt and ground black pepper

1 Blend the ginger, garlic, jerk seasoning, soy sauce and chilli together in a large, shallow dish. Add the chicken drumsticks and turn to coat in the marinade. Cover and leave in the refrigerator for at least 30 minutes, or up to 4 hours, if time allows.

2 Heat 15ml/1 tbsp oil in the open pressure cooker, add the onion and sauté for 3–4 minutes until golden. Use the Sauté, Poultry or Meat setting for the electric pressure cooker. Remove with a slotted spoon.

3 Add the remaining oil and chicken drumsticks and fry for 3–4 minutes, turning once or twice. Remove with a slotted spoon. Cook in batches, if easier. Stir in the stock, scraping the base of the cooker to remove any sediment. Add any remaining marinade and return the onion and drumsticks to the pressure cooker.

Electric: Close the lid and bring to High pressure using the Manual, Meat or Poultry setting. Cook for 8 minutes (10 minutes). Release the pressure quickly, making sure the 'keep warm' mode is switched off.
Stovetop: Close the lid and bring to High pressure. Cook for 8 minutes (10 minutes). Release the pressure quickly.

4 Meanwhile, make the salsa. Peel and dice the avocado and toss with the lime juice and rind. Add the corn, tomato, onion, coriander, parsley and olive oil and mix together. Season with Tabasco sauce, salt and pepper.

5 Remove the lid from the pressure cooker and carefully transfer the drumsticks to a warmed serving dish. Stir the honey into the sauce and boil for 4–5 minutes, to reduce, stirring occasionally. Use the Sauté or Meat setting for the electric pressure cooker. Return the chicken drumsticks to the pressure cooker and glaze with the sauce.

6 Transfer the chicken drumsticks to the warmed serving plate and sprinkle with shredded spring onion. Garnish with lime wedges and serve with the salsa.

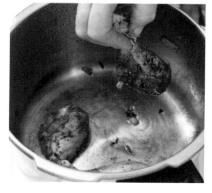

Energy 645kcal/2703kJ; Protein 77g; Carbohydrate 23.6g, of which sugars 10.3g; Fat 27.5g, of which saturates 5.6g; Cholesterol 362mg; Calcium 104mg; Fibre 7.2g; Sodium 1172mg.

Blue Cheese Stuffed Chicken Breasts

These stuffed chicken breasts are cooked in a wine sauce flavoured with mustard. When adding wine to your pressure cooker, bring to the boil in the open pressure cooker first, as this ensures there is no bitter flavour. Serve with broccoli and mashed potatoes.

Pressure: High
Time under Pressure: 6 minutes
   (8 minutes)
Release: Quick
Serves 4

4 skinless chicken breast fillets
75g/3oz blue cheese, such as
   Gorgonzola or Dolcelatte
4 sage leaves, chopped
4 slices prosciutto ham
25g/1oz/2 tbsp butter
1 onion, finely chopped
120ml/4fl oz/½ cup dry white wine
150ml/¼ pint/⅔ cup vegetable
   or chicken stock
30ml/2 tbsp single (light) cream
15ml/1 tbsp Dijon mustard
salt and freshly ground black pepper
mashed potatoes and green beans
   or broccoli, to serve

1 Cut a deep horizontal pocket lengthways in each chicken breast. Slice the cheese into four pieces and divide between the chicken pockets. Sprinkle with chopped sage and close.

2 Sprinkle the chicken breasts with freshly ground black pepper, then wrap each one in a slice of prosciutto ham. Secure each parcel with a wooden cocktail stick or toothpick.

3 Melt the butter in the open pressure cooker, add the onion and sauté until golden. Use the Sauté or Meat setting for the electric pressure cooker.

4 Add the chicken breasts, pour over the wine and bring to the boil. Add the stock.

Electric: Close the lid and bring to High pressure using the Meat or Poultry setting. Cook for 6 minutes (8 minutes). Release the pressure quickly, making sure the 'keep warm' mode is switched off.
Stovetop: Close the lid and bring to High pressure. Cook for 6 minutes (8 minutes). Release the pressure quickly.

5 Remove the chicken breasts with a slotted spoon and place on warmed serving plates. Stir the cream and mustard into the sauce and spoon a little over each chicken breast. Provide any remaining sauce separately. Serve immediately with mashed potatoes and green beans or broccoli.

Energy 321kcal/1343kJ; Protein 40.3g; Carbohydrate 3.5g, of which sugars 2.6g; Fat 16.3g, of which saturates 9g; Cholesterol 119mg; Calcium 118mg; Fibre 0.7g; Sodium 856mg.

Mediterranean Duck with Harissa

Harissa spices consist of a fiery blend of flavours from North Africa. Mixed with cinnamon, saffron and preserved lemons, they give this colourful casserole an unforgettable pungency. Pour off the excess fat from the duck in step 2, before cooking under pressure.

Pressure: High
**Time under Pressure: 10 minutes
  (12 minutes)**
Release: Natural/Slow
Serves 4

15ml/1 tbsp olive oil
4 duck portions
1 large onion, thinly sliced
1 garlic clove, crushed
2.5ml/½ tsp ground cumin
15ml/1 tbsp plain (all-purpose) flour
300ml/½ pint/1¼ cups chicken stock
juice of ½ lemon
5–10ml/1–2 tsp harissa spices
1 cinnamon stick
5ml/1 tsp saffron threads
rind of 1 preserved lemon, rinsed,
  drained and cut into fine strips
50g/2oz/½ cup black olives
50g/2oz/½ cup green olives
2–3 lemon slices
30ml/2 tbsp chopped fresh coriander
  (cilantro), plus extra leaves
  to garnish
salt and ground black pepper

1 Heat the oil in the open pressure cooker, add the duck portions and fry on both sides, to brown. Cook in batches, if easier. Use the Sauté or Meat setting for the electric pressure cooker.

2 Remove the duck with a slotted spoon and set aside. Pour off all but 15ml/1 tbsp of the fat. Add the onion and cook for 3–4 minutes, stirring occasionally. Add the garlic and ground cumin and cook for 1 minute.

3 Stir in the flour, then gradually add the stock and lemon juice. Bring to the boil, stirring well to remove any sediment from the base of the cooker. Add the harissa spices, cinnamon, saffron and preserved lemon rind.

4 Return the duck to the casserole.

Electric: Close the lid and bring to High pressure using the Manual, Meat or Poultry setting. Cook for 10 minutes (12 minutes). Release the pressure using natural release, making sure the 'keep warm' mode is switched off.
Stovetop: Close the lid and bring to High pressure. Cook for 10 minutes (12 minutes). Release the pressure slowly.

5 Carefully remove the lid and stir in the olives and lemon slices. Season with salt and pepper and leave to stand for 5 minutes, then reheat until bubbling. Use the Sauté or Meat setting for the electric pressure cooker. Stir in the chopped coriander and transfer to warmed serving plates. Garnish with coriander leaves.

Energy 396kcal/1649kJ; Protein 32.3g;
Carbohydrate 6.1g, of which sugars 2.2g; Fat
27.2g, of which saturates 7.4g; Cholesterol
104mg; Calcium 52mg; Fibre 1.8g; Sodium 962mg.

Duck Cassoulet

The pressure cooker greatly reduces the cooking time for this traditional French dish.
If time is really short, you can place the casserole under a preheated grill or broiler
to brown the topping, although the flavours will develop if finished in the oven.

Pressure: High
**Time under Pressure: 25 minutes
(32 minutes)**
Release: Natural/Slow
Serves 4

175g/6oz/1 cup dried cannellini
  beans
30ml/2 tbsp sunflower oil
115g/4oz/²⁄₃ cup unsmoked
  bacon lardons
2 boneless duck breast portions,
  about 350g/12oz
225g/8oz Toulouse or garlic sausages
1 onion, chopped
3 garlic cloves, finely chopped
1 celery stick, chopped
1 carrot, chopped
400g/14oz can chopped tomatoes
2 fresh thyme sprigs
350ml/12fl oz/1½ cups hot
  chicken stock
15ml/1 tbsp tomato purée (paste)
75g/3oz/1½ cups white breadcrumbs
salt and ground black pepper
fresh thyme sprigs, to garnish

Energy 768kcal/3192kJ; Protein 28.3g;
Carbohydrate 32.7g, of which sugars 7.7g; Fat
59.1g, of which saturates 17.8g; Cholesterol 106mg;
Calcium 119mg; Fibre 6.5g; Sodium 1314mg.

1 Place the beans in a bowl and cover with boiling water. Leave to stand for 1 hour. Drain.

2 Place 15ml/1 tbsp oil in the pressure cooker, add the lardons and fry for 3–4 minutes, to brown. Add the beans to the pressure cooker and 600ml/1 pint/2½ cups hot water.

Electric: Close the lid and bring to High pressure using the Manual, Beans, Pulses or Soup setting. Cook for 15 minutes (18 minutes). Release the pressure using natural release, making sure the 'keep warm' mode is switched off. After 10 minutes, quickly release the remaining pressure, if any.
Stovetop: Close the lid and bring to High pressure. Cook for 15 minutes (18 minutes). Release the pressure slowly. After 10 minutes, quickly release the remaining pressure, if any.

3 Drain in a sieve or strainer, transfer to a bowl and set aside.

4 Meanwhile, cut the duck portions into large pieces. Twist each sausage into three and cut into short lengths. In the cleaned pressure cooker, heat the remaining oil and fry the duck and sausages, until browned. Remove with a slotted spoon and drain on kitchen paper. Use the Sauté or Soup setting for the electric pressure cooker.

5 Add the onion to the open pressure cooker and cook, stirring for 2–3 minutes. Add 2 chopped garlic cloves, the celery and carrot and cook for 2–3 minutes. Add the tomatoes and thyme. Stir in the stock, scraping any sediment from the base of the pressure cooker.

6 Add the meat, sausages, beans and lardons to the pressure cooker.

Electric: Close the lid and bring to High pressure using the Manual or Meat setting. Cook for 10 minutes (14 minutes). Release the pressure using natural release, making sure the 'keep warm' mode is switched off. After 10 minutes, quickly release the remaining pressure, if any.
Stovetop: Close the lid and bring to High pressure. Cook for 10 minutes (14 minutes). Release the pressure slowly. After 10 minutes, quickly release the remaining pressure, if any.

7 Stir in the tomato purée and season with salt and ground black pepper. Remove the thyme sprigs. Transfer the cassoulet to an ovenproof dish. Mix the breadcrumbs and remaining chopped garlic together and sprinkle over the cassoulet. Place in a preheated oven at 160°C/325°F/Gas 3 and cook for 30–40 minutes, to lightly brown.

8 Remove the cassoulet from the oven and serve in warmed bowls, garnished with fresh thyme sprigs.

Turkey and Chickpea Tagine

Dried chickpeas, freshly cooked, always have a superior texture to the canned variety. Here, they are combined in the pressure cooker with turkey and apricots in a Moroccan-inspired sauce. This dish is delicious served with couscous, but you could serve it with rice.

Pressure: High
Time under Pressure: 32 minutes
(45 minutes)
Releases: Natural/Slow and Quick
Serves 4

115g/4oz/⅝ cup chickpeas
15ml/1 tbsp sunflower oil
1 onion, chopped
450g/1lb skinless, boneless turkey
    breast portions, cut into chunks
2 garlic cloves, chopped
5ml/1 tsp ground coriander
2.5cm/1in piece fresh root
    ginger, grated
5ml/1 tsp ground cinnamon
15ml/1 tbsp tomato purée (paste)
200ml/7fl oz/scant 1 cup
    chicken stock
100ml/3½fl oz/scant ½ cup
    orange juice
75g/3oz/⅓ cup ready-to-eat
    dried apricots
200g/7oz/generous 1 cup couscous
15ml/1 tbsp olive oil
45ml/2 tbsp pomegranate seeds
45ml/3 tbsp chopped fresh
    coriander (cilantro)
50g/2oz/½ cup toasted
    flaked almonds
salt and freshly ground black pepper

1 Place the chickpeas in a bowl. Cover with boiling water and leave to stand for 1 hour. Drain and place in the pressure cooker with 900ml/1½ pints/3¾ cups water.

Electric: Close the lid and bring to High pressure using the Manual, Beans or Pulses setting. Cook for 20 minutes (30 minutes). Release the pressure using natural release, making sure the 'keep warm' mode is switched off.
Stovetop: Close the lid and bring to High pressure. Cook for 20 minutes (30 minutes). Release the pressure slowly.

2 Drain the chickpeas and set aside. Heat the sunflower oil in the open pressure cooker, add the onion and sauté for 4–5 minutes, until soft. Add the turkey, garlic, coriander, ginger and cinnamon and cook for 2–3 minutes, stirring. Use the Sauté or Meat setting for the electric pressure cooker.

3 Stir in the tomato purée, stock and orange juice. Scrape the base of the cooker to remove any sediment. Stir in the apricots and chickpeas. Use the Sauté or Meat setting for the electric pressure cooker.

Electric: Close the lid and bring to High pressure using the Manual, Meat, Poultry or Soup setting. Cook for 12 minutes (15 minutes).
Stovetop: Close the lid and bring to High pressure. Cook for 12 minutes (15 minutes).

4 Just before the end of the cooking time, place the couscous in a bowl and cover with boiling water. Stir in the olive oil and cover. Leave to stand for 5 minutes, then stir to separate. Stir in the pomegranate seeds and half the coriander.

5 Reduce the pressure quickly, making sure the 'keep warm' mode is switched off for the electric pressure cooker. Remove the lid and stir in the almonds. Season with salt and black pepper and serve on warmed serving plates with the couscous. Sprinkle with the remaining coriander.

Energy 508kcal/2131kJ; Protein 36.6g;
Carbohydrate 52.5g, of which sugars 10.9g; Fat 18.3g, of which saturates 2.5g; Cholesterol 97mg; Calcium 122mg; Fibre 5.9g; Sodium 131mg.

Spicy Turkey and Potato Pie

This quick and easy pie is made with a spicy turkey mince, topped with mashed potato and cheese that is browned under the grill. The potatoes are cooked in the pressure cooker at the same time as the turkey filling, making this a complete meal in itself.

1 Heat the oil in the open pressure cooker, add the onion and sauté for 4–5 minutes or until lightly browned. Add the turkey mince and cook for 2–3 minutes, stirring, until browned. Use the Sauté or Meat setting for the electric pressure cooker.

2 Add the pepper and cook for 1 minute. Stir in the chilli powder, Worcestershire sauce, chopped tomatoes, tomato purée and chicken stock and bring to the boil.

3 Line the separator or steamer basket with foil. Place the potato quarters in the separator with 150ml/¼ pint/⅔ cup hot water. Place on top of the turkey mince.

Electric: Close the lid and bring to High pressure using the Meat or Poultry setting. Cook for 10 minutes (12 minutes). Release the pressure quickly, making sure the 'keep warm' mode is switched off.
Stovetop: Close the lid and bring to High pressure. Cook for 10 minutes (12 minutes). Release the pressure quickly.

4 Remove the lid carefully and check the potatoes are cooked. Remove the separator or steamer basket and stand it on a plate. Mix the flour with 30ml/2 tbsp water and stir into the turkey mixture. Bring back to the boil, stirring. Stir the peas, if using, into the turkey mixture and cook for 2 minutes. Use the Sauté or Meat setting for the electric pressure cooker.

5 Meanwhile, drain the potatoes and transfer to a bowl. Mash with the butter and milk and stir in half the cheese. Season to taste.

6 Check the seasoning for the turkey mixture, then spoon it into a shallow ovenproof dish. Top with the mashed potato and sprinkle over the remaining cheese. Place under a preheated grill to brown. Serve sprinkled with chopped parsley.

Pressure: High
Time under Pressure: 10 minutes (12 minutes)
Release: Quick
Serves 4

15ml/1 tbsp sunflower oil
1 onion, finely chopped
400g/14oz minced (ground) turkey
1 orange (bell) pepper, halved, seeded and chopped
5ml/1 tsp chilli powder
15ml/1 tbsp Worcestershire sauce
400g/14oz can chopped tomatoes
15ml/1 tbsp tomato purée (paste)
150ml/¼ pint/⅔ cup chicken stock
15ml/1 tbsp plain (all-purpose) flour
115g/4oz/1 cup frozen peas (optional)
salt and freshly ground black pepper
chopped fresh parsley, to garnish

For the topping
450g/1lb potatoes, peeled and cut into quarters
25g/1oz/2 tbsp butter
15ml/1 tbsp milk
40g/1½ oz mature (sharp) Cheddar cheese, grated
salt and ground black pepper

Cook's Tip
As the size of potatoes can vary, check they are tender before removing from the pressure cooker. If they are not ready, close the lid and return to High pressure for another 1–2 minutes.

Energy 367kcal/1543kJ; Protein 27.4g; Carbohydrate 31.1g, of which sugars 8.4g; Fat 15.7g, of which saturates 6.9g; Cholesterol 146mg; Calcium 127mg; Fibre 3.8g; Sodium 310mg.

Cider-braised Pheasants with Apple

The pressure cooker is ideal for tenderizing pheasants. They are cooked in an autumnal mix of apples and cider, flavoured with onions, bacon and tarragon, and the sauce is enriched with a dash of cream. Serve this dish with baby new potatoes.

Pressure: High
Time under Pressure: 12 minutes
  (15 minutes)
Release: Quick
Serves 4

4 streaky (fatty) bacon rashers (strips)
2 small pheasants
250g/1oz/2 tbsp butter
15ml/1 tbsp sunflower oil
1 onion, chopped
200ml/7fl oz/scant 1 cup dry cider
5 tarragon sprigs
150ml/¼ pint/⅔ cup chicken stock
2 eating apples
15ml/1 tbsp plain (all-purpose) flour
60ml/4 tbsp double (heavy) cream
salt and freshly ground black pepper

1 Cut the bacon rashers in half and use to cover the pheasant breasts, using cocktail sticks or toothpicks to secure. Season the pheasants with salt and black pepper.

2 Heat the butter and oil in the open pressure cooker, and place the pheasants breast side down and brown. Turn to brown on all sides, cooking one after the other, if necessary. Use the Sauté, Poultry or Meat setting for the electric pressure cooker. Transfer to a plate.

3 Add the onion to the pressure cooker and sauté for 3–4 minutes, to soften. Stir in the cider, making sure any sediment is removed from the base of the cooker. Bring to the boil.

4 Return the pheasants to the pressure cooker. Add 2 tarragon sprigs and the stock.

Electric: Close the lid and bring to High pressure using the Meat or Poultry setting. Cook for 12 minutes (15 minutes). Release the pressure quickly, making sure the 'keep warm' mode is switched off.
Stovetop: Close the lid and bring to High pressure. Cook for 12 minutes (15 minutes). Release the pressure quickly.

5 Cut the apples in half, core and cut into wedges. Carefully remove the lid from the pressure cooker and transfer the pheasants to a warmed serving dish. Remove the tarragon sprigs. Add the apple wedges and cook for 4–5 minutes, to soften. Use the Sauté or Meat setting for the electric pressure cooker. Meanwhile, mix the flour and cream together in a small bowl.

6 Gradually stir the cream mixture into the sauce and bring to the boil, stirring. Chop the remaining tarragon sprigs and stir into the sauce. Adjust the seasoning. Serve the pheasants with the apple wedges and spoon over a little sauce. Serve the remaining sauce separately.

Energy 660kcal/2752kJ; Protein 63.2g; Carbohydrate 12.8g, of which sugars 9.1g; Fat 38.9g, of which saturates 15.5g; Cholesterol 497mg; Calcium 88mg; Fibre 2.1g; Sodium 459mg.

Braised Guinea Fowl with Red Cabbage

The slightly gamey taste of guinea fowl is complemented perfectly by the sweet flavour of red cabbage, braised in apple juice and scented with juniper berries. This pressure cooker dish is also good made with either pheasant or chicken.

Pressure: High
Time under Pressure: 10 minutes
  (12 minutes)
Release: Natural/Slow
Serves 4

½ red cabbage, weighing about
  450g/1lb
15ml/1 tbsp butter
15ml/1 tbsp sunflower oil
1.3kg/3lb oven-ready guinea fowl,
  jointed
3 shallots, chopped
15ml/1 tbsp plain (all-purpose) flour
250ml/8fl oz/1 cup chicken stock
150ml/¼ pint/⅔ cup apple juice
15ml/1 tbsp soft light brown sugar
15ml/1 tbsp red wine vinegar
4 juniper berries, crushed
salt and freshly ground black pepper

Variation
Add to the fruity flavour of the cabbage by adding 15ml/1 tbsp sultanas (golden raisins) to the cooker with the red cabbage, before cooking.

1 Cut the cabbage into wedges, removing any tough outer leaves and the central core. Shred the wedges.

2 Heat the butter and oil in the open pressure cooker, add the guinea fowl and brown on all sides, cooking in batches, if necessary. Use the Sauté, Poultry or Meat setting for the electric pressure cooker. Transfer to a plate.

3 Add the shallots and sauté for 3–4 minutes, to brown. Stir in the flour, then gradually stir in the stock and apple juice. Bring to the boil, stirring continuously. Stir in the sugar, vinegar and juniper berries, then add the red cabbage.

4 Return the guinea fowl portions to the pressure cooker, nestling them into the cabbage.

Electric: Close the lid and bring to High pressure using the Poultry or Meat setting. Cook for 10 minutes (12 minutes). Release the pressure using natural release, making sure the 'keep warm' mode is switched off.
Stovetop: Close the lid and bring to High pressure. Cook for 10 minutes (12 minutes). Release the pressure slowly.

5 Carefully remove the lid and check the seasoning. Use a slotted spoon to place the guinea fowl portions on warmed serving plates. Serve with the red cabbage.

Energy 498kcal/2079kJ; Protein 48.8g;
Carbohydrate 14.7g, of which sugars 11.4g; Fat
27.4g, of which saturates 9.2g; Cholesterol 382mg;
Calcium 126mg; Fibre 3.9g; Sodium 143mg.

Rabbit with Red Wine and Prunes

This is a classic French dish with a wonderfully rich flavour, the prunes adding a delicious sweetness to the sauce. The pressure cooker is ideal for tenderizing the rabbit. Serve with fried potato cubes or new potatoes.

Pressure: High

Time under Pressure: 20 minutes (25 minutes)

Release: Natural/Slow

Serves 4

8 rabbit portions
30ml/2 tbsp sunflower oil
2 onions, finely chopped
2 garlic cloves, finely chopped
30m/2 tbsp Armagnac or brandy
300ml/½ pint/1¼ cups dry red wine
5ml/1 tsp soft light brown sugar
10ml/2 tsp cornflour (cornstarch)
90ml/3fl oz/6 tbsp double
   (heavy) cream
16 ready-to-eat prunes
salt and freshly ground black pepper

1 Season the rabbit portions liberally with salt and pepper. Heat the oil in the open pressure cooker, add the rabbit portions in batches and fry until they are golden brown on all sides. Use the Sauté, Poultry or Meat setting for the electric pressure cooker.

2 Remove the rabbit portions with a slotted spoon and set aside. Add the chopped onions and cook for 3–4 minutes, stirring occasionally, until softened. Add the garlic and cook for 1 minute.

3 Return the rabbit to the pressure cooker, add the Armagnac or brandy and bring to the boil. Add the wine and sugar and bring to the boil.

Electric: Close the lid and bring to High pressure using the Meat or Poultry setting. Cook for 20 minutes (25 minutes). Release the pressure using natural release, making sure the 'keep warm' mode is switched off.
Stovetop: Close the lid and bring to High pressure. Cook for 20 minutes (25 minutes). Release the pressure slowly.

4 Carefully remove the lid. Using a slotted spoon, transfer the rabbit pieces to a warmed serving dish and keep warm.

5 Mix the cornflour and 15ml/1 tbsp water together in a small bowl. Mix in the cream. Stir into the sauce with the prunes. Bring to the boil, stirring continuously. Simmer for 2–3 minutes. Use the Manual, Sauté or Soup setting for the electric pressure cooker. Season to taste, pour over the rabbit portions and serve.

Energy 615kcal/2571kJ; Protein 56.4g; Carbohydrate 23.6g, of which sugars 19.6g; Fat 26g, of which saturates 12.4g; Cholesterol 239mg; Calcium 147mg; Fibre 4.5g; Sodium 141mg.

Venison Sausage Casserole

This tasty supper dish can be prepared in minutes using your pressure cooker. The sausages are cooked with lentils and mixed vegetables in a mustard and wine sauce. You can serve the casserole with crusty bread and a tomato and onion salad, for a more substantial meal.

1 Heat the oil in the open pressure cooker and fry the sausages, until browned. Remove to a plate. Add the lardons and cook for 3–4 minutes, to brown lightly. Use the Sauté or Meat setting for the electric pressure cooker.

2 Add the leek, mushrooms and pepper and sauté for 4–5 minutes, until softened. Add the lentils, garlic, thyme and white wine and stir to remove any sediment from the base of the cooker. Bring to the boil.

3 Add the stock and return the sausages to the cooker.

Electric: Close the lid and bring to High pressure using the Manual or Meat setting. Sook for 10 minutes (12 minutes). Release the pressure quickly, making sure the 'keep warm' mode is switched off.
Stovetop: Close the lid and bring to High pressure. Cook for 10 minutes (12 minutes). Release the pressure quickly.

4 Open the cooker, removing the lid carefully. Stir the mustard and redcurrant jelly into the lentils and adjust the seasoning.

5 Divide the casserole between warmed plates and garnish with fresh thyme. Serve immediately.

Cook's Tip
Check if the lentils are cooked. The timing can vary from batch to batch, and with age. If they need more cooking, you can either return to pressure for a minute or so, or leave covered but not under pressure and cook for 3–4 minutes.

Pressure: High
Time under Pressure: 10 minutes (12 minutes)
Release: Quick
Serves 4

30ml/2 tbsp sunflower oil
400g/14oz venison sausages
115g/4oz//⅔ cup smoked bacon lardons
1 leek, cut into thick slices
115g/4oz/1½ cups mushrooms, halved or quartered
1 red (bell) pepper, halved, seeded and sliced
175g/6oz/¾ cup green lentils
1 garlic clove, crushed
2 fresh thyme sprigs, plus extra to garnish
125ml/4fl oz/½ cup dry white wine
225ml/8fl oz/1 cup vegetable stock
10ml/2 tsp Dijon mustard
15ml/1 tbsp redcurrant jelly
salt and ground black pepper

Energy 610kcal/2545kJ; Protein 27.4g; Carbohydrate 37.8g, of which sugars 8.5g; Fat 37.7g, of which saturates 12.7g; Cholesterol 62mg; Calcium 113mg; Fibre 8.8g; Sodium 1367mg.

Venison Pot Pies

The gamey flavour of venison is perfect for this dish, but boneless rabbit, hare or pheasant can be used instead. The meat filling is cooked in the pressure cooker until it is tender and succulent, before being topped with pastry and finished in the oven.

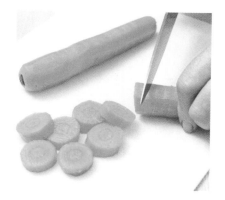  

Pressure: High

Time under Pressure: 20 minutes (25 minutes)

Release: Quick

Serves 4

675g/1½lb diced venison steak
30ml/2 tbsp plain (all-purpose) flour
30ml/2 tbsp sunflower oil
60ml/4 tbsp Madeira, port or sherry
300ml/½ pint/1¼ cups game or chicken stock
1 leek, sliced
225g/8oz parsnips, thickly sliced
225g/8oz carrots, thickly sliced
45ml/3 tbsp chopped fresh parsley
450g/1lb puff pastry
beaten egg yolk, to glaze
salt and freshly ground black pepper

Variation

You can make one large pie instead of the four individual ones, if you like.

Energy 757kcal/3176kJ; Protein 46.7g; Carbohydrate 62g, of which sugars 11.7g; Fat 35.7g, of which saturates 14.8g; Cholesterol 149mg; Calcium 133mg; Fibre 6.9g; Sodium 463mg.

1 Place the venison in a bowl. Add the flour and a little salt and pepper and toss together, to coat. Heat the oil in the open pressure cooker, then fry the venison, to brown. Use the Sauté, Poultry or Meat setting for the electric pressure cooker.

2 Stir in the Madeira, port or sherry and stock and stir well to remove any sediment from the base of the cooker. Bring to the boil.

3 Add the leek, parsnips and carrots and mix together.

Electric: Close the lid and bring to High pressure using the Manual, Soup or Meat setting. Cook for 20 minutes (25 minutes). Release the pressure quickly, making sure the 'keep warm' mode is switched off.
Stovetop: Close the lid and bring to High pressure. Cook for 20 minutes (25 minutes). Release the pressure quickly.

4 Carefully remove the lid and check the seasoning. Stir in the parsley and transfer to a bowl, cover and leave to cool.

5 To make the pies, preheat the oven to 220°C/425°F/Gas 7. Spoon the venison mixture into four individual dishes. Cut the pastry into quarters and roll out on a lightly floured surface to make the pie covers. Make the pieces larger than the pie dishes. Trim off any excess pastry and use to line the rim of each dish.

6 Dampen the pastry rims with cold water and cover with the pastry lids. Pinch the edges together to seal in the filling. Brush each pie with beaten egg yolk and make a small hole in the top of each one to allow steam to escape.

7 Stand the pies on a baking tray and bake for 25 minutes, or until the pastry is well risen and dark golden. If the pastry is browning too quickly, cover with foil after 15 minutes to prevent it from overbrowning. Serve with creamed potatoes and a green vegetable such as broccoli, if you wish.

Venison, Beef and Ale Pudding

Pressure cookers are ideal for cooking suet puddings. This one is filled with a tasty mixture of venison and beef cooked in ale and then encased in a suet pastry with leeks and mushrooms. Serve with green vegetables such as broccoli or green beans.

Pressure: High, then Low
Time under Pressure: 40 minutes (50 minutes) + pre-steaming
Releases: Quick and Natural/Slow
Serves 4

300g/11oz diced casserole or shoulder of venison
300g/11oz diced lean braising steak
25g/1oz/2 tbsp plain (all-purpose) flour
30ml/2 tbsp sunflower oil
300ml/½ pint/1¼ cups brown ale
15ml/1 tbsp Worcestershire sauce
1 leek, sliced
2 garlic cloves, chopped
15ml/1 tbsp tomato purée (paste)
115g/4oz/1½ cups mushrooms, thickly sliced
salt and freshly ground black pepper

For the pastry
200g/7oz scant 1 cup self-raising (self-rising) flour
2.5ml/½ tsp salt
100g/3½oz/⅔ cup shredded suet

Energy 469kcal/1979kJ; Protein 40.4g; Carbohydrate 45.5g, of which sugars 7.5g; Fat 11.8g, of which saturates 3g; Cholesterol 91mg; Calcium 220mg; Fibre 3.9g; Sodium 596mg.

1 Place the venison and steak in a large bowl. Add the flour and a little salt and pepper and toss together, to coat.

2 Heat the oil in the open pressure cooker, add the venison, steak and any remaining flour and fry until evenly browned. Use the Sauté or Meat setting for the electric pressure cooker. Add the ale and Worcestershire sauce and stir well to remove any sediment from the base of the cooker. Bring to the boil, stirring continuously. Add the leek and garlic and stir to combine.

Electric: Close the lid and bring to High pressure using the Manual or Meat setting. Cook for 15 minutes (20 minutes). Release the pressure quickly, making sure the 'keep warm' mode is switched off.
Stovetop: Close the lid and bring to High pressure. Cook for 15 minutes (20 minutes). Release the pressure quickly.

3 Carefully remove the lid and stir in the tomato purée. Transfer to a bowl, cover and leave to cool.

4 To make the pastry, sift the flour and salt together. Stir in the suet, then, using a round-bladed knife, gradually stir in about 120ml/4fl oz/ ½ cup cold water to mix to a soft dough.

5 Roll out two-thirds of the pastry on a lightly floured surface, into a circle. Use to line a lightly greased 1.5 litre/2½ pint/5 cup pudding basin, leaving any excess pastry hanging over the sides. Stir the mushrooms into the meat mixture and, using a slotted spoon, fill the basin with the mixture to within 2.5cm/1in of the top. Add 60ml/4 tbsp of the gravy, reserving the remainder.

6 Roll out the remaining pastry to make a lid. Brush the top edge of the pastry in the bowl with water and place the lid on top. Press and crimp the edges together. Cut off any excess pastry.

7 Cover the top of the pudding with a pleated double layer of greased greaseproof paper or a single layer of foil, and tie in place with string. Place the trivet or rack in the base of the pressure cooker and add 1.2 litres/ 2 pints/5 cups hot water. Carefully stand the basin on the trivet or rack.

Electric: Close the lid, leaving the steam vent open. Do not seal or bring to pressure; just steam for 20 minutes using the Manual or Soup setting. Refer to your manufacturer's handbook on how to do this; see also pages 44–5. Open the cooker and check there is still plenty of water. Bring to Low pressure and cook for 25 minutes (30 minutes). Release the pressure using natural release, making sure the 'keep warm' mode is switched off.
Stovetop: Close the lid, leaving the steam vent open. Do not seal or bring to pressure; just steam for 20 minutes. Refer to your manufacturer's handbook on how to do this; see also pages 44–5. Open the cooker and check there is still plenty of water. Bring to Low pressure and cook for 25 minutes (30 minutes). Release the pressure slowly.

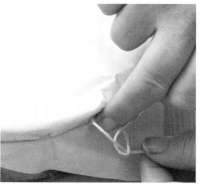

8 Heat the reserved gravy in a small pan. Carefully remove the pudding from the pressure cooker and turn it out on to a warmed serving plate.

GRAINS, PASTA AND PULSES

Freshly cooked grains and pulses are far superior to ready-prepared versions, and the pressure cooker cuts down the lengthy overnight soaking times and long cooking times associated with conventional cooking methods for pulses. Healthy, nutritious, meatless meals become easy to make. Try recipes such as mixed bean and tomato chilli, Tuscan baked beans, mixed bean and aubergine tagine with mint yogurt, or pease pudding. There is also a delicious black bean, chickpea and green bean salad in a honey, lemon and mustard dressing with basil. For a quick and easy supper dish, try chilli pasta or a risotto – either a traditional risotto with borlotti beans, or a barley risotto with asparagus and mushrooms. Another favourite is a quinoa-based salad with sun-dried tomatoes and mozzarella cheese, perfect for lunch, supper or even a packed lunch.

Basmati Rice and Nut Pilaff

Vegetarians will love this simple pilaff. Add wild or cultivated mushrooms, if you like. This dish can also be served with curries. Make sure you release the pressure slowly for at least 5 minutes, so that the rice settles in the pressure cooker before opening the lid.

Pressure: High
Time under Pressure: 4 minutes (5 minutes)
Release: Natural/Slow
Serves 4

30ml/2 tbsp sunflower oil
1 onion, finely chopped
1 garlic clove, crushed
225g/8oz/generous 1 cup
 basmati rice
1 large carrot, grated
5ml/1 tsp cumin seeds
10ml/2 tsp ground coriander
4 green cardamom pods
500ml/17fl oz/generous 2 cups
 hot vegetable stock
1 bay leaf
75g/3oz/½ cup cashew nuts or
 shelled walnuts
salt and ground black pepper
fresh parsley or coriander (cilantro)
 sprigs, to garnish

Variation
You can use whichever nuts you prefer, such as unsalted peanuts, almonds or pistachio nuts.

1 Heat the oil in the open pressure cooker, then add the onion and cook for 3–4 minutes, to soften. Add the garlic and cook for 1 minute. Use the Sauté or Soup setting for the electric pressure cooker.

2 Stir in the rice, carrot, cumin seeds and ground coriander and cook for 1 minute, stirring. Add the cardamom pods, stock and bay leaf and season with salt and pepper. Stir thoroughly to make sure nothing remains on the base of the cooker.

Electric: Close the lid and bring to High pressure using the Manual, Rice or Soup setting and cook for 4 minutes (5 minutes). Release the pressure using natural release, making sure the 'keep warm' mode is switched off. After 5 minutes, quickly release the remaining pressure, if any.
Stovetop: Close the lid and bring to High pressure. Cook for 4 minutes (5 minutes). Release the pressure slowly. After 5 minutes, quickly release the remaining pressure, if any.

3 Carefully remove the lid and take the cardamom pods and bay leaf out of the rice. Stir the cashew nuts or walnuts into the rice mixture. Taste to check the seasoning, adding more salt and pepper, if necessary. Spoon into warmed individual bowls, or on to a large platter, garnish with sprigs of parsley or coriander and serve immediately.

Energy 397kcal/1653kJ; Protein 9g; Carbohydrate 54.9g, of which sugars 4.4g; Fat 15.8g, of which saturates 2.6g; Cholesterol 0mg; Calcium 42mg; Fibre 2.1g; Sodium 11mg.

Brown Rice with Lime and Lemon Grass

It is unusual to find brown rice given the Thai treatment, but the nutty flavour of the grains is enhanced by the fragrant flavour of the limes and lemon grass in this delicious dish. Release the pressure slowly to avoid blocking the pressure cooker vents.

Pressure: High
Time under Pressure: 21 minutes (24 minutes)
Release: Natural/Slow
Serve 4

2 limes
1 lemon grass stalk
15ml/1 tbsp sunflower oil
1 onion, chopped
2.5cm/1in piece fresh root ginger, peeled and finely chopped
7.5ml/1½ tsp coriander seeds
7.5ml/1½ tsp cumin seeds
275g/10oz/1½ cups long grain brown rice
750ml/1¼ pints/3 cups hot vegetable stock
60ml/4 tbsp chopped fresh coriander (cilantro)
salt and ground black pepper
spring onions (scallions), toasted coconut strips and lime wedges, to garnish

1 Using a cannelle knife (zester) or fine grater, pare the rind from the limes, taking care not to remove any of the bitter white pith. Set the rind aside. Cut off the lower portion of the lemon grass stalk, discarding the papery top end of the stalk. Finely chop the lemon grass and set aside.

2 Heat the oil in the open pressure cooker, then add the onion and sauté for 3–4 minutes, to soften. Stir in the ginger, coriander and cumin seeds, lemon grass and lime rind and cook for 1–2 minutes, stirring. Use the Sauté or Soup setting for the electric pressure cooker.

3 Rinse the rice in cold water and drain. Stir in the rice and stock. Stir thoroughly to make sure no sediment remains on the base of the cooker.

Electric: Close the lid and bring to High pressure using the Manual or Soup setting. Cook for 21 minutes (24 minutes). Release the pressure using natural release, making sure the 'keep warm' mode is switched off.
Stovetop: Close the lid and bring to High pressure. Cook for 21 minutes (24 minutes). Release the pressure slowly.

4 Carefully remove the lid and stir the fresh coriander into the rice. Taste to check the seasoning, adding salt and pepper, as necessary. Fluff up the grains of rice and spoon into warmed individual bowls. Garnish with strips of spring onion, toasted coconut and lime wedges and serve immediately.

Energy 302kcal/1277kJ; Protein 6g; Carbohydrate 61g, of which sugars 3g; Fat 5.6g, of which saturates 0.9g; Cholesterol 0mg; Calcium 28mg; Fibre 2.5g; Sodium 5mg.

Asparagus, Mushroom and Barley Risotto

When making a risotto, pearl barley is a great alternative to rice, and will cook in around half the time in your pressure cooker. Here, it is flavoured with mushrooms, asparagus and Parmesan cheese. You could serve this delicious risotto with a green salad.

Pressure: High
Time under Pressure: 22 minutes (27 minutes)
Releases: Natural/Slow
Serves 3–4

15g/½oz/½ cup dried porcini
   mushrooms
100g/3¾oz asparagus tips
15ml/1 tbsp butter
15ml/1 tbsp olive oil
1 onion, finely chopped
1 garlic clove, crushed
250g/9oz/1½ cups pearl barley
75ml/2½fl oz/⅓ cup dry white wine
225g/8oz/3 cups chestnut
   mushrooms, thickly sliced
10ml/2 tsp fresh thyme leaves
750ml/1¼ pints/3 cups hot
   vegetable stock
50g/2oz/⅔ cup grated Parmesan
   cheese, plus extra to serve
   (optional)
salt and ground black pepper
fresh chopped chives, to garnish

1 Place the porcini mushrooms in a small bowl. Cover with boiling water and leave to soak for 30 minutes. Drain and reserve the liquid. Pour through a sieve or strainer to remove any grit, then chop the porcini.

2 Place the asparagus on a sheet of foil and wrap to enclose. Melt the butter in the pressure cooker and heat with the oil. Add the onion and cook for 3–4 minutes, to soften. Add the porcini mushrooms and garlic and cook for 1 minute. Use the Manual, Sauté or Soup setting for the electric pressure cooker.

3 Stir in the pearl barley and cook for 1 minute. Stir in the wine and cook for 1 minute. Add the chestnut mushrooms, thyme, stock and 100ml/3½fl oz/scant ½ cup of the reserved porcini mushroom liquid. Place the asparagus parcel on top.

Electric: Close the lid and bring to High pressure using the Manual or Soup setting. Cook for 4 minutes (5 minutes). Release the pressure using natural release, making sure the 'keep warm' mode is switched off. After 5 minutes, quickly release the remaining pressure, if any.
Stovetop: Close the lid and bring to High pressure. Cook for 4 minutes (5 minutes). Release the pressure slowly. After 5 minutes, quickly release the remaining pressure, if any.

4 Carefully remove the lid and take the asparagus out.

Electric: Close the lid and bring to High pressure using the Manual or Soup setting. Cook for 18 minutes (22 minutes). Release the pressure using natural release, making sure the 'keep warm' mode is switched off. After 5 minutes, quickly release the remaining pressure, if any.
Stovetop: Close the lid and bring to High pressure. Cook for 18 minutes (22 minutes). Release the pressure slowly. After 5 minutes, quickly release the remaining pressure, if any.

5 Carefully remove the lid and, if still watery, cook over a medium heat for a few minutes, stirring until thickened. Use the Sauté or Soup setting for the electric pressure cooker.

6 Cut the asparagus tips in half. Stir the Parmesan and asparagus pieces into the risotto and season with salt and pepper. Serve on warmed serving plates, sprinkled with chopped chives and ground black pepper. Serve with extra grated Parmesan, if you wish.

Energy 323kcal/1365kJ; Protein 8g; Carbohydrate 56.3g, of which sugars 3g; Fat 7.6g, of which saturates 2.6g; Cholesterol 8mg; Calcium 37mg; Fibre 2.8g; Sodium 32mg.

Tricolore Quinoa Salad

This is a quinoa-rich variation of the classic Italian salad. Good-quality sun-dried tomatoes are restored to plumpness after soaking, and when complemented by fresh tomatoes, this is a perfect salad to cook in your pressure cooker for *al fresco* dining on summer nights.

Pressure: High
Time under Pressure: 1 minute
    (1½ minutes)
Release: Natural/Slow
Serves 4

45ml/3 tbsp pine nuts
75g/3oz/½ cup quinoa
50g/2oz sun-dried tomatoes,
    rehydrated in boiling water
    for 2 hours
25g/1oz fresh basil leaves
225g/8oz mozzarella cheese,
    chopped or torn into small pieces
about 20 cherry tomatoes,
    or 8 ripe plum tomatoes,
    cut in half
salt and ground black pepper
cured Italian meats and
    ciabatta bread, to serve

For the dressing
90ml/6 tbsp balsamic vinegar
45ml/3 tbsp olive oil
2.5ml/½ tsp Dijon mustard
1 garlic clove, crushed
salt and ground black pepper

Cook's Tip
If you cannot programme your electric pressure cooker for this short cooking time, set a separate timer for the correct time and switch off the cooker after the given time.

1 Dry-fry the pine nuts in a heavy frying pan, stirring all the time, for about 4–5 minutes, until lightly browned. Be careful not to scorch the pine nuts. Set aside to cool.

2 Rinse the quinoa in cold water and drain well. Place it in the pressure cooker. Add 350ml/12fl oz/1½ cups water.

Electric: Close the lid and bring to High pressure using the Manual, Soup or Vegetable setting. Cook for 1 minute (1½ minutes). Release the pressure using natural release, making sure the 'keep warm' mode is switched off. After 10 minutes, quickly release the remaining pressure, if any.
Stovetop: Close the lid and bring to High pressure. Reduce the heat, making sure it is still under pressure, and cook over a low heat for 1 minute (1½ minutes). Release the pressure slowly. After 10 minutes, quickly release the remaining pressure, if any.

3 Drain and transfer to a bowl to cool.

4 Drain the sun-dried tomatoes, pat dry with kitchen paper, then cut with a sharp knife into long, thin strips.

5 Tear or chop one quarter of the basil leaves into pieces and place in a small jar or bowl. Add all the dressing ingredients and shake or whisk to mix.

6 Place the cooled quinoa, pine nuts, mozzarella, sun-dried tomatoes and cherry tomatoes in a bowl. Tear the remaining basil leaves, add to the bowl, pour in the dressing and toss gently to mix. Check the seasoning, adding more salt and pepper, if needed.

7 Serve alongside a cold platter of meats, accompanied by fresh ciabatta bread.

Energy 438kcal/1818kJ; Protein 16g; Carbohydrate 15.4g, of which sugars 5.4g; Fat 35.1g, of which saturates 10.5g; Cholesterol 33mg; Calcium 247mg; Fibre 1.8g; Sodium 370mg.

Rosemary Risotto with Borlotti Beans

It is possible to make risotto in the pressure cooker without the continual stirring of the traditional method. All the stock can be added at once, rather than ladleful by ladleful. This tasty rosemary-flavoured risotto is enriched with mascarpone and Parmesan cheeses.

1 Place the beans in a bowl. Cover with boiling water and leave to stand for 1 hour.

2 Drain and place in the pressure cooker. Add 600ml/1 pint/2½ cups hot water.

Electric: Close the lid and bring to High pressure using the Manual, Beans or Pulses setting. Cook for 20 minutes (30 minutes). Release the pressure using natural release, making sure the 'keep warm' mode is switched off.
Stovetop: Close the lid and bring to High pressure. Reduce the heat. Cook for 20 minutes (30 minutes). Release the pressure slowly.

3 Drain the beans in a sieve or strainer, rinse under cold running water and drain again. Place two-thirds in a food processor or blender and process to a coarse purée. Tip the remaining beans into a bowl and set aside.

4 Heat the butter and oil in the open cooker. Use the Sauté, Manual or Soup setting for the electric pressure cooker. Add the onion and cook for 4–5 minutes, stirring occasionally, to soften. Add the garlic and cook for 1 minute.

5 Stir in the rice and cook for 1 minute. Stir in the wine and cook for 1 minute. Add the stock, bean purée and rosemary.

Electric: Close the lid and bring to High pressure using the Manual, Rice or Soup setting. Cook for 6 minutes (8 minutes). Release the pressure using natural release, making sure the 'keep warm' mode is switched off.
Stovetop: Close the lid and bring to High pressure. Lower the heat, making sure it is still under pressure. Cook for 6 minutes (8 minutes). Release the pressure slowly.

6 Stir in the reserved beans, mascarpone and Parmesan cheese and season to taste with salt and pepper. Leave to stand for 5 minutes. Spoon into warmed individual serving bowls and serve immediately, sprinkled with extra Parmesan, if you wish.

Variation
Try using different herbs to vary the flavour. Fresh thyme or marjoram would make a good alternative to rosemary.

Pressure: High
Time under Pressure: 26 minutes (38 minutes)
Release: Natural/Slow
Serves 3–4

115g/4oz/⅔ cup dried borlotti beans
15ml/1 tbsp butter
15ml/1 tbsp olive oil
1 onion, finely chopped
2 garlic cloves, crushed
225g/8oz/1 cup risotto rice
120ml/4fl oz/½ cup dry white wine
600ml/1 pint/2½ cups hot vegetable stock
5ml/1 tsp chopped fresh rosemary
60ml/4 tbsp mascarpone
65g/2½oz/¾ cup grated Parmesan cheese, plus extra to serve (optional)
salt and ground black pepper

Energy 394kcal/1650kJ; Protein 12.5g; Carbohydrate 61.3g, of which sugars 3g; Fat 9g, of which saturates 4g; Cholesterol 15mg; Calcium 67mg; Fibre 6.7g; Sodium 82mg.

Chilli Pasta with Basil and Parmesan

This is a very quick and easy-to-make supper or lunchtime dish that can be prepared in minutes. Dried pasta cooks in around half the time using a pressure cooker. The pasta is infused with the flavour of tomatoes and chilli as it cooks.

1 Heat the oil in the open pressure cooker. Add the onion and fry for 3–4 minutes, to soften. Add the garlic and chilli and cook, stirring, for 1 minute. Use the Sauté or Soup setting for the electric pressure cooker.

2 Add 900ml/1½ pints/3¾ cups hot water and stir to remove any sediment from the base of the cooker. Add the pasta and top with the tomatoes. Do not stir.

Electric: Close the lid and bring to High pressure using the Manual, Soup or Rice setting. Cook for 4 minutes (6 minutes). Release the pressure quickly, making sure the 'keep warm' mode is switched off.
Stovetop: Close the lid and bring to High pressure. Cook for 4 minutes (6 minutes). Release the pressure quickly.

3 Stir in the tomato purée and season with salt and ground black pepper.

4 Divide the pasta between four warmed serving dishes, sprinkle with Parmesan shavings and fresh basil leaves and serve immediately. Top with extra grated Parmesan cheese, if you wish.

Pressure: High
Time under Pressure: 4 minutes (6 minutes)
Release: Quick
Serves 4

15ml/1 tbsp olive oil
1 onion, chopped
1 garlic clove, crushed
1 fresh red chilli, halved, seeded and finely chopped
350g/12oz/3 cups pasta shapes, such as penne or fusilli
400g/14oz can chopped tomatoes
30ml/2 tbsp tomato purée (paste)
salt and ground black pepper
Parmesan cheese shavings and shredded basil leaves, to garnish, plus extra grated Parmesan cheese (optional)

Energy 359kcal/1525kJ; Protein 12.3g; Carbohydrate 71.9g, of which sugars 8.9g; Fat 4.5g, of which saturates 0.6g; Cholesterol 0mg; Calcium 46mg; Fibre 5.3g; Sodium 61mg.

Spicy Tamarind Chickpeas

The pressure cooker is perfect for quickly cooking chickpeas, which make a good base for many vegetarian dishes. Here, they are tossed with sharp tamarind and spice to make a deliciously light vegetarian lunch or side dish.

Pressure: High

Time under Pressure: 25 minutes (30 minutes)

Release: Natural/Slow

Serves 4

225g/8oz dried chickpeas
25g/1oz tamarind paste
45ml/3 tbsp sunflower oil
2.5ml/½ tsp cumin seeds
1 onion, finely chopped
2 garlic cloves, crushed
2.5cm/1in piece fresh root ginger, peeled and grated
5ml/1 tsp ground cumin
5ml/1 tsp ground coriander
1.5ml/¼ tsp ground turmeric
1 fresh green chilli, finely chopped
2.5ml/½ tsp salt
225g/8oz tomatoes, skinned and chopped, or 220g/8oz can chopped tomatoes
2.5ml/½ tsp garam masala
chopped fresh chillies and chopped onion, to garnish

1 Place the chickpeas in a bowl. Cover with boiling water and leave to stand for 1 hour.

2 Drain the chickpeas and place in the pressure cooker. Add 1 litre/ 2½ pints/4 cups hot water.

Electric: Close the lid and bring to High pressure using the Manual, Beans, Pulses or Soup setting. Cook for 25 minutes (30 minutes). Release the pressure using natural release, making sure the 'keep warm' mode is switched off.
Stovetop: Close the lid and bring to High pressure. Cook for 25 minutes (30 minutes). Release the pressure slowly.

3 Meanwhile, place the tamarind paste in a bowl and add 120ml/4fl oz/ ½ cup water and mix together.

4 Drain the chickpeas and set aside. In the cleaned pressure cooker, heat the oil, then add the onion, garlic and ginger and sauté for 5 minutes. Use the Sauté or Soup setting for the electric pressure cooker.

5 Add the cumin, coriander, turmeric, chilli and salt and cook for 1 minute, stirring. Add the tomatoes, garam masala and tamarind mixture and bring to the boil. Add the chickpeas and simmer for 5 minutes. Spoon into a warmed serving dish and serve garnished with fresh chillies and onion.

Energy 288kcal/1208kJ; Protein 13.6g; Carbohydrate 33.9g, of which sugars 5.1g; Fat 11.9g, of which saturates 1.4g; Cholesterol 0mg; Calcium 113mg; Fibre 9.3g; Sodium 46mg.

Boston Baked Beans

The pressure cooker speeds up both the soaking time and the cooking of dried beans. The molasses or black treacle gives the beans a very rich flavour, but you could replace this with maple syrup. You can make this dish in advance if you wish.

1 Place the beans in a large bowl, cover with boiling water and leave to stand for 1 hour. Drain.

2 Place the beans in the pressure cooker. Stick the cloves in the onion and add to the pressure cooker, with the bay leaf.

3 In a bowl, blend together the tomato ketchup, molasses or black treacle, mustard and the stock. Pour over the beans. Bury the bacon in the beans.

Electric: Close the lid and bring to High pressure using the Manual, Beans, Pulses or Soup setting. Cook for 25 minutes (30 minutes). Release the pressure using natural release, making sure the 'keep warm' mode is switched off.

Stovetop: Close the lid and bring to High pressure. Cook for 25 minutes (30 minutes). Release the pressure slowly.

4 Remove the bacon from the beans, cool slightly, then, using a sharp knife, cut off any rind and fat and cut into chunks. Season the beans with salt and pepper. Add the chunks of bacon to the beans and serve.

Pressure: High
Time under Pressure: 25 minutes (30 minutes)
Release: Natural/Slow
Serves 4

225g/8oz/1¼ cups dried haricot (navy) beans
2 cloves
1 onion, peeled
1 bay leaf
45ml/3 tbsp tomato ketchup
15ml/1 tbsp molasses or black treacle
15ml/1 tbsp Dijon mustard
300ml/½ pint/1¼ cups vegetable stock
225g/8oz lean bacon joint
salt and ground black pepper

Energy 327kcal/1373kJ; Protein 21.9g; Carbohydrate 33.9g, of which sugars 9.4g; Fat 12.4g, of which saturates 4.2g; Cholesterol 33mg; Calcium 94mg; Fibre 12.6g; Sodium 1145mg.

Mixed Bean and Tomato Chilli

This is a great recipe to make with your pressure cooker. The beans need only be soaked for an hour in boiling water before cooking in the pressure cooker. Here, they are simmered in a fiery tomato sauce to make a delicious vegetarian chilli.

Pressure: High

Time under Pressure: 20 minutes (25 minutes)

Release: Natural/Slow

Serves 4

75g/3oz/generous ⅓ cup dried butter (lima) beans

75g/3oz/generous ⅓ cup dried cannellini beans

75g/3oz/generous ⅓ cup dried kidney beans

75g/3oz/generous ⅓ cup dried borlotti beans

15ml/1 tbsp sunflower oil

1 onion, chopped

2 garlic cloves, crushed

1 fresh red chilli

500g/1¼lb pack tomato passata (bottled strained tomatoes)

a large handful of fresh coriander (cilantro)

salt and ground black pepper

natural (plain) yogurt, to serve (optional)

1 Place the beans in a bowl. Cover with boiling water and leave to stand for 1 hour.

2 Drain and place in the pressure cooker. Add 1.2 litres/2 pints/5 cups water and bring to the boil in the open cooker. Use the Manual, Beans, Pulses or Soup setting for the electric pressure cooker. Once boiling, reduce the heat if using a stovetop pressure cooker. Remove any scum.

Electric: Close the lid and bring to High pressure. Use the Manual, Beans, Pulses or Soup setting and cook for 20 minutes (25 minutes). Release the pressure using natural release, making sure the 'keep warm' mode is switched off.

Stovetop: Close the lid and bring to High pressure. Cook for 20 minutes (25 minutes). Release the pressure slowly.

3 Drain the beans and set aside. Heat the oil in the open cooker. Use the Sauté or Soup setting for the electric pressure cooker. Add the onion and cook for 3–4 minutes, to soften. Add the garlic and chilli and cook for 1 minute.

4 Stir in the passata and add the beans. Simmer for 5 minutes. Adjust the seasoning. Stir in half the coriander. Ladle into warmed individual serving bowls and top with the remaining coriander. Top with a spoonful of yogurt, to serve, if you wish.

Energy 258kcal/1094kJ; Protein 18.3g; Carbohydrate 39.8g, of which sugars 7.5g; Fat 4g, of which saturates 0.5g; Cholesterol 0mg; Calcium 100mg; Fibre 17.6g; Sodium 64mg.

Tuscan Baked Beans

Beans are particularly popular in Tuscany, where they are cooked in many different ways. In this vegetarian dish, the beans are flavoured with fresh sage leaves. They will cook in the pressure cooker in under 30 minutes, as opposed to over 1½ hours in a pan.

1 Carefully pick over the beans, discarding any stones or other particles. Place the beans in a large bowl, cover with boiling water and leave to stand for 1 hour. Drain.

2 Place the beans in the pressure cooker and combine with the garlic, sage, leek and tomatoes. Add the stock.

Electric: Close the lid and bring to High pressure. Use the Manual, Beans, Pulses or Soup setting. Cook for 20 minutes (25 minutes). Release the pressure using natural release, making sure the 'keep warm' mode is switched off.
Stovetop: Close the lid and bring to High pressure. Cook for 20 minutes (25 minutes). Release the pressure slowly.

3 Season with salt and pepper. Stir in the tomato purée and simmer for 5 minutes. Use the Sauté or Soup setting for the electric pressure cooker. Allow to stand for 7–8 minutes. Serve hot or at room temperature.

Pressure: High
Time under Pressure: 20 minutes (25 minutes)
Release: Natural/Slow
Serves 4–6

300g/11oz/scant 1¾ cups dried beans, such as cannellini
2 garlic cloves, crushed
30ml/2 tbsp chopped fresh sage
1 leek, finely sliced
400g/14oz can plum tomatoes, chopped, with their juice
500ml/17fl oz/2 generous cups vegetable stock
30ml/2 tbsp tomato purée (paste)
salt and ground black pepper

Energy 154kcal/656kJ; Protein 12.4g; Carbohydrate 25.6g, of which sugars 4.5g; Fat 0.9g, of which saturates 0.1g; Cholesterol 0mg; Calcium 67mg; Fibre 12.1g; Sodium 48mg.

Mexican Refried Beans with Tostadas

Tostadas are crisp fried tortillas, popular in Mexico and South America. Here, refried beans are used for a classic tostada filling. Like all beans, they cook quickly in the pressure cooker. They are then finished in the frying pan, although you could use your pressure cooker for this.

Pressure: High

**Time under Pressure: 12 minutes
    (18 minutes)**

Release: Natural/Slow

Serves 4–6

115g/4oz/⅔ cup dried borlotti beans

3 garlic cloves, chopped

5ml/1 tsp ground cumin

30ml/2 tbsp sunflower oil

1 onion, chopped

2.5ml/½ tsp chilli powder

150ml/5fl oz/⅔ cup vegetable stock

15ml/1 tbsp tomato purée (paste)

30ml/2 tbsp chopped fresh
    coriander (cilantro)

salt and ground black pepper

6 wheat or corn tortillas

90ml/6 tbsp tomato salsa
    (see Cook's Tip)

30ml/2 tbsp sour cream

50g/2oz/½ cup grated Cheddar cheese

fresh coriander (cilantro) leaves,
    to garnish

Cook's Tip

To make a tomato salsa, mix together ½ small chopped onion with 1 small seeded and chopped chilli, 4 chopped tomatoes and 15ml/1 tbsp chopped fresh coriander (cilantro).

1 Place the beans in a large bowl, cover with boiling water and leave to stand for 1 hour. Drain.

2 Place the beans in the pressure cooker and combine with 1 chopped garlic clove and the cumin. Add 600ml/1 pint/2½ cups hot water.

Electric: Close the lid and bring to High pressure using the Manual, Beans, Pulses or Soup setting. Cook for 12 minutes (18 minutes). Release the pressure using natural release, making sure the 'keep warm' mode is switched off.

Stovetop: Close the lid and bring to High pressure. Cook for 12 minutes (18 minutes). Release the pressure slowly.

3 Drain the beans in a sieve or strainer.

4 While the pressure is releasing slowly, heat 15ml/1 tbsp oil in a frying pan and fry the onion, until softened. Add the remaining garlic and chilli powder and fry for 1 minute, stirring. Mix in the beans and mash very roughly with a potato masher. Add the stock, tomato purée, chopped coriander and seasoning and cook for a few minutes.

5 If you wish, fry the tortillas in hot oil for 1 minute, turning once, until crisp, then drain on kitchen paper, or alternatively warm them in the oven. Put a spoonful of beans on each tostada, spoon over some tomato salsa, the sour cream and sprinkle with cheese. Garnish with coriander leaves.

Energy 338kcal/1427kJ; Protein 12.5g; Carbohydrate 55.9g, of which sugars 3.5g; Fat 8.7g, of which saturates 3g; Cholesterol 11mg; Calcium 184mg; Fibre 7.3g; Sodium 289mg.

Mixed Bean and Aubergine Tagine with Mint Yogurt

In this Moroccan-inspired dish, the mixture of red kidney beans, black-eyed beans and aubergine provides both texture and flavour, enhanced by the herbs and chillies. This delicious bean recipe cooks very well in the pressure cooker.

Pressure: High
Time under Pressure: 13 minutes (17 minutes)
Release: Natural/Slow
Serves 4

115g/4oz/generous ½ cup dried red kidney beans
115g/4oz/generous ½ cup dried black-eyed beans (peas)
2 bay leaves
60ml/4 tbsp olive oil
1 aubergine (eggplant), about 225g/8oz, cut into chunks
1 onion, thinly sliced
3 garlic cloves, crushed
1–2 fresh red chillies, seeded and finely chopped
30ml/2 tbsp tomato purée (paste)
5ml/1 tsp paprika
2 large tomatoes, roughly chopped
200ml/⅓ pint/1¼ cups hot vegetable stock
15ml/1 tbsp each chopped fresh mint, parsley and coriander (cilantro)
salt and ground black pepper
fresh herb sprigs, to garnish

For the mint yogurt
150ml/¼ pint/⅔ cup natural (plain) yogurt
30ml/2 tbsp chopped fresh mint
2 spring onions (scallions), chopped

1 Place the beans in two separate bowls, then cover with boiling water. Leave to stand for 1 hour. Drain.

2 Place the beans and bay leaves in the pressure cooker and add 900ml/1½ pints/3¾ cups hot water.

Electric: Close the lid and bring to High pressure. Use the Manual, Beans, Pulses or Soup setting. Cook for 12 minutes (15 minutes). Release the pressure using natural release, making sure the 'keep warm' mode is switched off. After 10 minutes, quickly release the remaining pressure, if any.
Stovetop: Close the lid and bring to High pressure. Cook for 12 minutes (15 minutes). Release the pressure slowly. After 10 minutes, quickly release the remaining pressure, if any.

3 Drain, remove the bay leaves and set aside.

4 In the cleaned pressure cooker, add 45ml/3 tbsp oil. Add the aubergine and cook, stirring for 4–5 minutes, until browned. Use the Sauté or Soup setting for the electric pressure cooker. Remove with a slotted spoon and set aside.

5 Add the remaining oil and onion and cook, stirring, for 3–4 minutes, until softened. Add the garlic and chillies and cook for 2–3 minutes. Use the Manual, Sauté or Soup setting for the electric pressure cooker.

6 Stir in the tomato purée, paprika, tomatoes, aubergine and beans. Add the stock and stir thoroughly to make sure any sediment is removed from the base of the cooker.

Cook's Tip
If you cannot programme your electric pressure cooker for this short cooking time, set a separate timer for the correct time and switch off the cooker after the given time.

Energy 322kcal/1355kJ; Protein 17.1g; Carbohydrate 36.5g, of which sugars 9.8g; Fat 13.2g, of which saturates 2.1g; Cholesterol 0mg; Calcium 163mg; Fibre 15.1g; Sodium 60mg.

Electric: Close the lid and bring to High pressure using the Manual, Soup or Vegetable setting. Cook for 1 minute (2 minutes). Release the pressure using natural release, making sure the 'keep warm' mode is switched off. After 5 minutes, quickly release the remaining pressure, if any.

Stovetop: Close the lid and bring to High pressure. Cook for 1 minute (2 minutes). Release the pressure slowly. After 5 minutes, quickly release the remaining pressure, if any.

7 While the pressure is releasing, mix together the yogurt, mint and spring onions and place in a small serving bowl. Season the tagine with salt and pepper and mix in the chopped herbs. To serve, transfer to a warmed serving dish and garnish with fresh herb sprigs and serve with the yogurt.

Black Bean, Chickpea and Green Bean Salad

This is a mixed bean and chickpea salad made with dried black beans and fresh green beans, ideal for the pressure cooker. It is combined with a tasty mustard and honey dressing, and is perfect as a lunch dish. Serve with crusty bread for a more substantial meal.

1 Place the chickpeas in a bowl and cover with boiling water. Leave to stand for 1 hour. Drain, then place the chickpeas and black beans in the pressure cooker and combine. Add 900ml/1½ pints/3¾ cups hot water.

Electric: Close the lid and bring to High pressure using the Manual, Beans, Pulses or Soup setting. Cook for 25 minutes (30 minutes). Release the pressure using natural release, making sure the 'keep warm' mode is switched off. After 10 minutes, quickly release the remaining pressure, if any.
Stovetop: Close the lid and bring to High pressure. Cook for 25 minutes (30 minutes). Release the pressure slowly. After 10 minutes, quickly release the remaining pressure, if any.

2 While the pressure is releasing slowly, mix the olive oil and mustards together in a small bowl. Whisk in the lemon juice and honey. Stir in the garlic and season with salt and pepper.

3 Carefully remove the lid and add the green beans. Bring to the boil in the open cooker and cook for 3–4 minutes, until tender. Place the lid over to reduce the steam, but do not close. Use the Manual, Sauté or Soup setting for the electric pressure cooker.

4 Drain the beans and chickpeas in a sieve or strainer. Rinse under cold water and drain again. Transfer to a large bowl. Add the dressing and toss together. Leave to stand for 10 minutes, then mix in the onion and tomatoes. Transfer to a serving dish, sprinkle with basil leaves and serve.

Cook's Tip
Some electric pressure cookers do not have a programme that will complete the full cooking time. If this is the case, note the maximum time and reset the cooker for the remaining time as soon as the initial time has finished.

Pressure: High
Time under Pressure: 25 minutes (30 minutes)
Release: Natural/Slow
Serves 4

175g/6oz/1 cup dried chickpeas
175g/6oz/1 cup dried black turtle beans
225g/8oz/1½ cups fine green beans, cut into 4cm/1½in lengths
1 red onion, halved lengthwise and thinly sliced
6 small tomatoes, cut into wedges
a handful of fresh basil leaves

For the dressing
60ml/4 tbsp extra virgin olive oil
15ml/1 tbsp Dijon mustard
5ml/1 tsp wholegrain mustard
30ml/2 tbsp lemon juice
15ml/1 tbsp clear honey
1 garlic clove, crushed
salt and ground black pepper
fresh basil leaves, to garnish

Energy 386kcal/1627kJ; Protein 21.7g; Carbohydrate 48.1g, of which sugars 10.2g; Fat 13.3g, of which saturates 1.9g; Cholesterol 0mg; Calcium 125mg; Fibre 21.2g; Sodium 242mg.

Lentil Salad with Serrano Ham

A quick and easy lentil salad is possible using your pressure cooker. The lentils will not collapse when cooked, and will be ready in around 10 minutes. Combined with ingredients such as peppers, tomatoes, Serrano ham and blue cheese, this dish is difficult to resist.

Pressure: High
**Time under Pressure: 9 minutes
(11 minutes)**
Release: Natural/Slow
Serves 4

225g/8oz/1 cup Puy lentils
750ml/1¼ pints/3 cups hot
 vegetable stock
45ml/3 tbsp olive oil
30ml/2 tbsp balsamic vinegar
1 yellow (bell) pepper
10 cherry tomatoes
50g/2oz walnuts, chopped
1 small red onion, halved and
 thinly sliced
15ml/1 tbsp lemon juice
6 slices Serrano ham, torn into pieces
50g/2oz blue cheese, such as
 Roquefort or Dolcelatte, crumbled
salt and ground black pepper
a few mixed salad leaves or rocket
 (arugula) and crusty bread,
 to serve (optional)

1 Place the Puy lentils in a sieve or strainer and rinse under cold running water, and drain. Place the lentils in the open pressure cooker and add the stock.

Electric: Close the lid and bring to High pressure using the Manual or Soup setting. Cook for 9 minutes (11 minutes). Release the pressure using natural release, making sure the 'keep warm' mode is switched off.
Stovetop: Close the lid and bring to High pressure. Cook for 9 minutes (11 minutes). Release the pressure slowly.

2 Drain the lentils and place in a bowl. Add the olive oil and balsamic vinegar and mix together. Season to taste with salt and pepper. Leave to stand for 15 minutes.

3 Cut the pepper in half, remove the seeds and slice. Cut the cherry tomatoes into halves or quarters. Mix the pepper, tomatoes and walnuts into the lentils, along with the onion and lemon juice.

4 Place the mixed salad leaves or rocket on a serving platter and top with the lentil mixture. Lightly mix the Serrano ham and blue cheese through the leaves and lentils, and serve with chunks of crusty bread, if you wish.

Energy 436kcal/1823kJ; Protein 24.5g; Carbohydrate 31.4g, of which sugars 4.5g; Fat 24.4g, of which saturates 5.6g; Cholesterol 9mg; Calcium 118mg; Fibre 8.5g; Sodium 589mg.

Pease Pudding

"Pease pudding hot, pease pudding cold, pease pudding in the pot, nine days old..." goes the old rhyme. This dish becomes easy to make with the help of your pressure cooker. Just soak for an hour in boiling water, then cook in the pressure cooker in under 10 minutes.

Pressure: High

Time under Pressure: 12 minutes (16 minutes)

Release: Natural/Slow

Serves 4

300g/10oz/scant 1¾ cups dried yellow split peas

40g/1½ oz/3 tbsp butter, cut into pieces

1 egg, lightly beaten

salt and ground black pepper

Cook's Tips

• The pease pudding can be placed in a buttered ovenproof dish and cooked in a preheated oven at 180°C/350°F/Gas 4 for about 30 minutes, until the pudding is set.

• A small handful of chopped fresh mint can be added to the purée in step 2.

1 Cover the split peas with boiling water and leave for 1 hour. Drain, then place in the pressure cooker. Add 900ml/1½ pints/3¾ cups cold water. Bring to the boil in the open pressure cooker and remove any scum, using the Manual, Beans, Pulses or Soup setting for the electric pressure cooker.

Electric: Close the lid and bring to High pressure using the Manual, Beans, Pulses or Soup setting. Cook for 5 minutes (8 minutes). Release the pressure using natural release, making sure the 'keep warm' mode is switched off.

Stovetop: Close the lid and bring to High pressure. Cook for 5 minutes (8 minutes). Release the pressure slowly.

2 Drain and purée the peas in a food processor or blender. Add the butter, egg and seasoning. Mix together and place in a greased pudding bowl. Cover with a pleated sheet of greaseproof paper and a layer of foil and tie securely. Place on a trivet or in the steamer basket in the pressure cooker. Add sufficient water to reach a quarter of the way up the bowl.

Electric: Close the lid and bring to High pressure using the Manual or Soup setting. Cook for 7 minutes (8 minutes). Release the pressure using natural release, making sure the 'keep warm' mode is switched off.

Stovetop: Close the lid and bring to High pressure. Cook for 7 minutes (8 minutes). Release the pressure slowly.

3 Carefully remove the cover, turn out the pease pudding and serve.

Energy 343kcal/1447kJ; Protein 18.5g; Carbohydrate 43.7g, of which sugars 1.5g; Fat 11.7g, of which saturates 6g; Cholesterol 79mg; Calcium 35mg; Fibre 6.3g; Sodium 110mg.

VEGETABLES

The pressure cooker is perfect for cooking vegetables as both accompaniments and main-course dishes. It cooks them extremely quickly, which helps to preserve their vitamins and minerals, and you can either cook individual vegetables on a rack or trivet, or a selection of vegetables in the steamer basket. The recipes in this section include potato Dauphinois, which will cook in less than half the time of oven-baking, and tasty accompaniments such as braised leeks and carrots, spicy red cabbage with apples and onions, and a classic ratatouille. For a substantial main course, try the vegetable korma, pumpkin and mushroom stew, or the vegetable Kashmiri.

Beetroot with Lemon Dressing

Often grown in large kitchen gardens or on allotments, beetroot regularly features on menus in summer. Use your pressure cooker to speed up the cooking process, which otherwise can be quite lengthy. Serve as a first course or side dish.

1 Twist the tops off the beetroot and trim the root. Do not break the skin. Place the steamer basket or trivet in the pressure cooker and add the beetroot. Add 600ml/1 pint/2½ cups water.

Electric: Close the lid and bring to High pressure using the Manual, Soup or Beans setting. Cook for 23 minutes (25 minutes). Release the pressure quickly, making sure the 'keep warm' mode is switched off.
Stovetop: Close the lid and bring to High pressure. Cook for 23 minutes (25 minutes). Release the pressure quickly.

2 Uncover and check to make sure the beetroot is cooked and tender. Pinch the skin between two fingers; when cooked, the skin will come away easily. Drain the beetroot and allow to cool.

3 Peel when cold, and cut into wedges. Add the lemon rind and juice, and the oil and season to taste. Mix gently in the dressing. Sprinkle with chopped fresh chives, if you wish.

Cook's Tip
Beetroots will vary slightly in cooking time, so if they are not quite cooked, return to pressure for 2–3 minutes more.

Pressure: High
Time under Pressure: 23 minutes (25 minutes)
Release: Quick
Serves 4

4 medium, approximately 450g/1lb, evenly sized raw beetroot (beets)
grated rind and juice of ½ lemon
about 150ml/¼ pint/⅔ cup extra virgin olive oil (or a mixture of olive oil and sunflower oil, blended to taste)
salt and ground black pepper
chopped fresh chives, to garnish (optional)

Energy 265kcal/1097kJ; Protein 1.9g; Carbohydrate 8.6g, of which sugars 7.9g; Fat 25.1g, of which saturates 3.6g; Cholesterol 0mg; Calcium 23mg; Fibre 2.9g; Sodium 74mg.

Red Cabbage with Apples and Onions

In the recipe, red cabbage is lightly spiced with nutmeg, cloves and cinnamon, with a tangy sweet flavour from the apples. If you wish, you can heat the cabbage in the open cooker for 5 minutes to reduce the liquid slightly, instead of leaving it to stand for 5 minutes.

Pressure: High

Time under Pressure: 5 minutes (7 minutes)

Release: Quick

Serves 6–8

900g/2lb red cabbage

2 cooking apples

2 onions, chopped

5ml/1 tsp grated nutmeg

1.5ml/¼ tsp ground cloves

1/5ml/¼ tsp ground cinnamon

15ml/1 tbsp soft dark brown sugar

100ml/3½fl oz/scant ½ cup vegetable stock

45ml/3 tbsp red wine vinegar

25g/1oz/2 tbsp butter, diced

salt and ground black pepper

chopped flat leaf parsley, to garnish

1 Using a large, sharp knife, cut away and discard the large, white ribs from the outer cabbage leaves. Finely shred the cabbage. Peel, core and coarsely grate the apples.

2 Layer the shredded cabbage in the pressure cooker with the onions, apples, spices and sugar. Pour over the stock and vinegar. Dot the butter over the top.

Electric: Close the lid and bring to High pressure using the Manual or Soup setting. Cook for 5 minutes (7 minutes). Release the pressure quickly, making sure the 'keep warm' mode is switched off.
Stovetop: Close the lid and bring to High pressure. Cook for 5 minutes (7 minutes). Release the pressure quickly.

3 Remove the lid and stir well. Season with salt and pepper, then leave to stand for 5 minutes. Serve garnished with the flat leaf parsley.

Energy 77kcal/321kJ; Protein 1.8g; Carbohydrate 11.3g, of which sugars 10g; Fat 3g, of which saturates 1.6g; Cholesterol 7mg; Calcium 79mg; Fibre 5g; Sodium 30mg.

Braised Leeks and Carrots

Leeks and carrots go together beautifully in this recipe, and they are good finished with a little chopped mint, chervil or parsley. This dish is an excellent accompaniment to roast pork, beef or chicken. Root vegetables cook well in the pressure cooker.

1 Heat 40g/1½oz/3 tbsp butter in the pressure cooker, add the carrots and cook, stirring for 2–3 minutes, until glossy and starting to brown. Add the leeks and cook for 1 minute. Use the Sauté or Soup setting for the electric pressure cooker.

2 Add the wine, 90ml/6 tbsp water, the bay leaves and half the chopped herbs and mix together.

Electric: Close the lid and bring to High pressure using the Manual or Soup setting. Cook for 4 minutes (5 minutes). Release the pressure quickly, making sure the 'keep warm' mode is switched off.
Stovetop: Close the lid and bring to High pressure. Cook for 4 minutes (5 minutes). Release the pressure quickly.

3 Uncover and transfer the vegetables to a warmed serving dish. Bring the juice back to the boil, and boil to reduce the liquid. Use the Sauté or Soup setting for the electric pressure cooker.

4 Stir in the remaining butter. Season with salt and pepper. Pour over the vegetables and sprinkle with the remaining herbs.

Pressure: High
Time under Pressure: 4 minutes (5 minutes)
Release: Quick
Serves 4–6

50g/2oz/4 tbsp butter
450g/1lb carrots, thickly sliced
450g/1lb leeks, cut into 4cm/1½in lengths
90ml/6 tbsp dry white wine
2 fresh bay leaves
30ml/2 tbsp chopped fresh mint, chervil or parsley
a pinch of sugar
salt and ground black pepper

Energy 115kcal/475kJ; Protein 1.7g; Carbohydrate 8.2g, of which sugars 7.3g; Fat 7.5g, of which saturates 4.5g; Cholesterol 18mg; Calcium 40mg; Fibre 4.6g; Sodium 71mg.

Sweet Potatoes with Orange and Coriander

These orange, creamy-textured sweet potatoes prepared in the pressure cooker make a lovely alternative to ordinary potatoes. Here, they are served with a buttery orange dressing, flavoured with fresh coriander. They are perfect for serving with roast meats.

Pressure: High
Time under Pressure: 6 minutes
 (8 minutes)
Release: Quick
Serves 4

750g/1½lb sweet potatoes
280ml/½ pint/1 cup orange juice
15ml/1 tbsp butter
15ml/1 tbsp light muscovado
 (brown) sugar
15ml/1 tbsp chopped fresh coriander
 (cilantro)
salt and ground black pepper

Energy 231kcal/982kJ; Protein 2.7g;
Carbohydrate 50.1g, of which sugars 20.8g; Fat
3.7g, of which saturates 2.2g; Cholesterol 8mg;
Calcium 54mg; Fibre 6.1g; Sodium 105mg.

1 Peel the sweet potatoes and cut into 1–2cm/½–¾in thick slices or small chunks of a similar size. Place in the pressure cooker. Add the orange juice.

Electric: Close the lid and bring to High pressure using the Manual, Soup or Fish setting. Cook for 6 minutes (8 minutes). Release the pressure quickly, making sure the 'keep warm' mode is switched off.
Stovetop: Close the lid and bring to High pressure. Cook for 6 minutes (8 minutes). Release the pressure quickly.

2 Uncover and transfer the sweet potatoes to a warmed serving dish. Add the butter and sugar to the pan juices and heat, stirring to melt the butter and dissolve the sugar. Boil for 4–5 minutes, until thickened and syrupy and to reduce the liquid. Use the Sauté or Soup setting for the electric pressure cooker.

3 Return the sweet potatoes to the sauce and toss to coat. Season with salt and pepper. Transfer to the warmed serving dish and sprinkle with fresh coriander.

Potato Dauphinois

This is a delightfully tasteful dish containing layers of potatoes cooked in a garlicky cream. It can be made in less than half the usual time using a pressure cooker, and is finished off under the grill. Serve as an accompaniment to roast meat dishes and casseroles.

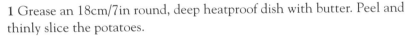

1 Grease an 18cm/7in round, deep heatproof dish with butter. Peel and thinly slice the potatoes.

2 Mix together the cream, garlic, nutmeg, salt and pepper. Place a third of the potatoes in the dish, then top with a third of the cream mixture. Repeat twice more.

3 Sprinkle over the grated cheese. Cover the dish with baking parchment and secure with string.

4 Place the trivet or rack in the base of the pressure cooker. Add 450ml/ ¾ pint/scant 2 cups water to the base of the pressure cooker and add the lemon juice. Place the dish on the trivet or rack.

Electric: Close the lid and bring to High pressure using the Manual or Soup setting. Cook for 20 minutes (25 minutes). Release the pressure using natural release, making sure the 'keep warm' mode is switched off. After 5 minutes, quickly release the remaining pressure, if any.
Stovetop: Close the lid and bring to High pressure. Cook for 20 minutes (25 minutes). Release the pressure slowly. After 5 minutes, quickly release the remaining pressure, if any.

5 Carefully take the dish out of the cooker. Remove the paper and brown the potatoes under the grill. Garnish with parsley sprigs and serve immediately.

Pressure: High
Time under Pressure: 20 minutes (25 minutes)
Release: Natural/Slow

Serves 4

15g/½oz/1 tbsp butter
450g/1lb potatoes
150ml/¼ pint/⅔ cup double (heavy) cream
1 garlic clove, crushed
2.5ml/½ tsp grated nutmeg
50g/2oz Gruyère or Emmenthal cheese, grated
5ml/1 tsp lemon juice
salt and ground black pepper
fresh parsley sprigs, to garnish

Cook's Tip

If your pressure cooker has a basket instead of a trivet, make sure the dish will fit in the basket first. If it doesn't, stand it on an upturned saucer.

Energy 344kcal/1427kJ; Protein 5.9g; Carbohydrate 18.8g, of which sugars 2.1g; Fat 27.7g, of which saturates 17.2g; Cholesterol 109mg; Calcium 145mg; Fibre 1.5g; Sodium 127mg.

Ratatouille

This is a highly versatile vegetable stew from France. Ratatouille is delicious served hot or cold, on its own or with eggs, pasta, fish or meat, particularly roast lamb. Release the pressure quickly to avoid overcooking the vegetables.

1 To skin the tomatoes, plunge them into a bowl of boiling water for about 30 seconds. Remove with a slotted spoon, then refresh in cold water. Peel away the skins and roughly chop the flesh.

2 Mix the oils together and heat 30ml/2 tbsp in the open pressure cooker. Add the onions and fry for 4–5 minutes. Use the Sauté or Soup setting for the electric pressure cooker. Add the peppers and cook for 2 minutes. Remove with a slotted spoon and set aside.

3 Add 15ml/1 tbsp oil and cook the aubergine for 2 minutes. Add the remaining oil and courgettes and cook for 2 minutes. Add the tomatoes and reserved vegetables.

4 Add 50ml/2fl oz/¼ cup water and the garlic, bay leaves, thyme and red wine vinegar.

Electric: Close the lid and bring to High pressure using the Manual, Soup or Vegetable setting. Cook for 3 minutes (4 minutes). Release the pressure quickly, making sure the 'keep warm' mode is switched off.
Stovetop: Close the lid and bring to High pressure. Cook for 3 minutes (4 minutes). Release the pressure quickly.

5 Season to taste with salt and pepper and serve warm or at room temperature, garnished with fresh thyme sprigs.

Pressure: High
Time under Pressure: 3 minutes (4 minutes)
Release: Quick
Serves 4–6

675g/1½lb/6 ripe, well-flavoured tomatoes
60ml/2 tbsp sunflower oil
60ml/2 tbsp olive oil
2 onions, thinly sliced
2 red (bell) peppers, cut into chunks
1 yellow or orange (bell) pepper, cut into chunks
1 aubergine (eggplant), cut into chunks
2 courgettes (zucchini), cut into thick slices
4 garlic cloves, crushed
2 bay leaves
15ml/1 tbsp chopped fresh thyme, plus extra sprigs to garnish
15ml/1 tbsp red wine vinegar
salt and ground black pepper

Cook's Tips
• If the sauce is quite thin, add 30–45ml/2–3 tbsp tomato purée (paste) and a pinch of sugar to the mixture at the end of cooking.
• Aubergines do not need to be salted to draw out the bitter juices, however the salting process helps prevent them from soaking up too much oil during frying. So, if you have time, sprinkle aubergine chunks with salt and leave in a colander over a bowl for 30 minutes, to drain. Rinse and pat dry with kitchen paper before frying.

Energy 149kcal/621kJ; Protein 3.8g; Carbohydrate 15.2g, of which sugars 13.6g; Fat 8.6g, of which saturates 1.2g; Cholesterol 0mg; Calcium 47mg; Fibre 6.3g; Sodium 17mg.

Butternut and Sage Purée

The butternut squash in this simple recipe is flavoured with sage and honey, and the pressure cooker greatly reduces its cooking time. This creamy side dish goes well served alongside a main meal of pork or chicken.

Pressure: High

Time under Pressure: 9 minutes (11 minutes)

Release: Quick

Serves 4

1.2kg/2½lb butternut squash
40g/1½oz/3 tbsp butter
250ml/8fl oz/1 cup vegetable stock or water
15ml/1 tbsp chopped fresh sage
15ml/1 tbsp clear honey
salt and ground black pepper
chopped parsley, to garnish (optional)

Energy 193kcal/817kJ; Protein 3.4g; Carbohydrate 27.8g, of which sugars 16.4g; Fat 8.5g, of which saturates 5.2g; Cholesterol 21mg; Calcium 146mg; Fibre 6.4g; Sodium 73mg.

1 Peel the butternut squash and cut it in half. Remove the seeds and cut the flesh into 4cm/1½in dice.

2 Melt the butter in the pressure cooker, add the squash and sauté for 3–4 minutes, until glossy. Use the Sauté or Soup setting for the electric pressure cooker.

3 Add the stock or water and chopped sage and mix together.

Electric: Close the lid and bring to High pressure using the Manual or Soup setting. Cook for 9 minutes (11 minutes). Release the pressure quickly, making sure the 'keep warm' mode is switched off.
Stovetop: Close the lid and bring to High pressure. Cook for 9 minutes (11 minutes). Release the pressure quickly.

4 Uncover and drain the squash in a colander.

5 Return the butternut squash to the cooker and mash to a rough purée. Add the honey and season to taste. Transfer to a warmed serving dish and serve immediately, sprinkled with black pepper and parsley, if you wish.

Pumpkin and Mushroom Stew

This tasty pressure cooker stew can just as easily be made with butternut squash if pumpkin is not available. It is delicious served hot with crusty bread and a green salad, or with jacket potatoes and mangetouts or broccoli.

1 Place the porcini mushrooms in a small bowl and cover with 300ml/½ pint/1¼ cups boiling water. Leave to soak for 15 minutes. Drain and reserve the water. Chop any large pieces of porcini.

2 Peel the onion and cut in half. Slice lengthways. Heat the oil in the open pressure cooker. Add the onion and fry for 4–5 minutes. Use the Sauté or Soup setting for the electric pressure cooker. Add the pumpkin and cook, stirring, for 3–4 minutes.

3 Add the porcini and chestnut mushrooms and sauté for 2 minutes. Add the garlic and sauté for 1 minute. Add 150ml/¼ pint/⅔ cup of the reserved porcini soaking liquor, vegetable stock, chopped sage and green beans and mix together.

Electric: Close the lid and bring to High pressure using the Manual, Soup or Vegetable setting. Cook for 5 minutes (6 minutes). Release the pressure quickly, making sure the 'keep warm' mode is switched off.
Stovetop: Close the lid and bring to High pressure. Cook for 5 minutes (6 minutes). Release the pressure quickly.

4 Carefully remove the lid and stir in the mustard and cream. Season to taste with salt and pepper, and serve immediately on warm plates.

Pressure: High
Time under Pressure: 5 minutes
  (6 minutes)
Release: Quick
Serves 4

25g/1oz porcini mushrooms
1 onion
60ml/2 tbsp sunflower oil
300g/11oz pumpkin, cut into
  2.5cm/1in cubes
200g/7oz/scant 2 cups chestnut
  mushrooms
2 garlic cloves, crushed
150ml/¼ pint/⅔ cup vegetable stock
5ml/1 tsp chopped fresh sage
115g/4oz/¾ cup green beans,
  cut in half
15ml/1 tbsp red wine vinegar
30ml/2 tbsp Dijon mustard
45ml/3 tbsp double (heavy) cream
salt and ground black pepper

Energy 152kcal/630kJ; Protein 3.1g; Carbohydrate 6.7g, of which sugars 4.9g; Fat 12.8g, of which saturates 4.6g; Cholesterol 15mg; Calcium 55mg; Fibre 3.3g; Sodium 227mg.

Vegetable Korma

The blending of spices is an ancient art in India. Here, the aim is to produce a subtle aromatic curry rather than an assault on the senses. Cooking it in your pressure cooker means that in less than 15 minutes you can have the finished dish on the table.

Pressure: High

Time under Pressure: 5 minutes (6 minutes)

Release: Quick

Serves 4

50g/2oz/4 tbsp butter

2 onions, sliced

2 garlic cloves, crushed

2.5cm/1in piece fresh root ginger

5ml/1 tsp ground cumin

5ml/1 tsp ground coriander

6 cardamom pods

5cm/2in piece cinnamon stick

5ml/1 tsp ground turmeric

1 fresh red chilli, seeded and chopped

1 potato, peeled and cut into 2.5cm/1in cubes

1 small aubergine (eggplant), chopped

115g/4oz mushrooms, thickly sliced

225ml/7fl oz/scant 1 cup water

115g/4oz green beans, cut into 2.5cm/1in lengths

60ml/4 tbsp natural (plain) yogurt

75ml/5 tbsp double (heavy) cream

5ml/1 tsp garam masala

salt and ground black pepper

fresh coriander (cilantro) sprigs, to garnish

poppadums, to serve

1 Melt the butter in the pressure cooker. Add the onions and cook for 4–5 minutes. Use the Sauté, Manual or Soup for the electric pressure cooker. Add the garlic and ginger and cook for 1 minute.

2 Add the cumin, coriander, cardamom, cinnamon stick, turmeric and chilli, and cook, stirring constantly for 30 seconds.

3 Add the potato, aubergine, mushrooms, water and green beans, and stir to mix.

Electric: Close the lid and bring to High pressure using the Manual or Soup setting. Cook for 5 minutes (6 minutes). Release the pressure quickly, making sure the 'keep warm' mode is switched off.
Stovetop: Close the lid and bring to High pressure. Cook for 5 minutes (6 minutes). Release the pressure quickly.

4 Uncover and transfer the vegetables to a warmed serving dish and keep hot. Boil the sauce to reduce a little. Use the Sauté, Manual or Soup setting for the electric pressure cooker.

5 Add the vegetables and mix together. Stir in the yogurt, cream and garam masala. Return to the warmed dish and garnish with fresh coriander. Serve with poppadums.

Energy 315kcal/1328kJ; Protein 8.3g; Carbohydrate 37.6g, of which sugars 2.9g; Fat 15.8g, of which saturates 8.3g; Cholesterol 5mg; Calcium 38mg; Fibre 0g; Sodium 405mg.

Vegetable Kashmiri

The pressure cooker quickly cooks these delicious vegetables in a spicy and aromatic sauce. They make a lovely vegetarian meal for two, or an accompaniment to a meat curry for four people. Release the pressure quickly to avoid overcooking the vegetables.

Pressure: High

Time under Pressure: 4 minutes
   (5 minutes)

Release: Quick

Serves 4

10ml/2 tsp cumin seeds

8 black peppercorns

2 green cardamom pods, seeds only

5cm/2in piece cinnamon stick

2.5ml/½ tsp grated nutmeg

30ml/2 tbsp sunflower oil

1 onion, finely chopped

2.5cm/1in piece fresh root ginger,
   peeled and grated

1 fresh red chilli, seeded and
   chopped

2.5ml/½ tsp salt

300ml/½ pint/1¼ cups
   vegetable stock

275g/10oz cauliflower florets

2 large potatoes, peeled and
   cut into 2.5cm/1in chunks

150ml/¼ pint/⅔ cup Greek
   (US strained plain) yogurt

toasted flaked (sliced) almonds
   and fresh coriander (cilantro)
   sprigs, to garnish

Energy 198kcal/826kJ; Protein 7.1g;
Carbohydrate 19.1g, of which sugars 6.3g; Fat
11g, of which saturates 3.5g; Cholesterol 27mg;
Calcium 86mg; Fibre 3.2g; Sodium 41mg.

1 Put the cumin seeds, peppercorns, cardamom seeds, cinnamon stick and nutmeg in a mortar or spice grinder, and grind to a fine powder.

2 Heat the oil in the pressure cooker. Add the onion and cook for 3–4 minutes. Add the ginger and chilli and fry for 2 minutes. Use the Sauté, Manual or Soup setting for the electric pressure cooker.

3 Add the ground spice mix and salt and cook for 1 minute, stirring constantly to prevent the spices from sticking to the base of the cooker.

4 Add the stock and mix thoroughly, making sure all the sediment is off the base of the cooker. Add the cauliflower and potatoes.

Electric: Close the lid and bring to High pressure using the Manual, Soup or Vegetable setting. Cook for 4 minutes (5 minutes). For crunchier vegetables, reduce by 1 minute. Release the pressure quickly, making sure the 'keep warm' mode is switched off.

Stovetop: Close the lid and bring to High pressure. Cook for 4 minutes (5 minutes). For crunchier vegetables, reduce by 1 minute. Release the pressure quickly.

5 In a bowl, stir 30ml/2 tbsp of the sauce into the yogurt, then pour over the vegetable mix and stir thoroughly to combine. Transfer the vegetables to a warmed serving dish. Sprinkle with toasted almonds and fresh sprigs of coriander, to garnish.

PUDDINGS AND DESSERTS

What could be more delightful and comforting than a steamed sponge pudding, a jam roly poly with custard, or a rich Christmas pudding? By using your pressure cooker, you can reduce the long steaming time associated with these types of puddings. Milk-based desserts also work well in the pressure cooker. Try dishes such as mocha-flavoured petits pots, crème caramel and crème brûlée, or traditional milk puddings such as semolina pudding and vanilla rice pudding. Dried fruits can be cooked without soaking overnight, and make delicious compotes or fruit fools, and fresh fruits such as pears can easily be poached in red wine. With steamed sponge and suet puddings, you need to pre-steam before cooking under pressure to give time for the raising agents to start working, so make sure you follow the instructions for each recipe. Steaming methods vary from manufacturer to manufacturer, so check your handbook to see which method they recommend before you begin.

Poached Pears in Red Wine

The pears take on a red blush from the wine and make a very pretty dish. This is a great dessert for making in advance, as the pears only improve by soaking in the wine syrup. The cooking time in the pressure cooker will vary according to size and ripeness.

1 Pour the red wine into the pressure cooker. Add the sugar, honey, cinnamon stick, vanilla pod, lemon or orange rind, cloves and peppercorns. Bring to the boil in the open pressure cooker. Use the Sauté or Soup setting for the electric pressure cooker.

2 Turn off the heat and leave to stand for 15 minutes. Meanwhile, peel the pears using a vegetable peeler, leaving the stems intact. Take a thin slice off the base of each pear so that it will stand square and upright. As each pear is peeled, toss it in lemon juice to prevent the flesh from browning. Place the pears upright in the spiced wine, making sure they do not touch the sides of the cooker. Spoon over the wine.

Electric: Close the lid and bring to High pressure using the Manual or Soup setting. Cook for 6 minutes (8 minutes). Release the pressure quickly, making sure the 'keep warm' mode is switched off.
Stovetop: Close the lid and bring to High pressure. Cook for 6 minutes (8 minutes). Release the pressure quickly.

3 The cooking time will vary according to the size and ripeness of the pears. Pierce with a cocktail stick or toothpick. If not tender, return to High pressure for another minute or so.

4 Transfer the pears to a serving dish, using a slotted spoon. Heat the syrup for about 10 minutes in the open cooker, to reduce and thicken a little, using the Manual or Soup setting for the electric pressure cooker. Leave to cool. Strain the cooled liquid over the pears and chill for at least 3 hours. Place the pears in serving dishes and spoon a little of the wine syrup over the top. Garnish with fresh mint and serve with whipped or sour cream.

Pressure: High
Time under Pressure: 6 minutes (8 minutes)
Release: Quick
Serves 4

1 bottle fruity red wine
150g/5oz/¾ cup caster (superfine) sugar
45ml/3 tbsp clear honey
1 cinnamon stick
1 vanilla pod (bean) split lengthways
large strip of lemon or orange rind
2 whole cloves
2 black peppercorns
4 firm ripe pears
juice of ½ lemon
mint leaves, to garnish
whipped cream or sour cream, to serve

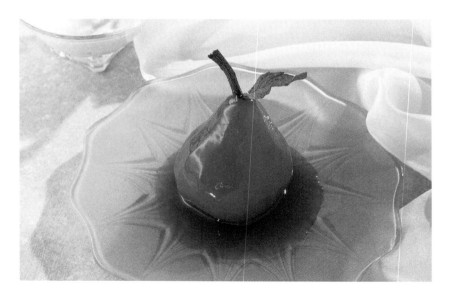

Energy 359kcal/1518kJ; Protein 0.9g; Carbohydrate 63.1g, of which sugars 63.1g; Fat 0.2g, of which saturates 0g; Cholesterol 0mg; Calcium 40mg; Fibre 4.4g; Sodium 20mg.

Apricot Fool

This is a quick and easy dessert that can be made in advance, if you wish. The apricots are easily tenderized by cooking in the pressure cooker. The dish can be served topped with whipped cream and Amaretti or shortbread as an accompaniment.

Pressure: High

Time under Pressure: 12 minutes (15 minutes)

Release: Natural/Slow

Serves 4

225g/8oz/1 cup dried apricots

50g/2oz/4 tbsp caster (superfine) sugar

juice of 1 lemon

150ml/¼ pint/⅔ cup double (heavy) cream

whipped cream, to decorate (optional)

Amaretti or shortbread, to serve (optional)

Energy 341kcal/1427kJ; Protein 3.4g; Carbohydrate 38.1g, of which sugars 38.1g; Fat 20.5g, of which saturates 12.5g; Cholesterol 51mg; Calcium 74mg; Fibre 5.8g; Sodium 41mg.

1 Place the apricots in a bowl and cover with boiling water. Leave to soak for 30 minutes, then drain.

2 Place the apricots and sugar in the pressure cooker with the lemon juice and 280ml/½ pint/generous 1 cup water.

Electric: Close the lid and bring to High pressure using the Manual, Soup or Dessert setting. Cook for 12 minutes (15 minutes). Release the pressure using natural release, making sure the 'keep warm' mode is switched off.
Stovetop: Close the lid and bring to High pressure. Cook for 12 minutes (15 minutes). Release the pressure slowly.

3 Leave to cool for 20 minutes.

4 Transfer the apricots and syrup to a food processor or blender and process to a purée. When the purée is cold, whip the cream until it just starts to thicken. Gently swirl through the apricot purée.

5 Spoon into four serving dishes or glasses and chill for 30 minutes. Serve topped with a dollop of cream, if you wish. Crispy Amaretti or shortbread are also good to serve with this dessert.

Dried Fruit Compote

After a few minutes' soaking, dried fruits can be cooked in the pressure cooker instead of the traditional method of soaking overnight. This makes for a speedy dessert, which is delicious served with a dollop of yogurt. Use dried fruits rather than ready-to-eat varieties.

1 Place the dried fruits in a bowl, cover with boiling water and leave to soak for 10 minutes. Drain off the soaking liquid into a measuring jug. Make the liquid up to 350ml/12fl oz/1½ cups.

2 Place the fruits and liquid in the pressure cooker. Add the lemon rind or juice and the cinnamon stick.

Electric: Close the lid and bring to High pressure using the Manual, Soup or Vegetable setting. Cook for 5 minutes (8 minutes). Release the pressure using natural release, making sure the 'keep warm' mode is switched off.

Stovetop: Close the lid and bring to High pressure. Cook for 5 minutes (8 minutes). Release the pressure slowly.

3 Transfer the fruit to a bowl using a slotted spoon.

4 Return the syrup to the boil and cook for a few minutes to reduce slightly, then pour over the fruit. Use the Sauté or Soup setting for the electric pressure cooker. Serve warm or cold, with yogurt.

Pressure: High
Time under Pressure: 5 minutes (8 minutes)
Release: Natural/Slow
Serves 8

450g/1lb/2½ cups mixed dried fruits, such as apricots, apples, prunes, figs, pears and large raisins
475ml/16fl oz/2 cups water
thinly pared rind of 1 small lemon or 20ml/2 tbsp lemon juice
1 cinnamon stick
low-fat natural (plain) yogurt, to serve

Energy 106kcal/451kJ; Protein 2.7g; Carbohydrate 24.4g, of which sugars 24.4g; Fat 0.4g, of which saturates 0g; Cholesterol 0mg; Calcium 52mg; Fibre 5.8g; Sodium 32mg.

Semolina Pudding

Made from durum wheat, semolina is milled to produce a small grain which is then cooked with milk to make a satisfying pudding. Some milk-based puddings tend to catch on the base of an electric pressure cooker, so use semi-skimmed (low-fat) milk to minimize this.

Pressure: High

Time under Pressure: 7 minutes (8 minutes)

Release: Natural/Slow

Serves 4

15g/½oz/1 tbsp butter
570ml/1pint/2½ cups milk
40g/1½oz/¼ cup semolina
a few drops of vanilla extract
25g/1oz/2 tbsp caster (superfine) sugar
ground cinnamon, to dust
pistachio nuts or fresh berries, to serve

Cook's Tip

If you would like a slightly thicker pudding, at the end of cooking and before stirring in the sugar, bring to the boil in the open cooker and cook for 2–3 minutes, stirring continuously. Use the Manual, Sauté or Soup setting for the electric pressure cooker.

1 Melt the butter in the pressure cooker to grease it. Add the milk and bring to the boil in the open cooker. Use the Sauté or Soup setting for the electric pressure cooker.

2 Add the semolina and vanilla, and stir into the milk.

Electric: Close the lid and bring to High pressure using the Manual, Soup or Rice setting. Cook for 7 minutes (8 minutes). Release the pressure using natural release, making sure the 'keep warm' mode is switched off.
Stovetop: Close the lid and cook for 7 minutes (8 minutes) on the lowest heat that will still maintain pressure, to prevent the pudding from catching on the base of the cooker. Release the pressure slowly.

3 Open the cooker and stir in the sugar. Leave to cool and thicken. Serve warm or cold. To serve, divide between four serving bowls, dust the top with ground cinnamon, and top with pistachio nuts or mixed berries.

Energy 178kcal/750kJ; Protein 5.9g;
Carbohydrate 27.8g, of which sugars 20.1g; Fat 5.6g, of which saturates 3.5g; Cholesterol 18mg; Calcium 163mg; Fibre 0.3g; Sodium 96mg.

Stuffed Baked Apples

These tasty baked apples are filled with cranberries, sultanas and pecan nuts. You can vary the filling to suit your wishes. Make sure you cut around the middle of the apples before cooking in your pressure cooker, to prevent the pressure from building up under the skin.

1 Wipe the apples and remove the cores, using an apple corer. Make a shallow cut around the middle of each apple.

2 Mix together the pecans, sultanas, cranberries, sugar and cinnamon or mixed spice, and use to fill the apple cavities. Dot the butter over the top of the filling.

3 Place each apple on a square of foil and wrap. Place the steamer basket or upturned steam rack in the pressure cooker. Add 275ml/½ pint/1¼ cups water. Place the apples in the basket or on the rack.

Electric: Close the lid and bring to High pressure using the Manual or Soup setting. Cook for 12 minutes (13 minutes). Release the pressure quickly, making sure the 'keep warm' mode is switched off.
Stovetop: Close the lid and bring to High pressure. Cook for 12 minutes (13 minutes). Release the pressure quickly.

4 Leave the apples to stand for 5 minutes. Meanwhile, chop the stem ginger and fold into the crème fraîche. Serve the apples with the ginger cream.

Cook's Tip
Every apple will vary on cooking time. The type and age of each apple causes variations. Check them with a skewer, and if they are still firm, return to the pressure cooker for an additional 1–2 minutes. If they are slightly larger than suggested, allow a little more time.

Pressure: High
Time under Pressure: 12 minutes (13 minutes)
Release: Quick
Serves 4

4 firm cooking apples, about 175g/6oz each
25g/1oz/¼ cup pecans, chopped
25g/1oz/¼ cup sultanas (golden raisins)
25g/1oz/¼ cup dried cranberries
25g/1oz/2 tbsp brown sugar
2.5ml/½ tsp ground cinnamon or mixed spice
15ml/1 tbsp butter
3 pieces preserved stem ginger
150ml/¼ pint/⅔ cup crème fraîche

Energy 292kcal/1215kJ; Protein 2g; Carbohydrate 21.7g, of which sugars 21.5g; Fat 22.6g, of which saturates 12.5g; Cholesterol 50mg; Calcium 38mg; Fibre 1.8g; Sodium 35mg.

Vanilla and Nutmeg Rice Pudding

A quick and easy-to-make milk dish, this rice pudding is flavoured with vanilla and nutmeg. You can make it with coconut milk, or flavour with rose water to ring the changes. If using a stovetop cooker, cook on the lowest heat possible that will still maintain pressure.

1 Melt the butter in the open pressure cooker. Add the milk and bring to the boil. Use the Manual, Dessert or Soup setting.

2 Stir in the rice and bring to a simmer, while stirring. Make sure the mixture is just simmering.

Electric: Close the lid and bring to High pressure using the Manual, Soup or Desserts setting. Cook for 12 minutes (15 minutes). Release the pressure using natural release, making sure the 'keep warm' mode is switched off. **Stovetop**: Close the lid and bring to High pressure. Cook for 12 minutes (15 minutes). Release the pressure slowly.

3 Stir in the sugar and vanilla, and transfer to individual serving dishes. Leave to stand for 15 minutes. Decorate with kiwi slices and sprinkle with nutmeg, if you wish, before serving. If you like, you can brown the top under the grill first.

Energy 199kcal/836kJ; Protein 6.1g; Carbohydrate 32.3g, of which sugars 17.3g; Fat 5.4g, of which saturates 3.5g; Cholesterol 18mg; Calcium 161mg; Fibre 0g; Sodium 93mg.

Pressure: High
Time under Pressure: 12 minutes
 (15 minutes)
Release: Natural/Slow
Serves 4

15g/½oz/1 tbsp butter
560ml/1 pint/2½ cups milk
75g/3oz/scant ½ cup short grain
 pudding rice
40g/1½oz/3 tbsp caster
 (superfine) sugar
a few drops of vanilla extract
kiwi slices and freshly grated
 nutmeg, to serve (optional)

Cook's Tips

• Milk can foam and bubble in a pressure cooker, so make sure you release the pressure slowly to avoid blocking the pressure valve.
• Some electric cookers are more fierce than others. If you find that foods tend to catch in your model, either use semi-skimmed (low-fat) milk or reduce the cooking time by a minute or so, and then cook in the open cooker for a couple of minutes, stirring continuously. Likewise, if you want a thicker rice pudding, cook for a couple more minutes in the open cooker, stirring continuously.

Petits Pots de Crème au Mocha

Whether electric or stovetop, your pressure cooker is ideal for making custard-based recipes. Here, the addition of coffee gives the dessert an even richer, more indulgent flavour. Check that your pots will fit into the pressure cooker before you start.

Pressure: High

Time under Pressure: 4 minutes (5 minutes)

Release: Natural/Slow

Serves 4

5ml/1 tsp instant coffee powder

15ml/1 tbsp brown sugar

300ml/½ pint/1¼ cups milk

150ml/¼ pint/⅔ cup double (heavy) cream

115g/4oz plain (semi-sweet) chocolate, broken into pieces

4 egg yolks

whipped cream and candied cake decorations, to decorate (optional)

Cook's Tip

It is important in step 3 to strain the custard mixture, to ensure a completely smooth custard, free from any lumps.

Energy 443kcal/1841kJ; Protein 7.4g;
Carbohydrate 26.5g, of which sugars 26.2g;
Fat 34.9g, of which saturates 19.8g; Cholesterol
260mg; Calcium 135mg; Fibre 1g; Sodium 57mg.

1 Put the instant coffee and sugar in a pan and stir in the milk and cream. Bring to the boil over a medium heat, stirring constantly, until the coffee and sugar have dissolved completely.

2 Remove the pan from the heat and add the chocolate pieces. Stir until the chocolate has melted.

3 In a bowl, whisk the egg yolks, then slowly whisk in the chocolate mixture until well blended. Strain the custard mixture into a large jug or pitcher and divide equally among the pots de crème or ramekins, first checking that they will fit in the pressure cooker.

4 Cover each pot de crème or ramekin with a piece of foil and seal. Place the trivet, steam rack or basket without leg extension in the pressure cooker. Add 300ml/½ pint/1¼ cups water. Place the dishes in the pressure cooker, making sure they do not touch the sides.

Electric: Close the lid and bring to High pressure using the Manual, Poultry or Fish setting. Cook for 4 minutes (5 minutes). Release the pressure using natural release, making sure the 'keep warm' mode is switched off. **Stovetop:** Close the lid and bring to High pressure. Cook for 4 minutes (5 minutes). Release the pressure slowly.

5 Carefully remove the pots from the cooker and leave to cool. Chill until ready to serve, then decorate with whipped cream and candied cake decorations, if you wish.

Crème Caramel

This classic baked egg custard with caramel sauce can be made in individual ramekin or soufflé dishes quite easily in the pressure cooker. It saves both time and power compared to traditional oven baking. Chill the desserts until ready to serve.

Pressure: High
Time under Pressure: 4 minutes (5 minutes)
Release: Natural/Slow
Serves 4

For the caramel
60ml/4 tbsp granulated (white) sugar
60ml/4 tbsp water

For the custard
280ml/½ pint/1¼ cups milk
vanilla pod (bean) or a few drops
    of vanilla extract
2 eggs
25g/1oz/2 tbsp caster (superfine)
    sugar
1 tsp lemon juice

Cook's Tip
If the custards will not sit in one layer, either cook them in two batches or place one dish on top of the others, provided the dishes are stable. If you are not sure, cook in two batches.

1 Warm four ramekin or soufflé dishes. Place the sugar and water for the caramel in a heavy pan and heat gently until the sugar has dissolved. Bring to the boil and cook without stirring, until the caramel is golden. Quickly divide between the dishes. Using oven gloves, tilt the dishes to coat evenly.

2 To make the custard, heat the milk in a small pan with the vanilla pod, if using. In a bowl, lightly whisk the eggs and sugar together. Remove the vanilla pod and scrape the seeds into the hot milk and whisk into the eggs, or add vanilla extract, if using.

3 Strain the custard into the dishes. Place 300ml/½ pint/1¼ cups water in the base of the pressure cooker and add the lemon juice. Add the trivet or steamer basket and place the ramekins on top, or inside. Lay a double thickness of baking parchment on top.

Electric: Close the lid and bring to High pressure using the Manual, Soup or Fish setting. Cook for 4 minutes (5 minutes). Release the pressure using natural release, making sure the 'keep warm' mode is switched off.
Stovetop: Close the lid and bring to High pressure. Cook for 4 minutes (5 minutes). Release the pressure slowly.

4 Carefully remove the dishes from the cooker and leave to cool. Chill until ready to serve. To serve, free the edges by pressing gently on each custard. Place a small serving dish over the top and invert. Remove the dish and serve.

Energy 161kcal/681kJ; Protein 6.2g;
Carbohydrate 25.6g, of which sugars 25.6g;
Fat 4.5g, of which saturates 1.7g; Cholesterol
120mg; Calcium 100mg; Fibre 0g; Sodium 78mg.

Crème Brûlée

There is no need to switch on the oven with this irresistible recipe for crème brûlée. It will cook in just 6 minutes or so in the pressure cooker, rather than an hour in the oven. Keep the custards in the refrigerator until you are ready to complete the brûlée topping.

1 With a small, sharp knife, split the vanilla pod lengthways and scrape the black seeds into a medium pan. Add the cream and bring just to the boil over a medium-high heat. Remove from the heat and cover. Set aside for 15–20 minutes.

2 In a bowl, lightly whisk the egg yolks and 50g/2oz/4 tbsp sugar together. Whisk in the cream and strain into a jug or pitcher. Divide between four ramekins. Cover each ramekin with foil.

3 Place 300ml/½ pint/1¼ cups water in the base of the pressure cooker and add the lemon juice. Add the trivet or steamer basket and place the ramekins on top, or inside.

Electric: Close the lid and bring to High pressure using the Manual or Soup setting. Cook for 6 minutes (7 minutes). Release the pressure using natural release, making sure the 'keep warm' mode is switched off. **Stovetop**: Close the lid and bring to High pressure. Cook for 6 minutes (7 minutes). Release the pressure slowly.

4 Carefully remove the dishes from the cooker. Remove the foil and leave to cool. Chill.

5 Preheat the grill or broiler. Sprinkle the remaining sugar over the surface of each custard and grill or broil for 30–60 seconds until the sugar melts and caramelizes. (Do not allow the sugar to burn, or the custard with curdle). Place in the refrigerator to set the crust, and chill completely before serving.

Pressure: High

Time under Pressure: 6 minutes (7 minutes)

Release: Natural/Slow

Serves 4

1 vanilla pod (bean)

450ml/¾ pint/scant 2 cups double (heavy) cream

4 egg yolks

125g/4oz/scant ¾ cup caster (superfine) sugar

1 tsp lemon juice

Energy 742kcal/3074kJ; Protein 4.9g; Carbohydrate 34.6g, of which sugars 34.6g; Fat 65.9g, of which saturates 39.1g; Cholesterol 356mg; Calcium 88mg; Fibre 0g; Sodium 35mg.

Pumpkin Pie

This spicy, sweet pie is an American favourite, traditionally served at Thanksgiving. It is also made at Halloween to use up the pulp from the hollowed-out pumpkin lantern. Use your pressure cooker to tenderize the pumpkin before finishing it in the oven.

Pressure: High
Time under Pressure: 7 minutes (9 minutes)
Release: Quick
Serves 8

200g/7oz/1¾ cups plain
  (all-purpose) flour
2.5ml/1/2 tsp salt
90g/3½oz/scant ½ cup unsalted
  butter
1 egg yolk

For the filling
900g/2lb piece pumpkin
2 large eggs
75g/3oz/6 tbsp light brown sugar
60ml/4 tbsp golden (light corn) syrup
250ml/8fl oz/1 cup double
  (heavy) cream
15ml/1 tbsp mixed spice
2.5ml/½ tsp salt
icing (confectioners') sugar,
  for dusting (optional)
crème fraîche, to serve

1 Sift the flour and salt into a mixing bowl. Rub in the butter until the mixture resembles fine breadcrumbs, then mix the egg yolk and enough iced water (about 15ml/1 tbsp) to make a dough. Roll the dough into a ball, wrap it in clear film and chill for at least 30 minutes.

2 Make the filling. Peel the pumpkin and remove the seeds. Cut the flesh into 4cm/1½in chunks. Place in the pressure cooker. Add 450ml/¾ pint/scant 2 cups water.

Electric: Close the lid and bring to High pressure using the Manual or Soup setting. Cook for 7 minutes (9 minutes). Release the pressure quickly, making sure the 'keep warm' mode is switched off.
Stovetop: Close the lid and bring to High pressure. Cook for 7 minutes (9 minutes). Release the pressure quickly.

3 Remove the lid and drain the pumpkin. Mash until completely smooth, then leave in a sieve or strainer over a bowl, to drain thoroughly.

4 Roll out the pastry on a lightly floured surface and use to line a 23–25cm/9–10in fluted, loose-bottomed flan tin. Prick the base and line with baking parchment and baking beans. Chill for 15 minutes.

5 Preheat the oven to 200°C/400°F/Gas 6. Bake the flan case for 10 minutes, then remove the paper and beans. Return the flan case to the oven and bake for 5 minutes more.

6 Lower the oven temperature to 190°C/375°F/Gas 5. Tip the pumpkin pulp into a bowl and beat in the eggs, sugar, syrup, cream, mixed spice and salt. Pour the mixture into the pastry case. Bake for 40 minutes or until the filling has set. Dust with icing sugar, if you wish, and serve at room temperature with a dollop of crème fraîche.

Energy 428kcal/1785kJ; Protein 6g; Carbohydrate 38.2g, of which sugars 18.6g; Fat 29g, of which saturates 17.1g; Cholesterol 150mg; Calcium 100mg; Fibre 2.5g; Sodium 119mg.

Banoffee Pie

A classic and irresistible dessert, this dish has layers of delicious crunchy cookie topped with toffee, banana and cream. The pressure cooker makes light work of making the toffee, which is cooked in the condensed milk can.

1 Place the trivet, rack or basket in the base of the pressure cooker. Remove the paper label, if any, from the condensed milk. Place the can on its side in the cooker and add sufficient hot water to cover the can without passing the maximum ⅔ mark on the side of the pressure cooker.

Electric: Close the lid and bring to High pressure using the Manual, Soup, Meat, Beans or Pulses setting. Cook for 30 minutes (50 minutes). You may need to reset the cooker if your programmes will not set for this long. Release the pressure using natural release, making sure the 'keep warm' mode is switched off.

Stovetop: Close the lid and bring to High pressure. Cook for 30 minutes (50 minutes). Release the pressure slowly.

2 Leave to cool in the water until lukewarm.

3 Meanwhile, mix together the biscuits, butter and nuts and press over the base and up the sides of a 23cm/9in fluted tart tin. Chill.

4 Open the can and spread the toffee over the base. Slice the bananas and arrange on top. Whip the cream and spread or pipe over the bananas. Sprinkle with grated chocolate and serve.

Pressure: High
Time under Pressure: 30 minutes (50 minutes)
Release: Natural/Slow
Serves 8

400g/14oz can sweetened condensed milk
200g/7oz digestive biscuits (graham crackers)
115g/4oz/½ cup butter, melted
25g/1oz chopped hazelnuts
3 bananas
300ml/½pint/1¼ cups double (heavy) cream
grated chocolate, to sprinkle

Energy 623kcal/2594kJ; Protein 7.3g; Carbohydrate 52.3g, of which sugars 37.9g; Fat 44.2g, of which saturates 25.6g; Cholesterol 110mg; Calcium 195mg; Fibre 0.7g; Sodium 316mg.

Lemon Mascarpone Cheesecake

Check that your springform tin or pan will fit in your pressure cooker before making this rich lemon cheesecake. It has a ginger biscuit base, topped with crème fraîche and fruits. Vary the fruits according to the seasons, or replace the fresh fruit with a raspberry coulis.

Pressure: High
**Time under Pressure: 25 minutes
(30 minutes)**
Release: Natural/Slow
Serves 6–8

115g/4oz ginger nut biscuits
(gingersnaps)
25g/1oz/¼ cup toasted flaked
(sliced) almonds
50g/2oz/4 tbsp butter, melted
400g/14oz/1¾ cup mascarpone
cheese
75ml/2½fl oz/5 tbsp sour cream
115g/4oz/generous ½ cup caster
(superfine) sugar
2 eggs
1 egg yolk
juice of 2 lemons
grated rind of 1 lemon
100ml/3½fl oz/½ cup crème fraîche
30ml/2 tbsp lemon curd
blueberries or redcurrants,
to decorate

Cook's Tip

If there is a little water condensation on top of the cheesecake when you open the lid, gently dab with kitchen paper to remove.

Variation

For a lighter cheesecake, replace up to half the crème fraîche with ricotta cheese.

1 Lightly grease an 18cm/7in springform cake tin (pan). Line the base with silicone paper. Place the tin on a sheet of foil about 38cm/15in square and wrap the exterior tightly, to prevent water entering the base of the tin.

2 Tie a piece of string tightly around the top of the tin, under the lip, to make a handle, or prepare a long piece of foil, folded to form a strip, which can go under the middle of the pan and up the sides to make a handle.

3 Place the ginger nut biscuits in a food processor and process to a crumb. Add the almonds and briefly process, to chop. Transfer to a bowl, add the melted butter and mix together. Press over the base of the prepared tin.

4 Place the mascarpone cheese, sour cream and sugar in a large bowl and whisk together. Whisk in the eggs, egg yolk and lemon juice. Fold in the lemon rind and pour over the biscuit base.

5 Place a trivet or round cooling rack in the base of the pressure cooker. Add 300ml/½ pint/1¼ cups water. Check that the rack is high enough so that the base of the pan is above the water level. Lower the tin into the pan, using the string or foil handle.

Electric: Close the lid and bring to High pressure using the Manual, Soup or Pulses setting. Cook for 25 minutes (30 minutes). Release the pressure using natural release, making sure the 'keep warm' mode is switched off.
Stovetop: Close the lid and bring to High pressure. Cook for 25 minutes (30 minutes). Release the pressure slowly.

6 Carefully remove the tin from the pressure cooker and leave to cool on a rack, then chill. To serve, remove from the tin and spread the crème fraîche over the top. Drizzle the lemon curd over and marble through the crème fraîche. Decorate with blueberries or redcurrants, then serve.

Energy 392kcal/1634kJ; Protein 9.3g;
Carbohydrate 31.4g, of which sugars 22.5g;
Fat 26.3g, of which saturates 14.9g; Cholesterol
141mg; Calcium 109mg; Fibre 0g; Sodium 291mg.

Mocha Cheesecake

Release the pressure slowly when making this dessert, so that the mocha filling settles before the lid is opened. Here, dark and white chocolate are used, but you can vary these depending on your favourite chocolate. Why not try an orange-flavoured chocolate?

1 Lightly grease an 18cm/7in springform cake tin (pan). Line the base with silicone paper. Place the tin on a sheet of foil about 38cm/15in square and wrap the exterior tightly, to prevent water entering the base of the tin.

2 Tie a piece of string tightly around the top of the tin, under the lip, to make a handle, or prepare a long piece of foil, folded to form a strip, which can go under the middle of the pan and up the sides to make a handle.

3 Place the digestive biscuits in a food processor and process to a crumb. Add the pecan nuts, and pulse, to chop. Transfer to a bowl, add the melted butter and mix together. Press the biscuit mixture evenly on top, over the base of the prepared tin.

4 Place the cream cheese, ricotta cheese, cream and sugar in a large bowl and, using an electric mixer, whisk together. Gradually beat in the eggs, then the melted chocolate and vanilla. Dissolve the coffee in 30ml/2 tbsp hot water and stir into the cheesecake mix. Pour over the biscuit base.

5 Place a trivet or round cooling rack in the base of the pressure cooker. Add 300ml/½ pint/1¼ cups water. Make sure the base of the tin will sit above the water. Lower the tin into the pan, using the string or foil handle.

Electric: Close the lid and bring to High pressure using the Manual, Soup or Pulses setting. Cook for 20 minutes (25 minutes). Release the pressure using natural release, making sure the 'keep warm' mode is switched off.
Stovetop: Close the lid and bring to High pressure. Cook for 20 minutes (25 minutes). Release the pressure slowly.

6 Carefully remove the tin from the pressure cooker and leave to cool on a rack, then chill. To serve, remove from the tin and sprinkle over the grated chocolate and transfer to a serving plate.

Pressure: High
Time under Pressure: 20 minutes (25 minutes)
Release: Natural/Slow
Serves 6–8

115g/4oz digestive biscuits (graham crackers)
25g/1oz/⅓ cup pecan nuts
40g/1½oz/3 tbsp butter, melted
300g/11oz/1⅔ cups cream cheese
100g/3¾oz/scant ½ cup ricotta cheese
90ml/3fl oz/6 tbsp double (heavy) cream
75g/3oz/⅓ cup caster (superfine) sugar
3 eggs
175g/6oz plain (semisweet) chocolate, melted
2.5ml/½ tsp vanilla extract
10ml/2 tsp instant coffee
grated plain (semisweet) and white chocolate, to decorate

Cook's Tip
If there is a little water condensation on top of the cheesecake when you open the lid, gently dab with kitchen paper to remove it.

Energy 547kcal/2271kJ; Protein 7.7g; Carbohydrate 34.2g, of which sugars 26.1g; Fat 43.1g, of which saturates 24.2g; Cholesterol 162mg; Calcium 111mg; Fibre 0.9g; Sodium 277mg.

Syrup Sponge Pudding

Always a winter-time favourite, sponge puddings can be made more speedily in your pressure cooker. Serve with custard, ice cream or cream. There are lots of different flavours you can make using this basic sponge pudding recipe – try some of the variations below.

Pressure: High

Time under Pressure: 25 minutes (35 minutes) + pre-steaming

Release: Natural/Slow

Serves 4

45ml/3 tbsp golden (light corn) syrup

115g/4oz/½ cup butter

115g/4oz/generous ½ cup caster (superfine) sugar

2 eggs, lightly beaten

175g/6oz/1½ cups self-raising (self-rising) flour

a few drops of vanilla extract

30ml/2 tbsp milk

custard, cream or ice cream, to serve (optional)

Variations

Marmalade

Replace the golden syrup with 30ml/2 tbsp marmalade and fold 15ml/1 tbsp marmalade into the sponge mix with the flour.

Coconut and Cherry

Replace the golden syrup with 45ml/3 tbsp cherry jam and replace 25g/1oz flour with 40g/1½oz desiccated (dry unsweetened shredded) coconut.

Chocolate

Omit the syrup. Blend 60ml/4 tbsp cocoa powder with 30ml/2 tbsp hot water, then beat into the mix in step 2, before beating in the eggs. Serve with a chocolate sauce.

1 Grease a 1 litre/1¾ pint/4 cup pudding basin and place the golden syrup in the base. Place a trivet, rack, metal pastry cutter or upturned saucer in the base of the pressure cooker.

2 Cream the butter and sugar together in a bowl, until pale and fluffy. Beat in the eggs, one at a time.

3 Using a metal spoon, fold in the flour. Stir in the vanilla extract and milk. Spoon the mixture into the prepared pudding basin.

4 Cover the basin with a pleated square of greased baking parchment or foil. Tie tightly to secure with string, making a handle for easy removal. Add 900ml/1½ pints/3¾ cups hot water to the pressure cooker.

5 Carefully place the pudding in the pressure cooker. Cover with the lid, but do not seal or bring to pressure; just steam for 20 minutes. See pages 44–5.

Electric: Close the lid and bring to High pressure using the Manual, Soup or Pulses setting. Cook for 25 minutes (35 minutes). Reset the timer, if necessary, to complete the cooking time. Release the pressure using natural release, making sure the 'keep warm' mode is switched off. **Stovetop**: Close the lid and bring to High pressure. Cook for 25 minutes (35 minutes). Release the pressure slowly.

6 Open the cooker and carefully remove the pudding. Remove the baking parchment or foil and place a warmed serving plate over the pudding. Upturn and remove the basin. Serve with custard, cream or ice cream, as you wish.

Energy 554kcal/2324kJ; Protein 8.3g; Carbohydrate 72.6g, of which sugars 40.1g; Fat 27.6g, of which saturates 16.1g; Cholesterol 177mg; Calcium 194mg; Fibre 1.8g; Sodium 409mg.

Upside-down Fruit Sponge

You can vary this pudding by using different fruits. When opening the pressure cooker after cooking, some condensation will have settled on the baking parchment cover. Dab this with kitchen paper to avoid it running on to the sponge when removing the cover.

  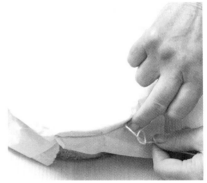

Pressure: High
**Time under Pressure: 25 minutes
(35 minutes) + pre-steaming**
Release: Natural/Slow
Serves 4
For the topping
40g/1½oz/3 tbsp butter
40g/1½oz/3 tbsp light brown
   soft sugar
4 pineapple rings, in fruit juice,
   drained and juice reserved

For the sponge
115g/4oz/½ cup butter
115g/4oz/generous ½ cup golden
   caster (superfine) sugar
2 eggs, lightly beaten
115g/4oz/1 cup self-raising
   (self-rising) flour
5ml/1 tsp baking powder
a few drops of vanilla extract
custard, cream or ice cream,
   to serve (optional)

Cook's Tip
Some electric pressure cookers
have a vented glass lid. Use this
for steaming, then replace it
with the pressure cooker lid
to cook under pressure.

1 Place the trivet, rack, metal pastry cutter or upturned saucer in the base of the pressure cooker. Place the butter and sugar for the topping in a bowl and beat together. Spread over the base and slightly up the sides of an 18cm/7in non-stick cake tin (pan). Do not use a loose-bottomed tin.

2 Arrange the pineapple slices on the base of the tin. Cream the butter and sugar, for the sponge, together in a bowl, until pale and fluffy. Beat in the eggs, one at a time.

3 Sift the flour and baking powder together. Using a metal spoon, fold in the flour and stir in the vanilla extract and 30ml/2 tbsp of the reserved fruit juice. Spoon the mixture into the cake tin, and spread over the fruit.

4 Cover the tin with a double layer of greased baking parchment. Tie tightly around the rim of the tin with string, to secure. Use sufficient string to make a handle for easy removal. Alternatively, use a foil strip. See page 19.

5 Add 750ml/1¼ pints/3 cups hot water to the pressure cooker. Carefully place the pudding in the pressure cooker. Cover with the lid, but do not seal or bring to pressure; just steam for 15 minutes. Refer to your manufacturer's handbook on how to do this. Also see pages 44–5. Use the Manual or Soup setting for the electric pressure cooker.

Electric: Close the lid and bring to High pressure using the Manual, Soup or Pulses setting. Cook for 25 minutes (35 minutes). Reset the timer, if necessary, to complete the cooking time. Release the pressure using natural release, making sure the 'keep warm' mode is switched off.
Stovetop: Close the lid and bring to High pressure. Cook for 25 minutes (35 minutes). Release the pressure slowly.

6 Open the cooker and carefully remove the sponge. Dab any moisture on the parchment lid with kitchen paper. Leave to stand for 5 minutes.

7 Remove the baking parchment and run a round bladed knife around the edge of the sponge. Place a warmed serving plate over the pudding and invert. Remove the tin. Serve with custard, cream or ice cream, as you wish.

Energy 595kcal/2489kJ; Protein 6.8g; Carbohydrate 66.1g, of which sugars 44.8g; Fat 35.6g, of which saturates 21.2g; Cholesterol 198mg; Calcium 138mg; Fibre 1.4g; Sodium 383mg.

Raspberry Jam Roly Poly

This classic British pudding is traditionally made with suet pastry. This recipe uses a mix of butter and suet for a lighter pastry. The pudding needs to be steamed for 20 minutes before cooking under pressure, to give the raising agents in the pastry time to rise first.

Pressure: Low

Time under Pressure: 25 minutes (30 minutes) + pre-steaming

Release: Natural/Slow

Serves 4

200g/7oz/1¾ cups self-raising (self-rising) flour
40g/1½oz/3 tbsp butter
50g/2oz/½ cup shredded suet (US chilled, grated shortening)
150ml/¼ pint/⅔ cup water or milk
2.5ml/½ tsp vanilla extract
115g/4oz raspberry jam
custard, to serve

Cook's Tips
• Some electric pressure cookers have a vented glass lid. Use this for steaming, then replace with the pressure cooker lid to cook under pressure.
• Make sure that the short width of the pastry is shorter than the width of your pressure cooker or pressure cooker basket.

Variations
Try mincemeat or a different variety of jam such as plum, apricot or black cherry.

1 Place the trivet, rack or steamer basket in the base of the pressure cooker.

2 Sift the flour into a bowl. Add the butter and rub in until it forms fine breadcrumbs. Stir in the suet, using a flat-bladed knife.

3 Add the water or milk and vanilla extract and work together with the knife to make a soft dough. Tip on to a lightly floured surface and roll out into a rectangle about 35 x 18cm/14 x 7in. Spread the jam over the top, leaving a gap along each edge.

4 Dampen the edges with water, using a pastry brush. Roll up from the short end and pinch the jam-free edge into the dough, to seal. Crimp each end.

5 Butter a sheet of foil and make a pleat in the centre, to allow for expansion. Wrap the roly poly loosely in the foil and secure the ends.

6 Add 900ml/1½ pints/3¾ cups hot water to the pressure cooker. Carefully place the roly poly on to the trivet. Cover with the lid, but do not seal or bring to pressure; just steam for 20 minutes. Refer to your manufacturer's handbook on how to do this. Also see pages 44–5. Use the Manual or Soup setting for the electric pressure cooker.

Electric: Close the lid and bring to Low pressure using the Manual, Soup or Pulses setting. Cook for 25 minutes (30 minutes). Reset the timer, if necessary, to complete the cooking time. Release the pressure using natural release, making sure the 'keep warm' mode is switched off.
Stovetop: Close the lid and bring to Low pressure. Cook for 25 minutes (30 minutes). Release the pressure slowly.

7 Open the cooker and carefully remove the parcel. Unwrap and place on a warmed serving plate. Serve sliced, with custard.

Energy 418kcal/1756kJ; Protein 4.6g; Carbohydrate 59.3g, of which sugars 20.7g; Fat 19.7g, of which saturates 11.6g; Cholesterol 32mg; Calcium 180mg; Fibre 2.2g; Sodium 254mg.

Christmas Pudding

Although this type of festive pudding is only made once a year, the benefits of a pressure cooker are enormous. It greatly reduces the hours of steaming that is otherwise required for a Christmas pudding. Serve with cream, custard or brandy butter.

Pressure: High
Time under Pressure: 1¾ hours
   (2¼ hours) + pre-steaming
Release: Natural/Slow
Makes 2 x 675g/1½lb puddings

175g/6oz/1 cup sultanas
   (golden raisins)
150g/5oz/1 cup raisins
75g/3oz/½ cup currants
50g/2oz/⅓ cup chopped mixed peel
50g/2oz/¼ cup ready-to-eat dried
   apricots, chopped
25g/1oz/¼ cup blanched almonds
50ml/2floz/¼ cup brandy or rum
150ml/¼ pint/⅔ cup barley wine
   or dark ale
115g/4oz/1 cup plain (all-purpose)
   flour
75g/3oz/1½ cups fresh white
   breadcrumbs
115g/4oz/½ cup light muscovado
   (brown) sugar
5ml/1 tsp mixed spice
50g/2oz carrots, grated
115g/4oz/½ cup butter, chilled
   and grated
grated rind and juice of ½ lemon
2 eggs
15ml/1 tbsp treacle (molasses)
holly sprig, to decorate (optional)
brandy or rum, and cream, custard
   or brandy butter, to serve

1 In a large bowl, combine the sultanas, raisins, currants, mixed peel, apricots and almonds. Pour over the brandy or rum and barley wine, and leave to soak overnight.

2 Mix the flour, breadcrumbs, sugar and mixed spice together in a bowl. Add to the fruit with the carrots, butter, grated lemon rind and juice, eggs and treacle, and mix together thoroughly.

3 Divide between two greased 1.2 litre/2 pint/5 cup pudding basins. Cover each with a layer of greased baking parchment and foil, and tie securely with string.

4 Place the trivet, rack or steamer basket in the pressure cooker. Pour in 1.6 litres/2¾ pints/6½ cups hot water and add a squeeze of lemon juice if the pressure cooker is aluminium. Place one pudding on the trivet.

5 Cover with the lid, but do not seal or bring to pressure. Leave the steam release vent open and just steam for 15 minutes. Refer to your manufacturer's handbook on how to do this. Also see pages 44–5. Use the Manual or Soup setting for the electric pressure cooker.

Electric: Close the lid and bring to High pressure using the Manual, Soup or Pulses setting. Cook for 1¾ hours (2¼ hours). Reset the timer, as necessary, to complete the cooking time. Release the pressure using natural release, making sure the 'keep warm' mode is switched off.
Stovetop: Close the lid and bring to High pressure. Cook for 1¾ hours (2¼ hours). Release the pressure slowly.

6 Open the cooker and carefully remove the pudding. Repeat with the second pudding in the same way. Leave to cool completely, then wrap in fresh baking parchment and foil.

7 Store for at least 1 month, until required. To reheat, place on the trivet, rack or steamer basket in the pressure cooker with 750ml/1½ pints/3 cups water and a dash of lemon juice.

Electric: Close the lid and bring to High pressure using the Manual, Soup or Pulses setting. Cook for 25 minutes (30 minutes). Release the pressure using natural release, making sure the 'keep warm' mode is switched off.
Stovetop: Close the lid and bring to High pressure. Cook for 25 minutes (30 minutes). Release the pressure slowly.

8 Turn out on to a warmed serving dish and decorate with holly, or flame with brandy or rum, as you wish. Serve with cream, custard or brandy butter.

Cook's Tip
Check the water level in the pressure cooker after steaming, if using an electric pressure cooker. If necessary, add a little more hot water.

Energy 1943kcal/8179kJ; Protein 28.1g; Carbohydrate 312.1g, of which sugars 239.6g; Fat 63.8g, of which saturates 32.6g; Cholesterol 354mg; Calcium 465mg; Fibre 14.2g; Sodium 880mg.

Fruity Croissant Pudding

A twist on the traditional bread and butter pudding, this recipe uses croissants, which are flakier and lighter than bread. It works best with day-old croissants, so is ideal for using up leftovers. Make sure your dish fits in the pressure cooker before layering with the ingredients.

Pressure: High

Time under Pressure: 8 minutes (10 minutes)

Release: Natural/Slow

Serves 4

3 large day-old croissants

40g/1½oz/3 tbsp butter, at room temperature

25g/1oz/⅛ cup sultanas (golden raisins)

25g/1oz/⅛ cup ready-to-eat dried apricots, chopped

250ml/8fl oz/1 cup milk

150ml/¼ pint/⅔ cup single (light) or double (heavy) cream

2 large eggs, lightly beaten

a few drops of vanilla extract

25g/1oz/2 tbsp caster (superfine) sugar

15g/½oz/1 tbsp soft light brown sugar

1 Slice each croissant thickly into about 6 slices. Butter a 900ml/ 1½ pint/3¾ cup, 18cm/7in round ovenproof dish, which will fit into the pressure cooker. Use the remaining butter to spread on one cut side of the croissant slices.

2 Arrange the croissant slices butter side up in the prepared dish, scattering with sultanas and apricots as you place them in the dish.

3 Pour the milk and cream into a pan and warm. Put the eggs, vanilla extract and sugar into a bowl and whisk together. Whisk in the milk. Pour over the croissants and leave to stand for 15 minutes.

4 Place the trivet or rack in the base of the pressure cooker. Add 300ml/ ½ pint/1¼ cups water. Cover the dish with greased foil and tie to secure. Carefully place the dish in the pressure cooker, using a foil strip to lower the dish into the pressure cooker, if necessary. See page 19.

Electric: Close the lid and bring to High pressure using the Manual, Soup or Meat setting. Cook for 8 minutes (10 minutes). Release the pressure using natural release, making sure the 'keep warm' mode is switched off.
Stovetop: Close the lid and bring to High pressure. Cook for 8 minutes (10 minutes). Release the pressure slowly.

5 Open the cooker and carefully lift out the pudding. Remove the foil and sprinkle with brown sugar. Place under a preheated grill until lightly browned. Leave to stand for 5–10 minutes and serve warm.

Energy 458kcal/1914kJ; Protein 11.1g; Carbohydrate 41.6g, of which sugars 24.5g; Fat 28.7g, of which saturates 15.7g; Cholesterol 185mg; Calcium 166mg; Fibre 2.2g; Sodium 345mg.

Chocolate and Raspberry Torte

This is a seriously rich and decadent chocolate torte. Made with ground almonds, which help to keep it moist, it is extremely quick and easy to make in the pressure cooker. The rich chocolate is offset by the fresh raspberries sprinkled over the top.

1 Grease and line an 18cm/7in cake tin (pan). Do not use a loose-bottomed tin. Place the butter, sugar, golden syrup and chocolat patissier in a pan. Heat gently until dissolved, and stir to combine. Cool.

2 Sift the flour into a large bowl with the bicarbonate of soda and baking powder. Stir in the ground almonds and make a well in the centre. Beat in the melted chocolate mixture with the egg and milk. Spoon into the prepared tin and cover the top tightly with foil.

3 Place the trivet or rack in the pressure cooker. Add 750ml/1¼ pints/3 cups hot water. Carefully lower the tin into the pressure cooker. Use a foil strip to assist you, if necessary. See page 19. Cover with the lid, but do not seal or bring to pressure; just leave the steam vent open and steam for 15 minutes. Refer to your manufacturer's handbook on how to do this. Also see pages 44–5. Use the Manual or Soup setting for the electric pressure cooker.

Electric: Close the lid and bring to High pressure using the Manual, Soup or Pulses setting. Cook for 25 minutes (35 minutes). Reset the timer, if necessary, to complete the cooking time. Release the pressure using natural release, making sure the 'keep warm' mode is switched off.
Stovetop: Close the lid and bring to High pressure. Cook for 25 minutes (35 minutes). Release the pressure slowly.

4 Open the cooker and carefully remove the torte. Place on a cooling rack and leave to cool. After 15 minutes, turn out on to the cooling rack and leave until cold.

5 Remove the paper and place on a serving plate. Bring the cream to the boil in a small pan. Stir in the chocolate and vanilla. Stir until smooth and starting to thicken. Spread over the top of the torte. Leave to cool and firm. To serve, top with fresh raspberries in the centre and dust with icing sugar, if you wish.

Pressure: High
Time under Pressure: 25 minutes (35 minutes) + pre-steaming
Release: Natural/Slow
Serves 4

75g/3oz/6 tbsp butter
40g/1½oz/3 tbsp soft light brown sugar
40g/1½oz golden (light corn) syrup
75g/3oz dark (bittersweet) Swiss chocolat patissier cooking chocolate, broken into pieces
130g/4½oz/1⅛ cups self-raising (self-rising) flour
1.2ml/¼ tsp bicarbonate of soda (baking soda)
2.5ml/½ tsp baking powder
40g/1½oz/⅜ cup ground almonds
1 egg
30ml/2 tbsp milk
75ml/2½fl oz/½ cup double (heavy) cream
75g/3oz 70% solids dark (bittersweet) chocolate
a few drops of vanilla extract
fresh raspberries, to decorate
icing (confectioners') sugar, for dusting (optional)

Energy 688kcal/2872kJ; Protein 9.5g; Carbohydrate 68.2g, of which sugars 43.5g; Fat 43.8g, of which saturates 23.4g; Cholesterol 126mg; Calcium 184mg; Fibre 2.6g; Sodium 291mg.

PRESERVES AND CHUTNEYS

Home-made marmalades, jam and chutneys are such a delight, and are far superior to many commercially prepared alternatives. Whether you grow your own fruit and vegetables, visit pick-your-own farms or just buy when in plentiful supply, preserving is the perfect way to extend the season. The pressure cooker saves so much time when making marmalade, as it quickens the tenderizing process necessary for the peel. Try either a traditional marmalade with Seville oranges or a tangy red grapefruit and ginger marmalade, which can be made throughout the year. Plum membrillo is a perfect recipe to make when there is a glut of plums, as it contains a high fruit content. There are also lots of chutneys and relishes to try. If you like them spicy, try mango chutney, red hot relish or fiery Bengal chutney, or for a milder flavour, try beetroot preserve or green tomato chutney. Whichever you choose, your pressure cooker will help speed up the process.

Lemon Curd

This rich, tangy curd is easy to make in the pressure cooker. It is delicious when spread thickly on crusty white bread or served with American-style pancakes. It also makes a tasty topping for milk puddings, or a zesty sauce when poured over fresh fruit tarts.

Pressure: High
Time under Pressure: 10 minutes (11 minutes)
Release: Natural/Slow
Makes about 550g/1¼lb

3–4 lemons
200g/7oz/1 cup caster (superfine) sugar
75g/3oz/6 tbsp butter, softened
2 eggs plus 2 yolks

1 Grate the rind from 1 lemon. Halve and squeeze the lemons, to give 150ml/¼ pint/⅔ cup lemon juice.

2 Place the sugar and butter in a 1.75 litre/3 pint/7½ cup heatproof bowl and whisk together, until soft and creamy. Beat in the eggs and egg yolks, then beat in the lemon juice and grated rind.

3 Place the bowl on a trivet, in the steamer basket or upturned rack. Add 600ml/1 pint/2½ cups water to the pressure cooker.

Electric: Close the lid and bring to High pressure using the Manual, Soup or Meat setting. Cook for 10 minutes (11 minutes). Release the pressure using natural release, making sure the 'keep warm' mode is switched off. After 10 minutes, quickly release the remaining pressure, if any.
Stovetop: Close the lid and bring to High pressure. Cook for 10 minutes (11 minutes). Release the pressure slowly. After 10 minutes, quickly release the remaining pressure, if any.

4 Open the cooker and whisk the lemon curd until thick, creamy and well blended. Pour into small, warm, sterilized jars. Cover, seal and label. Store in the refrigerator and use within 4 weeks.

Energy 331kcal/1389kJ; Protein 4.5g; Carbohydrate 42.2g, of which sugars 42.2g; Fat 17.2g, of which saturates 9.2g; Cholesterol 205mg; Calcium 39mg; Fibre 0g; Sodium 130mg.

Plum Cheese

This wonderfully rich, firm jelly is also known as *membrillo*. It can be served whole on a cheese board, or sliced with cheeses and cold meats. The pressure cooker quickly tenderizes the plums. Use low pressure to ensure the pectin is not reduced while under pressure.

1 Halve the plums. Place in the pressure cooker with 280ml/½ pint/ 1⅛ cups water.

Electric: Close the lid and bring to Low pressure using the Manual or Soup setting. Cook for 6 minutes (8 minutes). Release the pressure using natural release, making sure the 'keep warm' mode is switched off. After 10 minutes, quickly release the remaining pressure, if any.
Stovetop: Close the lid and bring to Low pressure. Cook for 6 minutes (8 minutes). Release the pressure slowly. After 10 minutes, quickly release the remaining pressure, if any.

2 Leave to cool slightly. Strain the fruit and any juices through a nylon sieve or strainer, pushing through as much pulp as possible. Weigh the fruit pulp, return to the pressure cooker and add an equal quantity of sugar.

3 Heat, stirring to dissolve the sugar. Bring to the boil and cook over a medium heat for about 20–30 minutes, until thick. As the mixture thickens, stir frequently to prevent the fruit from catching on the base of the pan. The paste should leave a groove for a couple of seconds when a spoon is drawn across the top. Use the Sauté or Soup setting for the electric pressure cooker. If this is too fierce, use the 'keep warm' function.

4 Pour into small, sterilized jars and seal. You may use ramekins and cover with greaseproof (waxed) paper and clear film or plastic wrap if you wish to turn out as a whole cheese. Keep refrigerated and use within 2 weeks if in unsealed pots, or up to 6 months in sealed jars.

Pressure: Low
**Time under Pressure: 6 minutes
   (8 minutes)**
Release: Natural/Slow
Makes about 5 x 150g/5oz pots
1kg/2¼lb plums
approximately 550g/1¼lb/2¾ cups
   jam sugar with added pectin

Energy 483kcal/2063kJ; Protein 1.6g;
Carbohydrate 126.8g, of which sugars 126.8g;
Fat 0.2g, of which saturates 0g; Cholesterol 0mg;
Calcium 46mg; Fibre 2.7g; Sodium 8mg.

Redcurrant Jelly

This is one of the best fruit jellies you can make. Use a low setting on your pressure cooker to ensure the pectin content of the redcurrants is not reduced while cooking under pressure. Serve with meats such as lamb or venison, or try with goat's cheese.

1 Place the redcurrants still on their stalks in the pressure cooker with the water.

Electric: Close the lid and bring to Low pressure using the Manual, Soup or Fish setting. Cook for 3 minutes (4 minutes). Release the pressure using natural release, making sure the 'keep warm' mode is switched off. After 15 minutes, quickly release the remaining pressure, if any.
Stovetop: Close the lid and slowly bring to the boil. Cook on Low pressure for 3 minutes (4 minutes). Release the pressure slowly. After 15 minutes, quickly release the remaining pressure, if any.

2 Mash the fruit, then strain the pulp through a scalded jelly bag suspended over a large bowl. If you do not have a jelly bag, line a large sieve, strainer or colander with a double layer of muslin (cheesecloth) or scalded dish towel, and place over a bowl.

3 Leave to drip for several hours or overnight. Do not squeeze the bag.

4 Measure the juice extract and return to the cleaned pressure cooker pan. For the electric pressure cooker, use the cooker or a large pan. Add 500g/1¼lb/2½ cups sugar for each 600ml/1 pint/2½ cups juice.

5 Bring to the boil, stirring to dissolve the sugar. Boil until setting point is reached, 105°C/221°F. Use the Sauté or Soup setting for the electric pressure cooker. Remove from the heat, or switch off. Skim with a slotted spoon to remove any scum and pour into warm, sterilized jars. Cover, seal and label.

Pressure: Low
Time under Pressure: 3 minutes (4 minutes)
Release: Natural/Slow
Makes 4 small pots, but will vary

1.3kg/3lb ripe redcurrants
450ml/¾ pint/scant 2 cups water
preserving sugar (see step 4 for quantity)

Cook's Tips

• Keep an eye on the pressure cooker when cooking the redcurrants, as some fruit can foam up and splutter out of the pressure valve. If this happens, reduce the heat or briefly remove from the heat, or switch off the electric pressure cooker.
• Some pressure cooker manufacturers do not recommend cooking redcurrants; check your manufacturer's handbook before making this recipe.

Energy 561kcal/2391kJ; Protein 4.2g; Carbohydrate 144.9g, of which sugars 144.9g; Fat 0g, of which saturates 0g; Cholesterol 0mg; Calcium 153mg; Fibre 14.7g; Sodium 13mg.

Seville Orange Marmalade

Real home-made marmalade tastes delicious, and as Seville oranges are only available in winter, this is a great preserve to make in the pressure cooker during the colder months. The flavour is much more intense than shop-bought marmalades.

1 Scrub the oranges using a nylon scrubbing brush, and pick off the disc at the stalk end. Cut the oranges in half and squeeze the juice, retaining the pips. Quarter the rind, cut away and reserve any thick pith and shred the rind, thickly or thinly, depending on how you prefer the finished marmalade.

2 Cut up the reserved pith roughly and tie it up with the orange and lemon pips in a square of muslin (cheesecloth) using a piece of string. Tie the bag loosely, so that water can circulate in the bag during cooking and will extract the pectin from the pith and pips.

3 Add the cut rind, strained juices, muslin bag and 900ml/1½ pints/3¾ cups water to the pressure cooker.

Electric: Close the lid and bring to High pressure using the Manual, Soup or Beans setting. Cook for 12–18 minutes (25–30 minutes), depending on the thickness of the rind. Release the pressure using natural release, making sure the 'keep warm' mode is switched off.
Stovetop: Close the lid and bring to High pressure. Cook for 12–18 minutes (25–30 minutes), depending on the thickness of the rind. Release the pressure slowly.

4 Release the lid and lift out the bag of pith and pips. Squeeze it between two plates over the pan, to extract as much pectin as possible. Add the remaining water and sugar to the pan and stir until the sugar has dissolved. Use the Sauté or Soup setting for the electric pressure cooker.

5 Bring to the boil in the open cooker, and boil until setting point is reached. To test, put a spoonful of marmalade on a cold saucer. Allow to cool slightly, then push the surface of the marmalade with your finger. Setting point has been reached if a skin has formed. If not, boil a little longer and keep testing, or use a sugar thermometer 105°C/221°F.

6 Skim, if necessary, and leave to cool for about 15 minutes, then stir to redistribute the rind. Using a small heatproof jug or pitcher, pour the marmalade into warm, sterilized jars. Cover and seal while hot. Label and store in a cool, dark place until required. The marmalade will keep well for at least 6 months.

Pressure: High
Time under Pressure: 12–18 minutes (25–30 minutes)
Release: Natural/Slow
Makes 2kg/4½lb
900g/2lb Seville oranges
juice and pips (seeds) of 2 lemons
1.2 litres/2 pints/5 cups water
1.3kg/3lb/6¾ cups preserving sugar, warmed

Energy 5455kcal/23275kJ; Protein 16.4g; Carbohydrate 1435g, of which sugars 1435g; Fat 0.9g, of which saturates 0g; Cholesterol 0mg; Calcium 800mg; Fibre 20.4g; Sodium 110mg.

Red Grapefruit and Ginger Marmalade

The red grapefruits give this marmalade a lovely rich colour and flavour, and the preserved stem ginger gives a kick at the end. The pressure cooker is a great help when making marmalade, as it reduces the lengthy cooking process of tenderizing the rind.

Pressure: High
Time under Pressure: 10 minutes (14 minutes)
Release: Natural/Slow
Makes about 2.75kg/6lb

1kg/2¼lb/approximately 3 red grapefruits
2 lemons
900ml/1½ pints/3¾ cups water
900g/2lb/4½ cups preserving sugar, warmed
6 pieces preserved stem ginger, chopped

1 Wash the grapefruits and remove the stalk ends. Remove the rind from the grapefruits and cut into thin shreds.

2 Remove the pith from the grapefruits and roughly chop the flesh, reserving any pips (seeds). Place the flesh in the pressure cooker, with the shredded rind. Squeeze the lemon juice, reserving any pips, and add to the pressure cooker.

3 Tie the grapefruit pith and pips and lemon pips in a square of muslin (cheesecloth), using a piece of string. Tie the bag loosely, so that water can circulate in the bag during cooking and will extract the pectin from the pith and pips.

4 Add the muslin bag and half the water to the pressure cooker.

Electric: Close the lid and bring to High pressure using the Manual, Soup or Fish setting. Cook for 10 minutes (14 minutes). Release the pressure using natural release, making sure the 'keep warm' mode is switched off.
Stovetop: Close the lid and bring to High pressure. Cook for 10 minutes (14 minutes). Release the pressure slowly.

5 Release the lid and lift out the bag of pith and pips. Squeeze it between two plates over the pan, to extract as much pectin as possible. Add the remaining water and sugar to the pan and stir until the sugar has dissolved. Add the chopped ginger. Use the Sauté or Soup setting for the electric pressure cooker.

6 Bring to the boil in the open cooker, and boil until setting point is reached. To test, put a spoonful of marmalade on a cold saucer. Allow to cool slightly, then push the surface of the marmalade with your finger. Setting point has been reached if a skin has formed. If not, boil a little longer and keep testing, or use a sugar thermometer 105°C/221°F.

7 Leave to cool for about 15 minutes, then stir to redistribute the rind and ginger. Using a small heatproof jug or pitcher, pour the marmalade into warm, sterilized jars. Cover and seal while hot. Label and store in a cool, dark place until required. The marmalade will keep well for at least 6 months.

Energy 3846kcal/16389kJ; Protein 12.5g; Carbohydrate 1008.5g, of which sugars 1008.5g; Fat 1g, of which saturates 0g; Cholesterol 0mg; Calcium 491mg; Fibre 17.3g; Sodium 75mg.

Fresh Berry Jam

This is a wonderful jam to make when summer produce is ripe. You can vary the quantities of fruits, depending on which ones you have in plentiful supply. Make sure you use a low pressure setting to cook the berries for this jam, so they soften without over-cooking.

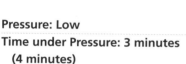

Pressure: Low

Time under Pressure: 3 minutes (4 minutes)

Release: Natural/Slow

Makes about 1.2kg/2½lb

300g/11oz/scant 3 cups strawberries, halved if large
150g/5oz/scant 1 cup raspberries
300g/11oz/scant 3 cups blackberries
150g/5oz/1½ cups blueberries
750g/1lb 11oz/3¾ cups jam sugar, with pectin
1 lemon

1 Place the fruits and sugar in a large bowl and mix together. Squeeze the lemon juice, reserving any pips (seeds). Add to the fruit and leave to stand for 1 hour. Tie any lemon pips in a small piece of muslin (cheesecloth).

2 Transfer the fruit and sugar mix to the pressure cooker with the muslin bag, and add 60ml/4 tbsp water. Bring nearly to the boil, stirring frequently, to dissolve any remaining sugar.

Electric: Close the lid and bring to Low pressure using the Manual, Soup or Fish setting. Cook for 3 minutes (4 minutes). If you cannot set your electric pressure cooker for this short cooking time, set a separate timer for the correct time and switch off the cooker after the given time. Release the pressure using natural release, making sure the 'keep warm' mode is switched off. After 15 minutes, quickly release the remaining pressure, if any.

Stovetop: Close the lid and bring to Low pressure. Cook for 3 minutes (4 minutes). Release the pressure slowly. After 15 minutes, quickly release the remaining pressure, if any.

3 Bring to the boil in the open cooker and boil until setting point is reached at 105°C/221°F. Use the Sauté or Soup setting for the electric pressure cooker. Remove from the heat, or switch off. Skim with a slotted spoon to remove any scum, and pour into warm, sterilized jars. Cover, seal and label.

Energy 3243kcal/13813kJ; Protein 9.8g;
Carbohydrate 851.3g, of which sugars 844.5g;
Fat 1.2g, of which saturates 0g; Cholesterol 0mg;
Calcium 338mg; Fibre 15.8g; Sodium 84mg.

Apricot Jam

This richly flavoured jam can be made at any time of year, so even if you miss the short apricot season, you can still enjoy the irresistible taste of sweet, tangy apricot jam. Using the pressure cooker for dried apricots reduces the soaking time required.

1 Put the apricots in a bowl, pour over boiling water and leave to soak for 5 minutes. Drain. Place the apricots and apple juice in the pressure cooker. Add the lemon juice and rind.

Electric: Close the lid and bring to High pressure using the Manual, Soup or Fish setting. Cook for 7 minutes (8 minutes). Release the pressure using natural release, making sure the 'keep warm' mode is switched off. After 10 minutes, quickly release the remaining pressure, if any.
Stovetop: Close the lid and bring to High pressure. Cook for 7 minutes (8 minutes). Release the pressure slowly. After 10 minutes, quickly release the remaining pressure, if any.

2 Add the sugar to the open cooker and stir until dissolved. Bring to the boil in the open cooker and boil until setting point is reached at 105°C/221°F. Use the Sauté or Soup setting for the electric pressure cooker. Remove from the heat, or switch off.

3 Stir in the almonds and leave to stand for a few minutes. Pour into warm, sterilized jars. Cover, seal and label. Store in a cool, dark place.

Pressure: High
Time under Pressure: 7 minutes (8 minutes)
Release: Natural/Slow
Makes about 2kg/4lb

675g/1½lb dried apricots, halved
900ml/1½ pints/3¾ cups apple juice
juice and grated rind of 2 unwaxed lemons
675g/1½lb/3½ cups preserving sugar
50g/2oz/½ cup blanched almonds, coarsely chopped

Energy 4576kcal/19503kJ; Protein 47.2g; Carbohydrate 1090.9g, of which sugars 1089.5g; Fat 33.5g, of which saturates 2.2g; Cholesterol 0mg; Calcium 1000mg; Fibre 69.3g; Sodium 437mg.

Rhubarb and Ginger Compote

This pressure cooker compote is delicious served by itself or topped with yogurt or ice cream. It is an ideal accompaniment for porridge, rice pudding or with Madeira or sponge cake as a dessert. It can also be used to flavour fools and parfaits.

Pressure: High

Time under Pressure: 30 seconds (1 minute)

Release: Quick

Serves 4

700g/1½lb rhubarb
rind and juice of 1 orange
100g/3½oz/½ cup caster (superfine) sugar
125ml/4fl oz/½ cup water
2 pieces preserved stem ginger

Cook's Tip

Sometimes rhubarb can splutter and block the vent, so keep an eye on the pressure cooker and make sure the heat is turned down if using a stovetop model. Watch the vent when releasing the pressure after cooking.

1 Cut the rhubarb into 2.5cm/1in lengths. Place in the pressure cooker and add the orange rind and juice, sugar and water, and leave to stand for 10 minutes. Chop the ginger and add.

2 Heat in the open pan for a couple of minutes and stir to dissolve any remaining sugar, using the Manual or Soup setting for the electric pressure cooker.

Electric: Close the lid and bring to High pressure using the Manual or Soup setting. Cook for 30 seconds (1 minute). If you cannot set your electric pressure cooker for this short cooking time, set a separate timer for the correct time and switch off the cooker after the given time. Release the pressure quickly, making sure the 'keep warm' mode is switched off.

Stovetop: Close the lid and bring to High pressure. Cook for 30 seconds (1 minute). Release the pressure quickly.

3 For a softer purée, release the pressure slowly, or use natural release for the electric pressure cooker.

4 Remove the pressure cooker lid and leave to cool. Either transfer to sterilized jars and refrigerate for up to 1 week, or serve immediately.

Energy 111kcal/476kJ; Protein 1.7g;
Carbohydrate 27.5g, of which sugars 27.5g; Fat
0.2g, of which saturates 0g; Cholesterol 0mg;
Calcium 170mg; Fibre 3.3g; Sodium 7mg.

Beetroot, Date and Orange Preserve

With its vibrant red colour and rich, earthy flavour, this distinctive chutney is good with salads, as well as full-flavoured cheeses such as mature Cheddar, Stilton or Gorgonzola. It is ideal for making in the pressure cooker.

1 Thinly peel the beetroot and cut into 1cm/½in pieces. Peel, quarter and core the apples. Cut into 1cm/½in pieces.

2 Place the beetroot, apples, onions, garlic, orange rind and vinegar in the pressure cooker and stir together to combine.

Electric: Close the lid and bring to High pressure using the Manual, Soup or Fish setting. Cook for 6 minutes (7 minutes). Release the pressure using natural release, making sure the 'keep warm' mode is switched off. **Stovetop**: Close the lid and bring to High pressure. Cook for 6 minutes (7 minutes). Release the pressure slowly.

3 Open the pressure cooker and stir in the sugar, allspice, salt and dates. Bring to the boil in the open pressure cooker, stirring until the sugar has dissolved. Boil in the open cooker until thickened, about 10–15 minutes. Use the Sauté or Soup setting for the electric pressure cooker. Stir from time to time as it thickens, to prevent it catching on the base of the cooker.

4 Spoon into hot, sterilized jars, cover and seal. Store in a cool, dark place and open within 5 months. Once opened, store in the refrigerator and use within 1 month.

Pressure: High
Time under Pressure: 6 minutes
  (7 minutes)
Release: Natural/Slow
Makes about 1.4kg/3lb

350g/12oz raw beetroots (beets)
350g/12oz eating apples
225g/8oz red onions, finely chopped
1 garlic clove, crushed
finely grated rind of 2 oranges
300ml/½ pint/1¼ cups malt vinegar
200g/7oz/1 cup granulated
  (white) sugar
5ml/1 tsp ground allspice
5ml/1 tsp salt
175g/6oz/1 cup chopped dried dates

Energy 1688kcal/7202kJ; Protein 16.6g; Carbohydrate 429.6g, of which sugars 422.4g; Fat 1.5g, of which saturates 0.2g; Cholesterol 0mg; Calcium 285mg; Fibre 29.9g; Sodium 2238mg.

Mango Chutney

No Indian meal would be complete without this classic chutney, which can be easily made in your pressure cooker. Its sweet, tangy flavour complements the warm taste of spices. It is also great served with chargrilled chicken breasts, and will liven up cheese sandwiches.

Pressure: High

Time under Pressure: 5 minutes (6 minutes)

Release: Natural/Slow

Makes about 450g/1lb

3 firm mangoes

280ml/½ pint/1⅛ cups cider vinegar

200g/7oz/scant 1 cup light muscovado (brown) sugar

1 fresh red chilli, halved, seeded and chopped

2.5cm/1in piece fresh root ginger, peeled and chopped

1 garlic clove, finely chopped

5 cardamom pods, bruised

1 bay leaf

2.5ml/½ tsp salt

Variation

If you prefer a milder mango chutney, you can omit the red chilli or reduce the quantity to half a chilli.

1 Peel the mangoes and cut out the stone (pit). Roughly chop the flesh. Place in the pressure cooker with the cider vinegar and stir together well.

Electric: Close the lid and bring to High pressure using the Manual, Soup or Fish setting. Cook for 5 minutes (6 minutes). Release the pressure using natural release, making sure the 'keep warm' mode is switched off.
Stovetop: Close the lid and bring to High pressure. Cook for 5 minutes (6 minutes). Release the pressure slowly.

2 Open the pressure cooker and add the sugar, chilli, ginger, garlic, cardamom, bay leaf and salt. Bring to the boil in the open pressure cooker over a medium heat, stirring occasionally. Use the Sauté or Soup setting for the electric pressure cooker. If this is too fierce, use the 'keep warm' function.

3 Cook until the chutney is reduced to a thick consistency, about 15 minutes, or until no excess liquid remains. Stir frequently as it thickens, to prevent it from catching on the base of the cooker. Remove and discard the bay leaf. Spoon into hot, sterilized jars and seal. Store for 1 week before eating, and use within 1 year. Once opened, store in the refrigerator and use within 1 month.

Energy 1058kcal/4519kJ; Protein 5g; Carbohydrate 274.6g, of which sugars 273.2g; Fat 1.1g, of which saturates 0.5g; Cholesterol 0mg; Calcium 120mg; Fibre 15.6g; Sodium 1008mg.

Apple Sauce

This sauce is perfect for serving with roast pork, or alternatively as a dessert with ice cream. When cooking apples, use the lowest possible heat setting after reaching pressure, and release the pressure slowly to prevent the purée from rising and blocking the vents.

1 Peel, quarter and core the apples. Cut into thick slices. Place in the pressure cooker and add the lemon juice and sugar. Depending on whether you want to make an apple sauce for a roast or a dessert, use the lesser or greater amount of sugar. Add the water.

2 Heat in the open cooker, to dissolve the sugar, using the Manual or Soup setting for the electric pressure cooker.

Electric: Close the lid and bring to High pressure using the Manual, Soup or Fish setting. Cook for 1 minute (2 minutes). If you cannot set your electric pressure cooker for this short cooking time, set a separate timer for the correct time and switch off the cooker after the given time. Release the pressure using natural release, making sure the 'keep warm' mode is switched off. After 5 minutes, release any remaining pressure quickly, taking care that the sauce does not splutter.

Stovetop: Close the lid and bring to High pressure. Cook for 1 minute (2 minutes). Release the pressure slowly. After 5 minutes, release any remaining pressure quickly, taking care that the sauce does not splutter.

3 Release the lid and stir the sauce with a wooden spoon. Stir in the ground cinnamon. Heat uncovered for a few minutes to thicken the sauce, if you wish. Serve either warm or cold.

Cook's Tip
Sometimes apples can splutter and block the vent, so keep an eye on the pressure cooker and make sure the heat is turned down if using a stovetop model.

Pressure: High
Time under Pressure: 1 minute (2 minutes)
Release: Natural/Slow
Serves 4–8
900g/2lb cooking apples
rind and juice of 1 lemon
either 25g/1oz/2 tbsp or 75g/3oz/
⅓ cup caster (superfine) sugar
200ml/7fl oz/scant 1 cup water
2.5ml/½ tsp ground cinnamon

Energy 66kcal/280kJ; Protein 0.3g; Carbohydrate 17g, of which sugars 17g; Fat 0.1g, of which saturates 0g; Cholesterol 0mg; Calcium 6mg; Fibre 1.7g; Sodium 2mg.

Green Tomato Chutney

This is the perfect chutney to make at the end of summer with leftover green tomatoes, which will not ripen before winter. The pressure cooker will not only quickly tenderize the tomatoes, but it is also an ideal vessel for finishing cooking your chutney.

Pressure: High
Time under Pressure: 5 minutes
  (7 minutes)
Release: Natural/Slow
Makes about 1.45kg/3¼lb
900g/2lb green tomatoes
450g/1lb cooking apples
450g/1lb onions
280ml/½ pint/1⅛ cups
  pickling vinegar
150g/5oz/1 cup sultanas
  (golden raisins)
5ml/1 tsp salt
2 garlic cloves
2.5cm/1in piece fresh root
  ginger, grated
225g/8oz/1 cup light muscovado
  (brown) sugar

1 Slice the tomatoes. Peel, core and chop the apples. Peel and chop the onions. Place in the pressure cooker with the vinegar, sultanas, salt, garlic and ginger.

Electric: Close the lid and bring to High pressure using the Manual, Soup or Fish setting. Cook for 5 minutes (7 minutes). Release the pressure using natural release, making sure the 'keep warm' mode is switched off. After 5 minutes, quickly release the remaining pressure, if any.
Stovetop: Close the lid and bring to High pressure. Cook for 5 minutes (7 minutes). Release the pressure slowly. After 5 minutes, quickly release the remaining pressure, if any.

2 Stir in the sugar and bring to the boil in the open pressure cooker. Cook over a low heat, stirring occasionally until most of the liquid has evaporated and the mixture has thickened, about 25 minutes. As it thickens, stir the chutney more frequently. Use the Sauté or Soup setting for the electric pressure cooker. If this is too fierce, use the 'keep warm' function.

3 Spoon into warm, sterilized jars, cover and seal. Store in a cool, dark place and leave to mature for at least 1 month before serving. Once opened, store in the refrigerator and use within 1 month.

Energy 1436kcal/6100kJ; Protein 17.4g;
Carbohydrate 353.1g, of which sugars 342.8g;
Fat 4.7g, of which saturates 0.9g; Cholesterol 0mg;
Calcium 329mg; Fibre 31g; Sodium 2100mg.

Barbecue Relish

Use your pressure cooker to make this relish, which captures the flavours of summer with tomatoes, cucumbers and peppers. As the name suggests, it is perfect for serving with barbecues, whether used inside a bun with a burger or served as a dressing for kebabs.

Pressure: High
Time under Pressure: 4 minutes (5 minutes)
Release: Natural/Slow
Makes about 1.4kg/3lb

2 onions, chopped
2 garlic cloves, crushed
2 orange (bell) peppers, seeded and chopped
1 cucumber, diced
900g/2lb firm tomatoes, skinned and quartered
200ml/7fl oz/scant 1 cup white malt vinegar, plus 15ml/1 tbsp extra
150g/5oz/¾ cup granulated (white) sugar
30ml/2 tbsp wholegrain mustard
15ml/1 tbsp Worcestershire sauce
15ml/1 tbsp tomato purée (paste)
5ml/1 tsp salt
30ml/2 tbsp cornflour (cornstarch)

1 Place the onions, garlic, peppers, cucumber, tomatoes and 200ml/7fl oz/1 cup vinegar in the pressure cooker and stir together to combine.

Electric: Close the lid and bring to High pressure using the Manual, Soup or Vegetable setting. Cook for 4 minutes (5 minutes). Release the pressure using natural release, making sure the 'keep warm' mode is switched off. After 5 minutes, quickly release the remaining pressure, if any.
Stovetop: Close the lid and bring to High pressure. Cook for 4 minutes (5 minutes). Release the pressure slowly. After 5 minutes, quickly release the remaining pressure, if any.

2 Open the pressure cooker and stir in the sugar, mustard, Worcestershire sauce, tomato purée and salt. Bring to the boil in the open pressure cooker, then boil to reduce the liquid until slightly thickened, about 10–15 minutes. Use the Sauté or Soup setting for the electric pressure cooker.

3 Mix the cornflour with the remaining 15ml/1 tbsp vinegar. Stir into the relish and cook for 2 minutes, until thickened.

4 Spoon into hot, sterilized jars, cover and seal. Store in a cool, dark place and open within 4 months. Once opened, store in the refrigerator and use within 1 month.

Cook's Tip
If your electric pressure cooker does not have a short cooking time, set a separate timer for the correct time and switch off the cooker after the given time.

Energy 1152kcal/4885kJ; Protein 18.8g; Carbohydrate 268.1g, of which sugars 231.5g; Fat 7.7g, of which saturates 1.4g; Cholesterol 0mg; Calcium 318mg; Fibre 27.5g; Sodium 3166mg.

Red Hot Relish

Make this relish in summer when tomatoes and peppers are plentiful. It enhances plain dishes such as cheese or mushroom omelette. Release the pressure slowly for 5 minutes to prevent the vegetables blocking the vent, then release quickly to ensure they do not overcook.

Pressure: High
Time under Pressure: 4 minutes (5 minutes)
Release: Natural/Slow
Makes about 1.2kg/2½lb

450g/1lb red onions, chopped
3 red (bell) peppers, seeded and chopped
800g/1¾lb ripe tomatoes, skinned and quartered
3 fresh red chillies, seeded and sliced
275ml/½ pint/scant 1 cup red wine vinegar
200g//7oz/1 cup granulated (white) sugar
30ml/2 tbsp mustard seeds
10ml/2 tsp celery seeds
15ml/1 tbsp paprika
5ml/1 tsp salt

Energy 1313kcal/5573kJ; Protein 29.9g; Carbohydrate 311.4g, of which sugars 294.1g; Fat 19.1g, of which saturates 2.3g; Cholesterol 0mg; Calcium 508mg; Fibre 31.3g; Sodium 2091mg.

1 Place the onions, peppers, tomatoes, chillies and vinegar in the pressure cooker and stir together to combine.

Electric: Close the lid and bring to High pressure using the Manual, Soup or Vegetable setting. Cook for 4 minutes (5 minutes). Release the pressure using natural release, making sure the 'keep warm' mode is switched off. After 5 minutes, release any remaining pressure quickly.
Stovetop: Close the lid and bring to High pressure. Cook for 4 minutes (5 minutes). Release the pressure slowly. After 5 minutes, release any remaining pressure quickly.

2 Open the pressure cooker and stir in the sugar, mustard seeds, celery seeds, paprika and salt. Bring to the boil, stirring occasionally until the sugar has dissolved completely. Use the Sauté or Soup setting for the electric pressure cooker. If this is too fierce, use the 'keep warm' function.

3 Cook the relish for about 30 minutes, or until most of the liquid has evaporated and the mixture has a thick but moist consistency. Stir frequently towards the end of the cooking time, to prevent the mixture from sticking to the pan.

4 Spoon into hot, sterilized jars, cover and seal. Store in a cool, dark place and leave to mature for at least 2 weeks before eating. Use the relish within 1 year of making.

Mediterranean Chutney

Reminiscent of the warm Mediterranean climate, this spiced vegetable chutney is mild and warm in flavour, and goes well with grilled meats and sausages. For a hotter, spicier dish, add a little cayenne pepper with the paprika when making this in your pressure cooker.

Pressure: High
Time under Pressure: 6 minutes (8 minutes)
Release: Natural/Slow
Makes about 1.3kg/3lb

350g/12oz Spanish onions, chopped
675g/1½lb ripe tomatoes, skinned and chopped
1 aubergine (eggplant), about 350g/12oz, trimmed and cut into 1cm/½in cubes
450g/1lb courgettes (zucchini), sliced
1 small yellow (bell) pepper, quartered, seeded and sliced
1 small red (bell) pepper, quartered, seeded and sliced
2 garlic cloves, crushed
1 small rosemary sprig
1 small thyme sprig
2 bay leaves
10ml/2 tsp salt
5ml/1 tsp paprika
275ml/½ pint/generous 1 cup distilled malt vinegar
300g/11oz/generous 1½ cups granulated (white) sugar

1 Put the chopped onions, tomatoes, aubergine, courgettes, peppers and garlic in the pressure cooker. Tie the rosemary, thyme and bay leaves in a piece of muslin (cheesecloth). Add to the cooker with the salt, paprika and vinegar.

Electric: Close the lid and bring to High pressure using the Manual, Soup or Fish setting. Cook for 6 minutes (8 minutes). Release the pressure using natural release, making sure the 'keep warm' mode is switched off.
Stovetop: Close the lid and bring to High pressure. Cook for 6 minutes (8 minutes). Release the pressure slowly.

2 Open the pressure cooker, add the sugar and stir until dissolved. Cook the chutney, uncovered, for about 30–40 minutes, or until most of the liquid has evaporated. Use the Sauté or Soup setting for the electric pressure cooker. If this is too fierce, use the 'keep warm' function. Stir occasionally as it thickens, to prevent it from catching on the base of the cooker.

3 When the chutney is reduced to a thick consistency and no excess liquid remains, discard the herbs, then spoon into warm, sterilized jars. Set aside until cool, then cover and seal with vinegar-proof lids.

4 Store in a cool, dark place and allow to mature for at least 2 months before eating. Use the chutney within 2 years. Once opened, store in the refrigerator and use within 2 months.

Energy 1597kcal/6788kJ; Protein 22.5g; Carbohydrate 386.9g, of which sugars 377.4g; Fat 6.2g, of which saturates 1.6g; Cholesterol 0mg; Calcium 374mg; Fibre 31.3g; Sodium 4033mg.

Fiery Bengal Chutney

Not for timid taste buds, this piquant chutney is the perfect choice for lovers of hot and spicy food. Although it can be eaten a month after making in your pressure cooker, it tastes even better if it is matured for a longer amount of time.

Pressure: High

Time under Pressure: 7 minutes (9 minutes)

Release: Natural/Slow

Makes about 1.3kg/3lb

75g/3oz fresh root ginger
675g/1½lb cooking apples
450g/1lb onions
4 garlic cloves, finely chopped
150g/5oz/1 cup raisins
275ml/½ pint/1⅛ cups malt vinegar
2 fresh red chillies
2 fresh green chillies
250g/9oz/1⅛ cups demerara (raw) sugar
10ml/2 tsp salt
5ml/1 tsp ground turmeric

Energy 1841kcal/7845kJ; Protein 14g; Carbohydrate 470.1g, of which sugars 454.9g; Fat 2.8g, of which saturates 0.1g; Cholesterol 0mg; Calcium 303mg; Fibre 26.8g; Sodium 4074mg.

1 Peel and finely shred the fresh root ginger. Peel, core and roughly chop the apples. Peel and quarter the onions, then slice as thinly as possible. Place in the pressure cooker with the garlic, raisins and vinegar.

Electric: Close the lid and bring to High pressure using the Manual, Soup or Fish setting. Cook for 7 minutes (9 minutes). Release the pressure using natural release, making sure the 'keep warm' mode is switched off.
Stovetop: Close the lid and bring to High pressure. Cook for 7 minutes (9 minutes). Release the pressure slowly.

2 Halve the chillies and remove the seeds, then slice them finely. Stir the sugar into the chutney, and bring to the boil in the open cooker. Use the Sauté or Soup setting for the electric pressure cooker. Simmer until the chutney is thick and pulpy, about 15–20 minutes, stirring frequently towards the end of the cooking time. If this is too fierce, use the 'keep warm' function. Add the chillies when the chutney starts to thicken.

3 When the chutney is reduced to a thick consistency and no excess liquid remains, turn off the heat and stir in the salt and turmeric. Spoon into warm, sterilized jars, cover and seal with vinegar-proof lids.

4 Store in a cool, dark place and allow to mature for at least 2 months before eating. Use the chutney within 2 years. Once opened, store in the refrigerator and use within 1 month.

Index

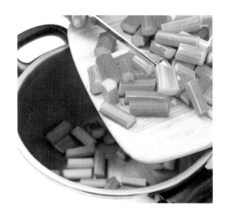

Acknowledgements and Cook's Notes

The publisher would like to thank the following for supplying equipment for recipe testing and photography.

Lakeland
Alexandra Buildings
Windermere
Cumbria
LA23 1BQ
Customer services 015394 88100
www.lakeland.co.uk

Flavormaster – Thane Direct
   UK Ltd
London WC2 3LH
www.thane.tv

Instant Pot UK – Early View Ltd
33a Walton Business Centre
44 Terrace Road
Surrey KT12 2SD
www.instantpot.co.uk

Kuhn Rikon UK Ltd
Landport Road
Wolverhampton
WV2 2QJ
01902 458 410
www.kuhnrikon.co.uk

Prestige – Meyer Group Ltd
Wirral International Business Park
Riverview Road
Bromborough
Wirral CH62 3RH
Customer services 0151 482 8282
www.prestige.co.uk

Tefal – Groupe SEB
Riverside House, Riverside Walk
Windsor SL4 1NA
+44 1753 835 014
www.groupeseb.com

Tower – RKW Ltd
Berry Hill Road
Stoke-on-Trent ST4 2Nl
Customer services 0333 220 6066
www.towerhousewares.co.uk

This edition is published by Lorenz Books, an imprint of Anness Publishing Ltd, 108 Great Russell Street, London WC1B 3NA; info@anness.com

www.lorenzbooks.com;
www.annesspublishing.com;
twitter: @Anness_Books

© Anness Publishing Ltd 2017

A CIP catalogue record for this book is available from the British Library.

Publisher: Joanna Lorenz
Senior Editor: Felicity Forster
Special Photography: Jon Whitaker
Food Styling: Jennie Shapter
Prop Styling: Pene Parker
Designer: Nigel Partridge

COOK'S NOTES

- Bracketed terms are intended for American readers.
- For all recipes, quantities are given in both metric and imperial measures and, where appropriate, in standard cups and spoons. Follow one set of measures, but not a mixture, because they are not interchangeable.
- Standard spoon and cup measures are level. 1 tsp = 5ml, 1 tbsp = 15ml, 1 cup = 250ml/8fl oz.
- Australian standard tablespoons are 20ml. Australian readers should use 3 tsp in place of 1 tbsp for measuring small quantities.

- American pints are 16fl oz/2 cups. American readers should use 20fl oz/2.5 cups in place of 1 pint when measuring liquids.
- The nutritional analysis given for each recipe is calculated per portion (i.e. serving or item), unless otherwise stated. If the recipe gives a range, such as Serves 4–6, then the nutritional analysis will be for the smaller portion size, i.e. 6 servings. The analysis does not include optional ingredients, such as salt added to taste.
- Medium (US large) eggs are used unless otherwise stated.